The Welsh Corgi Handbook

BY

LINDA WHITWAM

ISBN: 979-8651609147

Dedication

This book is dedicated to Her Royal Highness Queen Elizabeth II

in her Platinum Jubilee Year

Copyright

I am deeply grateful to the many passionate experts who have shared their extensive first-hand knowledge and love for the Pembroke Welsh Corgi and Cardigan Welsh Corgi. This book, the 20th in The Canine Handbooks series, would not have been possible without them.

Specialist Contributors

Linda Roberts

Fran Fricker

Piotr & Johnathan Mazur-Jones

Lucy Badham- Thornhill

Kevin Dover

Jo Evans

Lisa Thompson

Karen Hewitt

Sue Hardy

Kevin Egan

Alexandra Trefán-Török

Marian Your

Mary Ann Wehmueller

Maria Carter

Carole Turner

Margaret E. Leighton

Vicky Methuen

Eileen Eby

Robin Bruce

Tracy Irving

The Welsh Corgi League

The Cardigan Welsh Corgi Association

(Contributors' details appear at the back of the book)

Table of Contents

1. Meet the Corgi **6**

   History...8

2. Breed Standard **14**

3. All the Queen's Corgis **26**

4. Finding Your Puppy... **29**

   Family and Children...31

   Avoiding Bad Breeders...38

   Choosing a Healthy Corgi..45

   Advice from Corgi Experts...46

5. Bringing Puppy Home **50**

   Where Should the Puppy Sleep?...................................55

6. Crate and Housetraining.. **66**

   Using A Crate...66

   Housetraining Tips...73

   Bell Training..76

   Expert Opinion..77

7. Feeding a Corgi.. **81**

   Feeding Options...86

   What the Experts Feed...89

8. Typical Corgi Traits... **97**

   What To Expect..97

   Expert Views on The Corgi Temperament....................102

9. Basic Training.. **108**

   Teaching Basic Commands..113

   Collar and Lead (Leash) Training................................120

10. Specialist Training... **124**

   Dealing With Unwanted Behaviour..............................127

   Separation Anxiety..134

11. Exercise and Socialising.. **138**

   Socialisation...144

   What the Experts Say..148

12. Corgi Activities **151**

Pembrokes in Agility 151

Herd Mentality 155

The World's Your Oyster! 159

13. Corgi Health 163

Health Certificates for Puppy Buyers 165

Health Indicators 167

DM (Degenerative Myelopathy) 171

IVDD (Intervertebral Disc Disease) 172

14. Corgi Skin & Allergies 197

Types of Allergies 199

Parasites 204

Some Allergy Treatments 211

The Holistic Approach 214

15. The Corgi Coat and Grooming 217

Grooming Tips and Equipment 221

16. The Facts of Life 228

Pregnancy 232

Should I Breed From My Corgi? 235

Neutering - Pros and Cons 239

17. Corgi Rescue 244

18. Caring for Older Corgis 250

Helping Your Dog To Age Gracefully 252

What the Experts Say 255

Contributors 259

Useful Contacts 260

Disclaimer 261

Author's Notes: I have alternated between "he" and "she" in chapters to make this book as relevant as possible for all owners.

The Welsh Corgi Handbook uses British English, except where Americans have been quoted, when the original US English has been preserved.

This book has been printed in black and white to make it affordable for all new owners.

1. Meet the Corgi

There was a time a decade ago when Corgi numbers were worryingly low; the Cardigan was on the endangered breeds list and Pembrokes were headed that way. Then along came the Netflix series The Crown and the film The Queen's Corgi and the rest, as they say, is history!

While numbers increased 25% in a year in the UK, they positively exploded in the US where today the Pembroke Welsh Corgi is knocking on the door of top 10 breed status.

Those beautiful expressive eyes, big ears and undeniable good looks, coupled with intelligence, sociability and a good-natured temperament, have captured hearts and minds all over the world. The Pembroke is a firm favourite with families throughout North America, and while Cardigans still have some way to go, they are slowly moving up the rankings year on year.

With both the Pembroke and the Cardigan, you're getting a lot of dog in a medium-sized package. Don't expect a lapdog or a couch potato; you're getting a busy, sometimes bossy, spirited dog that was bred to work all day in tough conditions. With his love of a job or challenge and zest for life, the Welsh Corgi is here to stay.

....

A Lot of Dog in a Medium Package

There are hundreds of breeds registered with the Kennel Clubs and all of them are different, but the Corgi is truly unique - every dog is an individual and personalities vary from one Corgi to the next.

Along with other dogs bred to herd livestock, both the Pembroke and the Cardigan are in the Pastoral Group in the UK and the Herding Group in the USA.

Corgis are dwarf dogs, having been bred down from larger breeds to create a hardy, medium-sized dog to work on the farms in western Wales. However, nobody has told the Corgi he's not big!

These dogs are lively and tenacious with active minds and big personalities.

For an in-depth look at the Corgi temperament, see **Chapter 8. Typical Corgi Traits.** In the meantime, here is a brief description of both types.

The American Kennel Club says this of Pembroke: "Among the most agreeable of all small housedogs, the Pembroke Welsh Corgi is a strong, athletic, and lively little herder who is affectionate and companionable without being needy.

"They are one of the world's most popular herding breeds. At 10 to 12 inches at the shoulder and 27 to 30 pounds, a well-built male Pembroke presents a big dog in a small package. Short but powerful legs, muscular thighs, and a deep chest equip him for a hard day's work.

"Built long and low, Pembrokes are surprisingly quick and agile. They can be red, sable, fawn, and black and tan, with or without white markings. The Pembroke, *pictured,* is a bright, sensitive dog who enjoys play with his human family and responds well to training.

"As herders bred to move cattle, they are fearless and independent. They are vigilant watchdogs, with acute senses and a 'big dog' bark. Families who can meet the bold but kindly Pembroke's need for activity and togetherness will never have a more loyal, loving pet."

Linda Roberts, of Cherastayne Pembroke Welsh Corgis, and Breed Health Co-Ordinator for the Welsh Corgi League, adds: "The Pembroke Corgi is extremely intelligent and is often said to have the IQ of a seven-year-old child. I can say that some of mine have the IQ of a 16-year-old about to enter the correction system!

"They are very much a breed with which you have to have the upper hand at all times. If you're not up to running the show... your Pembroke will be in charge in no time at all!

"A well-bred Pembroke has a kind, outgoing confident temperament; that is a hallmark of the breed. Some are more outgoing than others and intent on getting up to any amount of mischief that they can find.

"In my opinion, the Pembroke is a very good house dog, very ready to alert their owner to a visitor at the door, or the telephone. Quite how effective they would be if an intruder was brandishing sausages is a different matter!

"It is remarkable how different even members of the same litter can be in terms of barking. I have some that hardly ever bark and the odd ones that can't keep their opinions to themselves. It is important to set firm guidelines when the dog is a youngster and to ensure that it learns in a kind and consistent way when barking is and is not appropriate."

In the US, the main visual difference between the two breeds is the Cardigan's long bushy tail, while the Pembroke's is docked. However, most Pembrokes in the rest of the world have tails.

There is also the fairly rare phenomenon of a Pembroke being born with a natural bobtail, *seen here on prizewinning UK Pembroke Marshall (Woodhenge Star Mariner), bred by Mr and Mrs Coulson. Photo by Robin Bruce.*

There are also personality differences between the two breeds, as summed up here by Tracy Irving, breeder and exhibitor of both Pembrokes and Cardigans:

"Pembrokes are much more outgoing than Cardigans; they go head-first into almost anything they do. Cardigans are more studious and need to see it, smell it or hear it a couple of times before deciding it might actually be safe."

Karen Hewitt, Chairperson of the Cardigan Welsh Corgi Association and breeder of Cardhew Cardigan Corgis, says: "Cardigans are very intelligent dogs, usually willing and eager to please, but they can also be stubborn and wilful. They are bright enough to work out how to get things done the way they want them done, which may not always be your way!

"All of the Cardis I have owned have been loving and affectionate, outgoing and even-tempered, they will have a go at anything if it means that they can spend time with their families. They are great with children, and all-round good family dogs.

"However, they are also working dogs, they have a strong instinct to protect their homes and owners. Our dogs at home will willingly get into the most alien situations because we ask them to, and they trust us."

Photo: Karen's Carrie and Sally enjoying their holiday at the seaside.

"We went on holiday to Devon last year and they carefully stepped onto a funicular railway carriage (a mountain railway operated by a cable). It was loud, rattly and bumpy, but as long as we were with them, that was just fine.

"I saw many other large, fearless-looking dogs refuse to enter or sit shivering whilst our girls took it in their stride.

"I have never owned a Pembroke, but I do know several. They are, I believe, everybody's friend, where a Cardi might sit back and decide whether or not they want to know you."

History

Although they are both Welsh, surprisingly the origins of the Pembroke and Cardigan are quite different. You'll see this if you look at them side by side; as well as the Pembroke's lack of tail in the US, there are other physical differences.

The Cardigan is a larger dog with big, rounded ears and a face more akin to a hound, while the Pembroke is descended from the Spitz breeds (Spitz, Pomeranian, Samoyed, Husky, etc.) and has a thicker coat, and more pointed ears and face, like a fox.

The Corgi is thought to be one of the oldest British native breeds. According to Encyclopædia Britannica, a dog resembling the Cardigan Welsh Corgi was brought to Cardiganshire (western Wales in the UK) by the Celts when they migrated around 1200 BC. The original type, known as the **Bronant**, was related to the Teckel, forefathers of the Dachshund.

The ancestors of the Pembroke Welsh Corgi are believed to be dogs brought to Pembrokeshire (the south west corner of Wales, just below Cardiganshire) by Flemish weavers in the 10th or 11th century AD.

Another theory is that around the same time, Viking raiders brought their Swedish Vallhunds when they invaded the British Isles, and the resulting interbreeding with native dogs produced the Pembroke. Although the specific details have been lost in the Welsh mists of time, it is not disputed that the Corgi has been around for over 1,000 years - perhaps as long as 3,000 in the case of the Cardigan. A Welsh cattle dog is mentioned in the Domesday Book of 1086.

Wales is steeped in folklore and according to Welsh legend, the origins of the Pembroke lie with the fairies and elves, who used the Welsh Corgi to pull their fairy coaches and take them into battle. One version says that the Pembrokes were also warriors and great helpers to the fairy folk.

Every time they flew over the land with their Corgis, the King and Queen of the Fairies saw a family working all hours just to feed themselves, with no time for rest. They felt sorry for them and gifted their Corgis to the family to help them on the farm. If you look closely, even today you can see the marks of the 'fairy saddle' over the shoulders in the Pembroke's coat, especially on sables.

The Farmer's Right-Hand Man

The word 'Corgi' derives from the Welsh language; its meaning is not entirely clear. *Cor* could mean dwarf or to watch over, *ci/gi* means dog. For a long time, the Welsh referred to both types of Corgi as either *'Ci-llathed'* meaning yard-long dog (a Welsh yard was 40 inches) or *'Ci Sawdlo,'* meaning heel dog.

The Corgi is a dwarf breed; they were bred down from larger working dogs. West Wales is wet and windy and some of the hilly terrain is rocky, so the early farmers and crofters needed a tough, honest dog that they could easily train and rely on to help them - but not too big to feed. The Corgi fitted the bill perfectly.

The Corgi's size and agility made him ideal for working with cattle because he could nip at the livestock's heels without being kicked. These plucky dogs were excellent herders, a trait that became particularly valuable with the Enclosure Acts of the 17th century.

The Acts abolished the open field system which had been the way people farmed for centuries. Fields were fenced and crofters had to use common land, which was often higher up and further afield, to graze their animals.

The Corgi's natural style of working is droving - moving or driving the herd from behind and the flanks - rather than herding them together (like the Border Collie). As competition among crofters for grazing land became fierce, Corgis were invaluable in helping them not only to drive their cattle to new pastures on common land, but also to guard the animals from predators and stop them from straying once there.

The Corgi was a Jack of All Trades and the crofter's right-hand man. These tenacious dogs guarded the farmyard as well as the stock. According to The Cardigan Welsh Corgi Club of America: "The Cardigan's original work was to go before his master's cattle herd and clear the way by chasing off potential predators as well as trespassing herds, providing an area for grazing.

"Later, the Cardi began to act as a herder, working behind the master's cattle and as a *'drover,'* driving cattle from the Welsh farms to the English markets."

Before the rail system was developed, cattle, sheep and even geese had to be driven on foot to market. For larger animals these markets could sometimes be as far away as the Midlands in England, well over 100 miles away from western Wales, and the journey could take weeks.

Sometimes the drovers were also employed to carry important documents or money across the country. It was common for them to use lesser-known paths across rough terrain in the mountains to avoid toll roads, and the hardy Corgis not only drove the animals, but also helped to protect their masters from highwaymen.

Amazingly, at the end of the drove the Corgis simply found their own way home! They retraced the route of the drove, stopping at the same inns to be fed by the innkeepers, who'd been paid to feed them by the drover on the way to market. How about that for intelligence?!

Two things happened to make the Corgi mostly redundant. Welsh farmers began to raise sheep in fenced pastures and the advent of steam trains in the 1800s meant that livestock could be delivered to the markets much quicker.

Droving became a thing of the past and the Welsh farmers turned to the Border Collie to herd the enclosed sheep. Corgis settled down very successfully into their new roles mainly as companions and household pets.

Development of the Breeds

In 1859, the first conformation dog show was held in Newcastle-Upon Tyne. It was tagged on to the cattle show and the only dogs represented were sporting dogs: Setters and Pointers. Fanciers of other breeds soon got involved, but the Corgi arrived late to the show scene.

It wasn't until 1925 that The Welsh Corgi Club was formed in Haverfordwest, Wales, to represent both the Pembroke and Cardigan - and the first Corgi was entered in a show later that year. The first Championship was awarded in 1928 to a red and white Pembroke bitch named Shan Fach at Cardiff.

For the next few years, the two breeds were interbred and shown in the same classes, but the exhibitors were unhappy as the result depended on whether the individual judge preferred Cardigans or Pembrokes!

In 1934 they got their wish when the UK Kennel Club recognised the Cardigan and Pembroke as two separate breeds. Some 59 Cardigans and 240 Pembrokes were initially entered in the pedigree register. Interestingly, the decision of which breed a dog belonged to was left to the owner!

The first Pembrokes, Little Madam and Captain William Lewis, arrived in America the same year with Mrs. Lewis Roesler of Massachusetts, a well-known breeder of Old English Sheepdogs.

It is said that she saw Little Madam, **pictured,** at Paddington Station while on a visit to a show in England, and bought her on the spot for £12!

Little Madam was the first Pembroke to be registered with the AKC and became the first American Champion Corgi Bitch in 1935, beaten to the overall Champion title by the male UK/Am Ch (Sierra) Bowhit Pivot who had been imported into California.

One of the earliest breed notes from the American Kennel Gazette in March 1935, described both types of Corgi as "the big little dog." The note continued: "In character and disposition each type is superlative, most affectionate and responsive, calm and obedient, and usually courteous to strangers, not noisy."

Unlike with some other breeds, the Corgi has remained largely true to his roots. Their indomitable spirit, loyalty to their owners and love of a challenge is still very much evident in today's Pembrokes and Cardigans.

The One and Only...

They'll make you laugh - and they might make you cry when they're driving you nuts as puppies, barking their heads off or disappearing in the opposite direction, deaf to your frantic calls! But whatever life throws at you, one thing is sure: your Corgi will be there for you through thick and thin.

The following people have all added their 100s of years of combined expertise to this book: leading breeders of both Pembrokes and Cardigans from the US, UK and Europe, several committee members of The Welsh Corgi League (WCL), Chairperson and committee members of the Cardigan Welsh Corgi Association (CWCA), a professional trainer of Corgis, three people who train their Corgis for canine competitions, a veterinary surgeon, Breed Health Co-ordinator, international exhibitors and show judges, and six highly experienced Pembroke owners.

And it's fair to say that they know a thing or two about Corgis! Here's a few of their stories of the unique traits of their Corgis.

Karen Hewitt, Cardhew Cardigan Welsh Corgis: "The right dog with the right trainer can go a long way. But be aware that they may be training you, rather than the other way around.

"We had a lovely little bitch call Cilla who needed to go out constantly. She would sit at the door over and over again; we were worried that she might have a bladder problem. Then we realised why...

"We had encouraged her to come in by giving her a small treat when she came back into the house after visiting the garden. By the time she was a few months old, she came to realise that there was an almost inexhaustible supply of biscuits if she went in and out enough. Clever girl!"

Lucy Badham-Thornhill: "I was walking and scrambling up around 300 feet of steep woody slope. Beaty, my Corgi, managed the first few yards then unfortunately went lame. I carried her up a bit, then put her down - still lame.

"This continued several times until, in the end, I carried her all the way up. When we got to the top, she scampered off without even a backward glance!"

Lucy added: "We have had a lot of different animals around over the years and never had any problems with Corgis being aggressive towards anything. One supervised introduction usually suffices to establish a new family member.

"My son used to have rats, which escaped periodically. Floss, the Corgi, would always find the escapee and sit quietly watching till one of us arrived to collect him!"

Kevin Egan describes his Pembroke Edward's quirky habits and enthusiastic approach to life: "Edward is our dog at home - or rather, it is his residence now, we are *his* people and he makes sure that we walk him and feed him on time - them's the rules!

"Our day starts at 7.30am for the walk to our local park. Edward has some playmates that he enjoys to run with, and his favourite is a white retriever called Charmer.

"When they meet, they adopt stances about 10 yards apart - similar to a couple of gunslingers in a cowboy Western. The retriever stands motionless trying to look nonchalant; whilst Edward crouches slightly, in the way that lions do while hunting for prey in a wildlife documentary!

"They both eye each other up for a few seconds then the retriever usually makes the first move by rushing past Edward, who then bursts into action like a small rapid ginger torpedo in pursuit of his quarry, sometimes catching him with a head butt to the ribs, but mostly missing by a fraction. They love it!"

The Corgi's love of food is notorious, and Kevin added: "Edward was sitting with me on the boundary watching a local cricket match one afternoon. At the 4pm tea interval, he turned around to look at both scorers as they prepared the players' drinks and sandwiches on the picnic table in front of the scorebox.

"Unwisely, both vacated their seats briefly and Edward leapt on the table seat in a flash, greedily devouring a tomato and getting stuck into some tuna and mayo spread. One of the scorers' guests appeared on the scene and screamed loudly: "Help!! There's a huge fox eating our tea!"

Best of friends: Edward, centre, with young Barney, left, and Mungo in Kevin's garden.

Many, but not all, Corgis like water. Hungarian breeder Alexandra Trefán-Török, of Born To Be Corgis, tells how her dogs follow their natural herding instincts - even when swimming:

"Most of my Corgis are water-addicted. They are very confident in the water and their tails help them to change direction. They also fetch the ball easily. We have a fresh water pond in our garden and my Cardigan Tsunami is the biggest fan.

"She goes to swim about five or six times every day; she is a very good swimmer, paddling smoothly without any effort. She just feels so well in the water. Some of my younger Pembrokes follow her, but they prefer to swim only during summer time.

"We are always laughing when we watch them in the water because they try to herd the goldfish while they are swimming. They are true fish herders and keep them in a circle; I can't explain how funny it is!"

Vicky Methuen tells a story that illustrates both the intelligence and herding instincts of these dogs: "My grandparents had a pub near Conwy in Wales, and a Pembroke called Billy Corgi.

"Regulars were always greeted by Billy, who would herd them over towards the bar where my grandfather was waiting to ask them what they were drinking.

"When they ordered a pint of best bitter, Billy would wander over to the beer pumps, and when they ordered a gin and tonic, Billy would walk towards the spirit optics.

"We can only assume that with the regulars who made a fuss of him, Billy somehow learnt to associate their voices with the actions of my grandfather; so, a male voice meant a trip to the pumps and a female voice meant the optics!"

Vicky's second story is a lovely example of the Corgi's big heart: "In my mother's final years, when she was over 90, I used to push her in the wheelchair on walks with Purdy, our Pembroke, sitting on her lap. Ears pricked and eyes focused on the path ahead, Purdy was the lookout!

"A few weeks after Mum died, I was walking Purdy on the same walk. Coming towards us from a distance was an elderly couple, the man pushing his wife in a wheelchair.

"Suddenly Purdy's ears pricked up, her trot turned into a canter and I realised she was heading full tilt towards this couple... I shouted a warning, but to my horror, this elderly lady suddenly found 16kg of Corgi jumping on to her lap!

"She listened to my explanation and took it all in good heart, saying how very touching it was."

Photo: Yes, Corgis do smile! Vicky's Brona, aged six, smiles for the camera (and a treat) on the command "Puppy, puppy, puppy!"

A Final Few Words...

And finally, we asked our experts to sum up the Corgi in a few words:

- ❖ Smart, Alert, Social, Honest
- ❖ Healthy, Intelligent, Outgoing
- ❖ Fun, Cheeky, Loyal
- ❖ Loyal, Smart, The Perfect Companion
- ❖ A Big Personality
- ❖ Affectionate, Intelligent, Loyal, Greedy
- ❖ Loyal, Active Companion
- ❖ Smart, Loyal, Sassy
- ❖ Lovable, Curious, Bold, Family
- ❖ Clever, Attractive, Energetic, Loyal
- ❖ Intelligent, Witty, Versatile, AWESOME
- ❖ A Friend Forever!
- ❖ Beautiful, Loyal and Loving... I could give you dozens more, all complimentary

Arm yourself with a waterproof coat, lots of time and patience and a sense of humour.

Then read on to learn how to understand, train and take best care of these wonderful dogs for the rest of their lives, and how to successfully build a deep bond that will become one of the most important things in your life - and certainly theirs.

2. Breed Standard

The Breed Standard is a blueprint not only for the ideal appearance of each breed, but also for character and temperament, how the dog moves and what colours are acceptable.

In other words, it ensures that a Pembroke looks and acts like a Pembroke, and a Cardigan looks and acts like a Cardigan, ensuring they are "fit for function, fit for life."

Although they are both Welsh Corgis, the Pembroke (Pem) and the Cardigan (Cardi) are two entirely separate breeds, each with their own Breed Standard.

....

The Breed Standard is administered by the Kennel Club in the UK. In the USA it is written by the national breed clubs and approved by the AKC (American Kennel Club). The Kennel Clubs then keep the register of purebred (pedigree) dogs. Dogs entered in conformation shows run under Kennel Club and AKC rules are judged against the Breed Standard.

Good breeders strive to breed their dogs to the Breed Standard. Breeders of Corgis that take part in canine competitions also want to ensure that the Corgi's natural herding instincts are passed down through their bloodlines from one generation to the next.

Responsible breeders select only the finest dogs for reproduction, based on the health, look and temperament of the parents and their ancestors. If you are looking to buy a puppy, have a good look at the parents - or at least the mother. Purebred puppies usually resemble their parents.

The Corgi was originally bred in Wales to herd farm animals. Both types are in the **Herding Group** in the US and the **Pastoral Group** in the UK.

The AKC says: "All Herding breeds share an instinctual ability to control the movement of other animals. These breeds were developed to gather, herd and protect livestock.

"The herding instinct in these breeds is so strong that Herding breeds have been known to gently herd their owners, especially the children of the family. In general, these intelligent dogs make excellent companions and respond beautifully to training exercises."

Photo: Pembroke (left) and Cardigan.

The Kennel Club says this about the Pastoral Group: "The Pastoral Group consists of herding dogs that are associated with working cattle, sheep, reindeer and other cloven-footed animals. Usually this type of dog has a weatherproof double coat to protect it from the elements when working in severe conditions.

"Breeds such as the Collie family, Old English Sheepdogs and Samoyeds, who have been herding reindeer for centuries, are but a few included in this group."

Differences

Breeders of the respective two types would say that there are numerous differences. However, the main ones can be summed up as:

- **Temperament** – Pembrokes tend to be spirited and outgoing by nature, while Cardigans can be more reserved and laid-back
- **Size** – Cardigans are slightly bigger with heavier bones and longer bodies
- **Tails** – The Cardi has a fox-like tail. In the US, Pems' tails are docked.

  Docking the tails of pet dogs is illegal in the UK and Europe, so Pems have a tail in these countries *(pictured)*, except a few that are born with a natural bobtail

- **Faces** – The Pembroke has more pointed ears and nose, similar to a fox
- **Ears** – The Cardigan's ears are longer and rounded
- **Eyes** – Both have black eye rims, but Cardigan Blue Merles may have pale blue, blue or blue-flecked eyes
- **Front Feet** – Straight on a Pembroke, turned out on a Cardigan
- **Colours** – Both types can be Red or Sable. The Pembroke can also be Fawn, or Black and Tan, but the Cardigan comes in a bigger range of colours, with Blue Merle, Brindle, Tricolour with Brindle, and Tricolour with Red all being acceptable

Characteristics

The AKC has this description: "Among the most agreeable of all small housedogs, the Pembroke Welsh Corgi is a strong, athletic, and lively little herder who is affectionate and companionable without being needy. They are one the world's most popular herding breeds.

"At 10 to 12 inches at the shoulder and 27 to 30 pounds, a well-built male Pembroke presents a big dog in a small package. Short but powerful legs, muscular thighs, and a deep chest equip him for a hard day's work. Built long and low, Pembrokes are surprisingly quick and agile.

"They can be red, sable, fawn, and black and tan, with or without white markings. The Pembroke is a bright, sensitive dog who enjoys play with his human family and responds well to training.

"As herders bred to move cattle, they are fearless and independent. They are vigilant watchdogs, with acute senses and a *'big dog'* bark. Families who can meet their bold but kindly Pembroke's need for activity and togetherness will never have a more loyal, loving pet."

The UK Kennel Club says: "Slightly smaller than the Cardigan, not quite as long in body and with a smaller ear and straighter front legs, the Pembroke was traditionally docked, but that differentiation no longer exists since the docking ban. However, some breeders have worked hard to produce natural bobtails.

"The Pembroke has always been the more popular breed, perhaps helped by the Royal patronage it has received since the reign of King George VI and carried on by our present monarch Queen Elizabeth II."

Photo: Pembroke with a full tail herding sheep.

The AKC's description of the Cardigan states: "The Cardigan Welsh Corgi is a masterpiece of the breeder's art. Every aspect of its makeup is perfectly suited to moving cattle, and yet it is so congenial and sweet-faced that it would be a cherished companion even if it never did a day's work.

"Long, low-set dogs with sturdy bone, short legs, and a deep chest, Cardigans are powerful workers of deceptive speed and grace. Cardis can weigh anywhere from 25 to 34 pounds, with females at the lower end of the scale. They come in several coat colors, from red to the popular blue-merle pattern.

"The quickest way to distinguish Cardis from their cousins, Pembroke Welsh Corgis, is to check out the hindquarters: Cardigans have tails; Pembrokes do not. Cardis are trainable, faithful, and vigilant guardians with a *'big dog'* bark. Well-socialized Cardis are especially fond of kids and agreeable with other pets.

"These athletic, rugged herders have a love for the outdoors, and they thrive on mental stimulation and physical activity."

The UK Kennel Club: "Of the two types of Corgi, the Cardigan is thought to be the older. The word Corgi is thought to be rooted in the Celtic 'cor' meaning dwarf and 'gi' – dog. They are both short legged which equips them well for the job of driving livestock forward.

"The Cardigan has always been undocked, and was once known affectionately as the Yard Dog (Ci Llatharid), because the measurement from his nose to the end of his tail was a Welsh yard (102 cm/40 in). He is the longer-bodied of the two breeds and his front legs are slightly bowed.

"The two breeds have traditionally been used as heelers, driving cattle by day and guarding them at night. At one time the Cardigan and the Pembroke were allowed to interbreed freely but in 1934 The Kennel Club recognised them as two separate breeds."

 If you haven't chosen your puppy yet, read the Breed Standard and Kennel Club descriptions of the breed. This is what you should be looking for in terms of appearance and natural temperament. Compare the mother of any litter you visit with this ideal list of attributes.

....

US Breed Standard - Pembroke

General Appearance: Low-set, strong, sturdily built and active, giving an impression of substance and stamina in a small space. Should not be so low and heavy-boned as to appear coarse or overdone, nor so light-boned as to appear racy.

Outlook bold, but kindly. Expression intelligent and interested. Never shy nor vicious. Correct type, including general balance and outline, attractiveness of headpiece, intelligent outlook and correct temperament are of primary importance.

Movement is especially important, particularly as viewed from the side. A dog with smooth and free gait has to be reasonably sound and must be highly regarded. A minor fault must never take precedence over the above desired qualities.

A dog must be very seriously penalized for the following faults, regardless of whatever desirable qualities the dog may present: oversized or undersized; button, rose or drop ears; overshot or undershot bite; fluffies, whitelies, mismarks or bluies.

Photo: Ch Heronsway Heartbeat, one of the USA's top winning bitches, bred by Mrs Anne Bowes.

Size, Proportion, Substance: Size - Height (from ground to highest point on withers) should be 10 to 12 inches. Weight is in proportion to size, not exceeding 30 pounds for dogs and 28 pounds for bitches.

In show condition, the preferred medium-sized dog of correct bone and substance will weigh approximately 27 pounds, with bitches approximately 25 pounds. Obvious oversized specimens and diminutive toylike individuals must be very severely penalized.

Proportions - Moderately long and low. The distance from the withers to the base of the tail should be approximately 40 percent greater than the distance from the withers to the ground. **Substance** - Should not be so low and heavy-boned as to appear coarse or overdone, nor so light-boned as to appear racy. Head: The head should be foxy in shape and appearance.

Expression - Intelligent and interested, but not sly. Skull - should be fairly wide and flat between the ears. Moderate amount of stop. Very slight rounding of cheek, not filled in below the eyes, as foreface should be nicely chiseled to give a somewhat tapered muzzle.

Distance from occiput to center of stop to be greater than the distance from stop to nose tip, the proportion being five parts of total distance for the skull and three parts for the foreface. Muzzle should be neither dish-faced nor Roman-nosed.

Eyes - Oval, medium in size, not round, nor protruding, nor deepset and piglike. Set somewhat obliquely. Variations of brown in harmony with coat color. Eye rims dark, preferably black. While dark eyes enhance the expression, true black eyes are most undesirable, as are yellow or bluish eyes.

Ears - Erect, firm, and of medium size, tapering slightly to a rounded point. Ears are mobile, and react sensitively to sounds. A line drawn from the nose tip through the eyes to the ear tips, and across, should form an approximate equilateral triangle. Bat ears, small catlike ears, overly large weak ears, hooded ears, ears carried too high or too low, are undesirable. Button, rose or drop ears are very serious faults.

Nose - Black and fully pigmented.

Mouth - Scissors bite, the inner side of the upper incisors touching the outer side of the lower incisors. Level bite is acceptable. Overshot or undershot bite is a very serious fault.

Lips - Black, tight with little or no fullness.

Neck, Topline, Body: Neck - Fairly long. Of sufficient length to provide over-all balance of the dog. Slightly arched, clean and blending well into the shoulders. A very short neck giving a stuffy appearance and a long, thin or ewe neck are faulty.

Topline - Firm and level, neither riding up to nor falling away at the croup. A slight depression behind the shoulders caused by heavier neck coat meeting the shorter body coat is permissible.

Body - Rib cage should be well sprung, slightly egg-shaped and moderately long. Deep chest, well let down between the forelegs. Exaggerated lowness interferes with the desired freedom of movement and should be penalized. Viewed from above, the body should taper slightly to end of loin. Loin short. Round or flat rib cage, lack of brisket, extreme length or cobbiness, are undesirable.

Tail - Docked as short as possible without being indented. Occasionally a puppy is born with a natural dock, which if sufficiently short, is acceptable. A tail up to two inches in length is allowed, but if carried high tends to spoil the contour of the topline.

Forequarters: Legs - Short, forearms turned slightly inward, with the distance between wrists less than between the shoulder joints, so that the front does not appear absolutely straight. Ample bone carried right down into the feet.

Pasterns firm and nearly straight when viewed from the side. Weak pasterns and knuckling over are serious faults. Shoulder blades long and well laid back along the rib cage. Upper arms nearly equal in length to shoulder blades. Elbows parallel to the body, not prominent, and well set back to allow a line perpendicular to the ground to be drawn from tip of the shoulder blade through to elbow.

Feet: Oval, with the two center toes slightly in advance of the two outer ones. Turning neither in nor out. Pads strong and feet arched. Nails short. Dewclaws on both forelegs and hindlegs usually removed. Too round, long and narrow, or splayed feet are faulty.

Hindquarters: Ample bone, strong and flexible, moderately angulated at stifle and hock. Exaggerated angulation is as faulty as too little. Thighs should be well muscled. Hocks short, parallel, and when viewed from the side are perpendicular to the ground.

Photo: "Reggie" aged 21 months, owned by Linda Roberts. UK Ch. Rosewood Sea Dragon of Cherastayne, bred by Lisa Coit in the USA and imported into the UK. Photo by Wendy McColl.

Barrel hocks or cowhocks are most objectionable. Slipped or double-jointed hocks are very faulty. Feet - as in front.

Coat: Medium length; short, thick, weather-resistant undercoat with a coarser, longer outer coat. Over-all length varies, with slightly thicker and longer ruff around the neck, chest and on the shoulders. The body coat lies flat. Hair is slightly longer on back of forelegs and underparts and somewhat fuller and longer on rear of hindquarters.

The coat is preferably straight, but some waviness is permitted. This breed has a shedding coat, and seasonal lack of undercoat should not be too severely penalized, providing the hair is glossy, healthy and well groomed. A wiry, tightly marcelled coat is very faulty, as is an overly short, smooth and thin coat.

Very Serious Fault - Fluffies - a coat of extreme length with exaggerated feathering on ears, chest, legs and feet, underparts and hindquarters. Trimming such a coat does not make it any more acceptable. The Corgi should be shown in its natural condition, with no trimming permitted except to tidy the feet, and, if desired, remove the whiskers.

Color: The outer coat is to be of self colors in red, sable, fawn, black and tan with or without white markings. White is acceptable on legs, chest, neck (either in part or as a collar), muzzle, underparts and as a narrow blaze on head.

Very Serious Faults -
Whitelies - Body color white, with red or dark markings.
Blues - Colored portions of the coat have a distinct bluish or smoky cast. This coloring is associated with extremely light or blue eyes, liver or gray eye rims, nose and lip pigment.
Mismarks - Self colors with any area of white on the back between withers and tail, on sides between elbows and back of hindquarters, or on ears.
Black with white markings and no tan present.

Gait: Free and smooth. Forelegs should reach well forward without too much lift, in unison with the driving action of the hind legs. The correct shoulder assembly and well-fitted elbows allow a long, free stride in front.

Viewed from the front, legs do not move in exact parallel planes, but incline slightly inward to compensate for shortness of leg and width of chest.

Hind legs should drive well under the body and move on a line with the forelegs, with hocks turning neither in nor out. Feet must travel parallel to the line of motion with no tendency to swing out, cross over or interfere with each other. Short, choppy movement, rolling or high-stepping gait, close or overly wide coming or going, are incorrect.

This is a herding dog, which must have the agility, freedom of movement, and endurance to do the work for which he was developed.

Temperament: Outlook bold, but kindly. Never shy or vicious. The judge shall dismiss from the ring any Pembroke Welsh Corgi that is excessively shy.

....

UK Breed Standard - Pembroke

NOTE: The Pembroke is officially referred to as: *"The Welsh Corgi Pembroke"* in the UK.

General appearance: Low set, strong, sturdily built, alert and active, giving impression of substance and stamina in small space.

Characteristics: bold in outlook, workmanlike.

Temperament: Outgoing and friendly, never nervous or aggressive.

Head and skull: Head foxy in shape and appearance, with alert, intelligent expression, skull fairly wide and flat between ears, moderate amount of stop. Length of foreface in proportion to skull 3 to 5. Muzzle slightly tapering. Nose black.

Eyes: Well set, round, medium size, brown, blending with colour of coat.

Ears: Pricked, medium sized, slightly rounded. Line drawn from tip of nose through eye should, if extended, pass through, or close to tip of ear.

Mouth: Jaws strong with perfect, regular and complete scissor bite, i.e. upper teeth closely overlapping lower teeth and set square to the jaws.

Neck: Fairly long.

Forequarters: Lower legs short and as straight as possible, forearm moulded round chest. Ample bone, carried right down to feet. Elbows fitting closely to sides, neither loose nor tied.

Shoulders well laid, and angulated at 90 degrees to the upper arm.

Body: Medium length, well-sprung ribs, not short coupled, slightly tapering, when viewed from above. Level topline. Chest broad and deep, well let down between forelegs.

Hindquarters: Strong and flexible, well-angulated stifle. Legs short. Ample bone carried right down to feet. Hocks straight when viewed from behind.

Feet: Oval, toes strong, well arched, and tight, two centre toes slightly advance of two outer, pads strong and well arched. Nails short.

Tail: Previously customarily docked short. **Undocked:** set in line with the topline. Natural carriage which may be above or below topline when moving or alert. Natural bobtails may occur, when the tail can be of any length, carried above or below topline when moving or alert.

Gait/movement: Free and active, neither loose nor tied. Forelegs move well forward, without too much lift, in unison with thrusting action of hindlegs.

Coat: Medium length, straight with dense undercoat, never soft, wavy or wiry.

Colour: Self colours in Red, Sable, Fawn, Black and Tan, with or without white markings on legs, brisket and neck. Some white on head and foreface permissible.

Size: Height: approximately 25-30 cms (10-12 ins) at shoulder. Weight: dogs: 10-12 kgs (22-26 lbs); bitches: 9-11 kgs (20-24 lbs).

....

US Breed Standard – Cardigan

General Appearance: Low set with moderately heavy bone and deep chest. Overall silhouette long in proportion to height, culminating in a low tail set and fox-like brush. General Impression - A handsome, powerful, small dog, capable of both speed and endurance, intelligent, sturdily built but not coarse.

Size, Proportion, Substance: Overall balance is more important than absolute size. Dogs and bitches should be from 10½ to 12½ inches at the withers when standing naturally. The ideal length/height ratio is 1.8:1 when measuring from the point of the breast bone (prosternum) to the rear of the hip (ischial tuberosity) and measuring from the ground to the point of the withers.

Ideally, dogs should be from 30 to 38 pounds; bitches from 25 to 34 pounds. Lack of overall balance, oversized or undersized are serious faults

Head: The head should be refined in accordance with the sex and substance of the dog. It should never appear so large and heavy nor so small and fine as to be out of balance with the rest of the dog. **Expression** alert and gentle, watchful, yet friendly.

Eyes medium to large, not bulging, with dark rims and distinct corners. Widely set. Clear and dark in harmony with coat color. Blue eyes (including partially blue eyes), or one dark and one blue eye permissible in blue merles, and in any other coat color than blue merle are a disqualification.

Ears large and prominent in proportion to size of dog. Slightly rounded at the tip, and of good strong leather. Moderately wide at the base, carried erect and sloping slightly forward when alert.

When erect, tips are slightly wide of a straight line drawn from the tip of the nose through the center of the eye. Small and/or pointed ears are serious faults. Drop ears are a disqualification.

Skull - Top moderately wide and flat between the ears, showing no prominence of occiput, tapering towards the eyes. Slight depression between the eyes. Cheeks flat with some chiseling where the cheek meets the foreface and under the eye. There should be no prominence of cheekbone.

Muzzle from the tip of the nose to the base of the stop should be shorter than the length of the skull from the base of the stop to the high point of the occiput, the proportion being about three parts muzzle to five parts skull; rounded but not blunt; tapered but not pointed. In profile the plane of the muzzle should parallel that of the skull, but on a lower level due to a definite but moderate stop.

Nose black, except in blue merles where black noses are preferred but butterfly noses are tolerated. A nose other than solid black in any other color is a disqualification. Lips fit cleanly and evenly together all around. Jaws strong and clean. Underjaw moderately deep and well formed, reaching to the base of the nose and rounded at the chin. Teeth strong and regular.

Scissors bite preferred; i.e., inner side of upper incisors fitting closely over outer side of lower incisors. Overshot, undershot, or wry bite are serious faults.

Neck, Topline, Body: Neck moderately long and muscular without throatiness. Well developed, especially in males, and in proportion to the dog's build. Neck well set on; fits into strong, well-shaped shoulders.

Topline level. Body long and strong. Chest moderately broad with prominent breastbone. Deep brisket, with well sprung ribs to allow for good lungs. Ribs extending well back. Loin - short, strong, moderately tucked up. Waist well defined. Croup - Slight downward slope to the tail set.

Tail - set fairly low on body line and reaching well below hock. Carried low when standing or moving slowly, streaming out parallel to ground when at a dead run, lifted when excited, but never curled over the back. High tail set is a serious fault.

Forequarters: The moderately broad chest tapers to a deep brisket, well let down between the forelegs. Shoulders slope downward and outward from the withers sufficiently to accommodate desired rib-spring. Shoulder blade (scapula) long and well laid back, meeting upper arm (humerus) at close to a right angle. Humerus nearly as long as scapula.

Elbows should fit close, being neither loose nor tied. The forearms (ulna and radius) should be curved to fit spring of ribs. The curve in the forearm makes the wrists (carpal joints) somewhat closer together than the elbows. The pasterns are strong and flexible. Dewclaws removed.

The feet are relatively large and rounded, with well filled pads. They point slightly outward from a straight-ahead position to balance the width of the shoulders. This outward point is not to be more than 30 degrees from center line when viewed from above. The toes should not be splayed.

The correct Cardigan front is neither straight nor so crooked as to appear unsound. Overall, the bone should be heavy for a dog of this size, but not so heavy as to appear coarse or reduce agility. Knuckling over, straight front, fiddle front are serious faults.

Hindquarters: Well-muscled and strong, but slightly less wide than shoulders. Hipbone (pelvis) slopes downward with the croup, forming a right angle with the femur at the hip socket. There should be moderate angulation at stifle and hock. Hocks well let down. Metatarsi perpendicular to the ground and parallel to each other. Dewclaws removed.

Feet point straight ahead and are slightly smaller and more oval than front. Toes arched. Pads well filled. Overall, the hindquarters must denote sufficient power to propel this low, relatively heavy herding dog efficiently over rough terrain.

Coat: Medium length but dense as it is double. Outer hairs slightly harsh in texture; never wiry, curly or silky. Lies relatively smooth and is weather resistant. The insulating undercoat is short, soft and thick. A correct coat has short hair on ears, head, the legs; medium hair on body; and slightly longer, thicker hair in ruff, on the backs of the thighs to form "pants," and on the underside of the tail. The coat should not be so exaggerated as to appear fluffy.

This breed has a shedding coat, and seasonal lack of undercoat should not be too severely penalized, providing the hair is healthy. Trimming is not allowed except to tidy feet and, if desired, remove whiskers. Soft guard hairs, uniform length, wiry, curly, silky, overly short and/or flat coats are not desired. A distinctly long or fluffy coat is an extremely serious fault.

Color: All shades of red, sable and brindle. Black with or without tan or brindle points. Blue merle, *pictured,* (black and gray; marbled) with or without tan or brindle points. There is no color preference.

White flashings are usual on the neck (either in part or as a collar), chest, legs, muzzle, underparts, tip of tail and as a blaze on head.

White on the head should not predominate and should never surround the eyes. Any color other than specified and/or body color predominantly white are disqualifications.

Gait: Free and smooth. Effortless. Viewed from the side, forelegs should reach well forward when moving at a trot, without much lift, in unison with driving action of hind legs. The correct shoulder assembly and well fitted elbows allow for a long free stride in front. Viewed from the front, legs do not move in exact parallel planes, but incline slightly inward to compensate for shortness of leg and width of chest.

Hind legs, when trotting, should reach well under body, move on a line with the forelegs, with the hocks turning neither in nor out, and in one continuous motion drive powerfully behind, well beyond the set of the tail.

Feet must travel parallel to the line of motion with no tendency to swing out, cross over, or interfere with each other. Short choppy movement, rolling or high-stepping gait, close or overly wide coming or going, are incorrect.

This is a herding dog which must have the agility, freedom of movement, and endurance to do the work for which he was developed.

Temperament: Even-tempered, loyal, affectionate, and adaptable. Never shy nor vicious.

Disqualifications: Blue eyes, or partially blue eyes, in any coat color other than blue merle. Drop ears. Nose other than solid black except in blue merles. Any color other than specified. Body color predominantly white.

....

UK Breed Standard – Cardigan

General appearance: Sturdy, tough, mobile, capable of endurance. Long in proportion to height, terminating in fox-like brush, set in line with body.

Characteristics: Alert, active and intelligent.

Temperament: Alert, intelligent, steady, not shy or aggressive.

Head and skull: Head foxy in shape and appearance, skull wide and flat between ears tapering towards eyes above which it is slightly domed. Moderate stop. Length of foreface in proportion to skull 3 to 5, muzzle tapering moderately towards nose which projects slightly and in no sense blunt. Underjaw clean cut. Strong but without prominence. Nose black.

Eyes: Medium size, clear, giving kindly, alert but watchful expression. Rather widely set with corners clearly defined. Preferably dark, to blend with coat, eye rims must be black. One or both eyes pale blue, blue or blue flecked, permissible only in blue merles.

Ears: Erect, proportionately rather large to size of dog. Tips slightly rounded, moderately wide at base and set about 9 cms (3½ ins) apart. Carried so that tips are slightly wide of straight line drawn from tip of nose through centre of eyes, and set well back so that they can be laid flat along neck.

Mouth: Teeth strong, with scissor bite, i.e. upper teeth closely overlapping lower teeth and set square to the jaws.

Neck: Muscular, well developed, in proportion to dog's build, fitting into well-sloping shoulders.

Forequarters: Shoulders well laid, angulated at approximately 90 degrees to upper arm; muscular, elbows close to sides. Strong bone carried down to feet.

Legs short but body well clear of the ground, forearms slightly bowed to mould round the chest. Feet turned slightly outwards.

Body: Chest moderately broad with prominent breast bone. Body fairly long and strong, with deep brisket, well-sprung ribs. Clearly defined waist. Topline level.

Hindquarters: Strong, well angulated and aligned with muscular thighs and second thighs, strong bone carried down to feet, legs short; when standing, hocks vertical, viewed from side and rear.

Feet: Round, tight, rather large and well padded.

Tail: Like a fox's brush, set in line with the body and moderately long (to touch or nearly touch ground). Carried low when standing but may be lifted a little above body when moving, not curled over back.

Gait/movement: Free and active, elbows fitting close to sides, neither loose nor tied. Forelegs reaching well forward without too much lift, in unison with thrusting action of hindlegs.

Coat: Short or medium of hard texture. Weather-proof, with good undercoat. Preferably straight.

Colour: Acceptable colours are blue merle, brindle, red, sable, tricolour with brindle points and tricolour with red points.

All of the above with or without the typical white markings on head, neck, chest, underparts, legs and feet, white tail tip. White should not predominate on body or head where it should never surround the eyes. Nose and eye rims must be black. Liver and dilute colours highly undesirable.

Size: Height: ideal 30 cms (12 ins) at shoulder. Weight in proportion to size with overall balance the prime consideration.

···

Glossary

Butterfly nose - patches of pink on the nose

Dewclaw - the extra nail on the upper, inner part of a dog's foot – usually on the front legs

Cobby - thickset

Cow-hocked - knock-kneed on the back legs

Croup - where the back meets the tail

Hock - joint on a dog's back leg below the stifle (knee); like the ankle joint of a human

Haw - the third eyelid or "nictitating membrane"

Occiput - bony bump seen at the top rear of the skull on some breeds

Pastern - the area just above the feet and below the wrist joint (front legs) or hock (back legs)

Roach - when the back is slightly humped rather than flat

Stop - area between a dog's eyes, below the skull

Withers - the ridge between the shoulder blades

3. All the Queen's Corgis

The Queen and her Corgis is the longest love affair in the 1,000-year history of the British Royal Family. It was love at first sight when young Elizabeth and sister Margaret saw their first Pembroke while visiting the children of the Marquess of Bath some 90 years ago.

First in a Long Line

So, in 1933, their beloved father King George VI (then Prince Albert, Duke of York) decided to purchase a Corgi as a gift for his daughters, and Thelma Gray of Rozavel Kennels brought three puppies to the family home.

The girls chose the red Dookie because of his slightly longer (docked) tail; after seven-year-old Elizabeth remarked: "I would like him to have something to wag, otherwise we won't know if he is pleased or not."

Thelma kept the puppy for a few weeks, until the family moved from their city home at 145 Piccadilly to Windsor Castle, where there was lots of space for a dog to run round.

Thelma's kennelman said that the puppy was so pleased with himself and his breed for being chosen, that he refused to eat out of the same dish as the rest of the litter! Jokingly they began to call him *'The Duke,'* which was shortened to *'Dukie'* and finally to *'Dookie.'* The Royals loved the name and it stuck.

Dookie (Rozavel Golden Eagle) became a beloved member of the family and was described as: "Unquestionably the character of the Princesses' delightful canine family," and "a born sentimentalist."

The Princesses loved their new companion and took him for long walks through Windsor Park. They taught Dookie lots of tricks, which he willingly performed for a (forbidden) piece of chocolate cake.

One of his most successful acts was to play leapfrog with Princess Margaret; he would jump over her as she kneeled down. The Princesses even fed Dookie by hand from a dish held by a footman. Like many Corgis, he had a habit of nipping at the heels of guests!

Three years later the family introduced a second Pembroke, Jane (Rozavel Lady Jane), so that Dookie could have an heir. However, the two Corgis remained 'just good friends' - there was no pitter-patter of tiny paws on the expensive carpets at Windsor Castle.

Photo: Princess Elizabeth with Jane (left) and Dookie. It's interesting to note that many of the Queen's early Corgis were almost completely red.

After Dookie's lack of romantic interest, Jane was mated with Rozavel Tafferteffy and produced two pups on Christmas Eve 1938. The Princesses gave them the festive names of Crackers and Carol. Sadly, Carol suffered from fits and had to be put to sleep.

The Queen Mother (as the Princesses' mother was known after Elizabeth became Queen) introduced a disciplined regime for the dogs; each was to have its own wicker basket, raised above the floor to avoid drafts.

Meals were served for each dog in its own dish, the diet approved by veterinary experts with no treats from the royal table. Meat dog biscuits were served in the morning, while the late afternoon meal consisted of dog meal with gravy. Extra biscuits were handed out for celebrations and rewards.

Crackers became the Queen Mother's favourite and retired with her to the Castle of Mey in Scotland, where he lived to the ripe old age of 15.

At that time, Corgis were a relatively rare breed and the general public knew almost nothing about them. But the arrival of Dookie into the Royal Family changed all that. Articles and photographs of him appeared in many of the major newspapers and magazines of the day - although the reports were not always accurate.

Dookie was described variously as "a Labrador puppy," a "Welsh Sheepdog" and, most commonly, a "Welsh Terrier." However, the public gradually came to understand that the dog who'd stolen the hearts of the Princesses was indeed a Pembroke Welsh Corgi - creating the first of several surges in the popularity of the breed due to its royal connections.

Coming of Age

On her 18th birthday on April 21st 1944, Princess Elizabeth was given her own Corgi, Susan, **pictured,** (Hickathrift Pippa by Glamorous Knight), who went on to become the future Queen's faithful companion for over 14 years.

Not many people know that when she and Prince Philip married at Westminster Abbey three years later, Elizabeth hid Susan under a pile of rugs in their open horse-drawn carriage during the celebratory procession through the streets of London.

Susan even joined the 21-year-old Princess and her new husband on their honeymoon at the Balmoral Estate - although, Prince Philip was less keen on the Corgis than his new bride, having been heard to describe them as "too yappy!"

Susan was much-loved by her mistress but less popular with the Royal Household, on whom she left her mark - literally! Susan bit the postman, various members of the royal staff, including the royal clockwinder and a chauffeur and two policemen.

Nearly all of the present royal Corgis can trace their ancestry back to Susan's first litter with Ch. Rozavel Lucky Strike in 1949. Queen Elizabeth was very upset when Susan passed away at the age of nearly 15, as revealed in a letter she wrote to the Sandringham vet, Harold Swann:

"I had always dreaded losing her as I had had her since she was six weeks old, but I am ever so thankful that her suffering was so mercifully short. Yours sincerely, Elizabeth R."

Despite her sadness, the Queen's humour is also portrayed in a separate note to Dr Swann. Replying to his question about how long the plump Susan had been increasing in size, Her Majesty replied: "No idea - she's always been fat!"

Susan is buried in the park of Sandringham estate, Norfolk, where all the royal Corgis are buried. Her gravestone, *pictured,* reads: "Susan, born 20.02.44, died 26.01.59 for almost 15 years the faithful companion of the Queen."

Long Reign

Princess Elizabeth became Queen Elizabeth II in 1952, taking on all the responsibilities that came with the title at the tender age of 25. She was in a game park on a Commonwealth Tour of Kenya when she heard the news of her father's death, and became the first Sovereign in over 200 years to accede to the throne while abroad.

Not only has the Queen continued her long reign, but the Corgis have too. Queen Elizabeth is known for her loyalty and she has stuck with Corgis as her favourite breed - despite owning many other breeds over the decades.

The Queen has had over 30 Corgis, many of which she bred herself; she stopped breeding in 2018. The Corgi roll call of honour includes everyday names mixed with the unusual: Emma, Willow, Linnet, Disco, Monty, Holly, Pharos, Windsor Spark, Heather and Brush, to name but a few.

Three of them, Monty, Willow and Holly, appeared alongside the Queen and Daniel Craig in a James Bond TV sketch set in Buckingham Palace shown during the London 2012 Olympics' opening ceremony.

Photo: The 2016 Vanity Fair magazine cover. Queen Elizabth II celebrates her 90th birthday with her Corgis and Dorgis.

Queen Elizabeth is thought to be the creator of the Dorgi when she mated her Corgi Tiny with Princess Margaret's Dachshund Pipkin.

The royal Corgis and Dorgis lack for nothing. For decades, and until after the death of her beloved husband, Prince Philip, the Queen very much looked forward to her daily walk with her dogs, and over the years she has been known to fill Christmas stockings with toys and treats for them. These days their meals are prepared by a personal chef.

The Corgi has climbed from obscurity to family favourite following films about The Royal Family and the Netflix drama series The Crown. At the end of the day, it's all down to one person.

Queen Elizabeth II's legendary devotion and loyalty to the Corgi over nine decades is unsurpassed.

On behalf of all Corgi lovers everywhere: Thank you, your Majesty.

Sources: Various, especially Wikipedia.

4. Finding Your Puppy

Finding a good puppy can be a minefield. If you haven't got yours yet, read this chapter before you commit to anything; it will increase your chances of finding a healthy, happy Corgi with a good temperament.

The best way to select a puppy is with your HEAD - not your heart! You'll soon find dozens of Corgi puppies advertised, but it requires a bit more time and research to find a first-rate breeder. If you already have your puppy, skip to the next chapter.

....

With their beautiful fluffy faces, expressive eyes, huge ears and inquisitive nature, there are few more appealing things on this Earth than Corgi puppies. If you go to view a litter, the pups are sure to melt your heart and it is extremely difficult - if not downright impossible - to walk away without choosing one.

If you haven't yet chosen your pup and take only one sentence from this entire book, it is this:

FIND AN ETHICAL, KNOWLEDGEABLE BREEDER WHO PRODUCES HEALTHY PUPPIES WITH GOOD TEMPERAMENTS

– even if that means waiting longer than you'd like. It will be worth it in the long run.

 Although both types of Corgi are considered healthy breeds, there are still genetic disorders that can be passed down. So, look for a breeder who health tests. See Chapter 13. Corgi Health for details.

Find a breeder who knows Corgis inside out and who does not offer lots of different breeds.

After all, apart from getting married or having a baby, getting a puppy is one of the most important, demanding, expensive and life-enriching decisions you will ever make.

Your Corgi will love you unconditionally - but there is a price to pay. In return for their devotion - you have to fulfil your part of the bargain.

In the beginning, you have to be prepared to devote much of your day to your new puppy. You have to feed her several times a day and housetrain virtually every hour, you have to give her your attention and start to gently introduce the rules of the house.

You also have to be prepared to part with hard cash for regular healthcare and pet insurance.

Puppies are high energy and hard work! If you are unable to devote the time and money to a new arrival, if you have a very young family, a stressful life or are out at work all day, then now might not be the right time for a puppy. Corgi puppies demand your attention and thrive on being involved. They are not couch potatoes, nor do they like being shut away from people or left alone for long periods, which can result in behaviour issues. This is a natural reaction and is not the dog's fault; they are simply responding to an environment that is failing to meet their needs.

Pick a healthy Corgi pup and they should live for well over a decade, maybe into their teens if you're lucky - so this is certainly a long-term commitment. Before taking the plunge, ask yourself some questions:

Do I Have Enough Time for a Puppy?

Even a strong-willed puppy will feel a bit lonely after leaving mother and littermates for the first time. Spend time with your new arrival to make them feel safe and sound. Ideally, for the first few days you will be around most of the time to help yours settle and to start bonding.

If you work, book time off if you can - although this is more difficult for some of our hardworking American readers who get short vacations - but don't just get a puppy and leave them all alone in the house a couple of days later. Start by leaving them a few minutes a day and gradually build up the time so they don't over-bond with you and develop separation anxiety.

Housetraining (potty training) starts the moment your pup arrives home. Then, after the first few days and once he or she's feeling more settled, make time for short sessions of a few minutes of behaviour training. Corgi puppies are lively, curious, playful and greedy and these traits can lead to mischief if not channelled.

You'll also have to find time to slowly start the socialisation process by taking your puppy out of the home to experience new places, strangers, other animals, loud noises, busy roads, etc. - but make sure you CARRY them until the vaccinations have taken effect.

FACT ❯ The importance of socialisation cannot be over-emphasised. Start as soon as possible, as that critical window up to four months of age is when your puppy is at their most receptive to all things new.

Under-socialised dogs may bark at the slightest thing; others become over-protective of their food, toys or humans. The more positive experiences a Corgi is introduced to early on, the better.

Photo: Lettice meets her first hedgehog, courtesy of Lucy Badham-Thornhill.

Get into the habit of taking your pup for a short walk every day - five minutes once fully vaccinated, increasing gradually to around 10 minutes at four months. While the garden or yard is fine, new surroundings stimulate interest and help to stop puppies becoming bored.

Gently introducing her to different people will help her to become more relaxed around people. Initially, get people to sit on the floor at her level.

Make time right from the beginning to get your pup used to being handled by all the family and dog-friendly visitors, gently brushed, ears checked, and later having their teeth touched and cleaned.

 We recommend you have your pup checked out by a vet within a couple of days of arriving home - many good breeders insist on it - but don't put your puppy on the clinic floor where she can pick up germs from other dogs.

How Long Can I Leave My Puppy?

This is a question we get asked a lot and one that causes much debate among new owners. All dogs are pack animals; their natural state is to be with others. So being alone for long periods is not normal for them - although many have to get used to it.

Another issue is the toilet; Corgi puppies have really tiny bladders. Forget the emotional side of it, how would you like to be left for eight hours without being able to visit the bathroom? So how many hours can you leave a dog alone?

 **In the UK, rescue organisations will not allow anybody to adopt if they regularly leave the dog alone for more than four or five hours a day.**

The Corgi was originally bred as a working dog to herd sheep or cattle for hours on end. They enjoy having a job to do, leaving one alone for too long can trigger unwanted behaviour.

A bored or lonely Corgi may display signs of unhappiness such as nuisance barking, peeing/pooping indoors, chewing, resource guarding, getting into things they shouldn't, stubbornness, aggression, disobedience, or just plain switching off.

 A general rule of thumb is that a puppy can last without urinating for one hour or so for every month of age.

So, provided your puppy has learned the basics, a three-month-old puppy should be able to last for around three hours without needing to go. If the breeder has done a lot of housetraining, the puppy will be able to last longer. But until housetraining kicks in, young puppies just pee at will!

Family and Children

Corgis really do make excellent family pets, with one big proviso: You have to be able and willing to devote enough time to meet your Corgi's needs in terms of attention, training, grooming and - once they are fully grown - exercise.

Corgi puppies may not be suitable for every family with very young children. Toddlers and young kids are uncoordinated and there can be a risk of injury if not well supervised. Corgis can and do form very strong and loving bonds with children - once both have learned respect for each other.

 Children (and adults) should be taught how to correctly handle Corgi puppies so as not to damage their tiny skeletons. Encourage youngsters to interact with the dog on the floor, rather than constantly picking them up to cuddle.

Puppies regard children as playmates - just like a child regards a puppy as a playmate. Both are playful and excitable, so it's important to teach them both the boundaries of play. A Corgi puppy wouldn't intentionally harm a child, or vice versa, but either could cause injury if they get over-excited. Your children will naturally be delighted with your new arrival, but kids and puppy should not be left unsupervised - no matter how well they get along in the beginning.

 Teach your children to be gentle with your dog and your dog to be gentle with your children.

 **FACT** ⟩ Corgis were bred to herd - and that is what many still like to do. Some will try and round up the children and, if they run away, nip the back of their legs.

This is not aggression; they are doing what comes naturally, but Corgis need to be taught right from the off that humans are not farm animals! Nipping the kids, or adults, is not acceptable, so take time to train them out of this habit - and teach your children not to run away from your Corgi. See **Training chapters 9 and 10** for more detailed information.

Your dog's early experiences with children should all be positive. If not, a dog may become nervous or mistrustful - and what you want around children is most definitely a relaxed dog that does not feel threatened by a child's presence.

Take things steady in the beginning and your Corgi will undoubtedly form a deep, lifelong bond that your children will remember throughout their lives.

Fran Fricker, breeder of Kerman Cardigan Welsh Corgis for over 40 years, says: "Young Pembrokes sometimes have a reputation for being a bit nippy, but this is often because a child gets excited and the play becomes rough. If guidelines are followed from the start this does not happen.

"Cardigans are more watchful and will weigh the situation up first. But both make fabulous child companions."

Photo: Fran's grandchildren Olive and Celyn in Welsh national costume with Juni (Ch Kerman Carbon Copy).

"Take it from me, who has not been without a Corgi for over 60 years, I would place one with a family with no worries. My Cardigans often accompany me in the workplace; I work with all disabilities and all ages and they provide a calming and soothing effect - even with the most distressed."

Alexandra Trefán-Török, of Born to Be Pembrokes and Cardigans, Hungary, thinks that adults have an important role to play: "Parents can do a lot to teach the puppy what is acceptable and what is not. Corgis will try to catch the back of the knees of running children, but it is easy to manage for parents who have prior experience with dogs.

"Otherwise, I recommend getting the Corgi first and children some years later when the dog is adult! This would make them perfect pals. Having small children with a puppy is a bit more difficult for beginners."

Kennel Club Assured Breeder Jo Evans has over 30 years' experience with her Cerdinen Pembroke Welsh Corgis: "My Corgis love children - however they have been known to grab small children around the bottom of their trousers and tip them up! My Cara still grabs me (gently) behind the knee when she is excited."

Kevin Dover, international show judge and breeder of Pemcader Pembrokes: "Welsh Corgis are great family pets as long as children fully understand that a puppy also needs its space when eating and time to rest when tired.

"The worst thing is allowing a child to continually harass a puppy as eventually something will have to give - and it is usually the child being snapped at. This is taken as being the dog at fault, when it's the parents' fault for allowing their children to ignore the rules.

"Corgis respond to a schedule, they like to get up and go out at a set time, be fed at the same time and be exercised at the same time. Just because it's raining is no reason for them not be exercised which all should be taken into consideration before buying any animal."

Lisa Thompson, who has 20 years' experience breeding Thompson's Pembroke Welsh Corgis in Wisconsin: "Yes, I would place a Corgi with a family with children, but kids need to know not to run or the Corgi will herd them! They also need to know not to tease a Corgi."

Photo of 12-week-old Nelson courtesy of Lisa.

Linda Roberts, Cherastayne Pembroke Welsh Corgis: "My Pembrokes are generally very eager to meet small children when out on walks, I am very careful to ensure that the children approach in a calm and sensible manner and don't let them jump all over the dogs.

"Most parents these days are well aware of how their children should behave around animals. I take these opportunities to educate people and children about the breed. Most have no idea they were bred to herd cows.

"I have placed puppies with families with children of around nine or 10 and upwards in the past with great success. As with all things, it is a matter of finding the right family for the right puppy. A family with very young children is likely to have quite enough to occupy their time without bringing a small needy puppy into their home and, in these circumstances, I would encourage them to wait until the children are a little bit older and more capable and responsible enough to take an active role in the raising of their dog."

Kevin Egan, long-term owner and Welsh Corgi League officer: "There is something about kids and Corgis! The Pembrokes react very positively amongst children.

"Our regular first-hand experience of this is breed stand duty at the bi-annual Discover Dogs event. Many young families attend the show in search of a new canine family member and when toddlers spot the Pembrokes, there is spontaneous fun and games, theoretically because the dogs and the kids are about the same size. Most importantly, the dogs are very fault-tolerant; this has much to do with their temperament and ability to cope with fairly robust handling."

Experienced owner Lucy Badham-Thornhill: "I first had my Corgis when my children were small and never had any problems. The dogs put up with anything. Now my family are grown up, my current two dogs are not used to small children and I am therefore more careful - this applies to dogs of all breeds. I think Corgis can be wonderful family dogs."

Single People

Many singles own dogs, but if you live alone, getting a puppy will require a lot of dedication on your part. There is nobody to share the responsibility, so taking on a determined, people-loving dog like the Corgi requires a commitment and a lot of your time if the dog is to have a decent life.

If you are out of the house all day, a Corgi is NOT a good choice. They enjoy being with you and, as is typical of dogs originally bred to do a job, they get bored quite easily. Corgis are also intelligent and left to their own devices, may become mischievous. Being alone all day is not much of a life for a dog. However, if you can afford to devote a lot of time on a daily basis to your Corgi, then he or she will undoubtedly become your best friend.

Older People

Corgis are affectionate and love being with their people. A Corgi may be a good choice for older people, provided they are able to meet the breed's need for regular exercise as well as playtime, games or some other activity to challenge their little grey cells.

Other Pets

However friendly your puppy is, other pets in your household may not be too happy at a new arrival. Socialised Corgis usually get on well with other animals, but it might not be a good idea to leave your pet hamster or rabbit running loose – at least until they have got used to each other.

Some Corgis have stronger prey/chase instincts than others. Most live very well with cats, but this may not stop them chasing other small animals once out of the house. If an animal or bird stands its ground, the Corgi will probably not chase, but if they try to get away, the Corgi's herding instinct may well kick in.

If you do have other pets, introduce them slowly to your Corgi. Puppies are naturally extremely curious and playful and will sniff and investigate other pets; they may even chase them inside the house. Depending on how lively your pup is, you may have to separate them initially, or put the pup into a pen or crate for short periods to allow the cat to investigate without being pestered by a hyperactive pup who thinks the cat is a great playmate.

This will also prevent your puppy from being injured. If the two animals are free and the cat lashes out, your pup's eyes could get scratched. A timid Corgi might need protection from a bold cat - or vice versa. A bold cat and a timid Corgi will probably settle down together quickest!

If things seem to be going well with no aggression, then let them loose together after one or two supervised sessions. Take the process slowly; if your cat is stressed or frightened, he may decide to leave. Our feline friends are notorious for abandoning home because the board and lodgings are better down the road...

Lucy Badham-Thornhill added: "We used to have chickens and hedgehogs and my son kept rats. The Corgis were fantastic with them all. A dog once lunged at the cat and our Corgi Mole immediately put herself between them to protect the cat. Lettice, our other Corgi, and the cat take turns to chase each other! I think they know who belongs in their household."

More than One Dog

Well-socialised Corgis have no problem sharing their home with other dogs. Introduce your puppy to other dogs and animals in a positive, non-frightening manner that will give her confidence. Supervised sessions help everyone to get along and for the other dog or dogs to accept your new pup.

If you can, introduce them for the first time outdoors on neutral ground, rather than in the house or in an area that one dog regards as her own. You don't want the established dog to feel they have to protect their territory, nor the puppy to feel she is in an enclosed space and can't get away.

If you are thinking about getting more than one pup, consider waiting until your first puppy is a few months old or an adult before getting a second.

Waiting means you can give your full attention to one puppy; get housetraining, socialisation and the basics of obedience training out of the way before getting your second.

Another benefit is that an older well-trained dog will help teach the new puppy some manners.

Vicky Methuen, who lives in Pembrokeshire, West Wales - where the Pembroke originated from - has owned the breed for over 40 years and says: "I have always had two dogs and try to overlap so that a newcomer is welcomed into the home by the incumbent resident.

"The last time this took place was when Billie-Corgi was four years old and greeted a seven-week-old Brona. All went well and the pup slept in a pre-prepared *'boudoir'* in the utility room. After about a week she settled into her basket in the kitchen."

 Think carefully before getting two puppies from the same litter. Apart from the time and expense involved, you want your new Corgi to learn to focus on YOU, and not her littermate.

Owning two dogs can be twice as nice; they will be great company for each other, but bear in mind that it's also double the training, food and vet's bills.

Plan Ahead

Choosing the right breeder is one of the most important decisions you will make. Like humans, your puppy will be a product of her parents and will inherit many of their characteristics. Appearance, natural temperament, size and how healthy your puppy is depends to a large extent on the genes of her parents.

Responsible breeders check the health history and temperament of the parents, carry out health tests where necessary and only breed from good, healthy stock with good temperaments.

The price of puppies of all breeds has shot up, so it's hard to say what a fair price is for a well-bred pedigree pup. Factors such as region, colour and markings can also affect price, and you'll pay more for a Corgi with show prospects, or one with ancestors with a proven track record in Agility or other canine competitions than for a pet Corgi.

Since Covid, price is no longer a reliable indication of the quality of the pup, but beware of **"bargain"** puppies, these are not top quality pups. Instead, spend the time to find a reputable breeder and read **Chapter 13. Corgi Health** to discover what to look for before buying.

 BE PATIENT. **Start looking months or even a year before your planned arrival. Good Corgi breeders with quality breeding dogs often have a waiting list for their pups, so get your name on a list in good time.**

Phone or email your selected breeder or breeders to find out about future litters and potential dates, but don't commit until you've asked lots of questions. A healthy Corgi will be your irreplaceable companion for over a decade so why buy one from a general ad?

Would you buy an old car or a house with potential structural problems just because it looked pretty in a website photo or was cheap? The answer is probably no, because you know you'd have stress and expense at some point in the future.

Visit the breeder personally at least once before picking the puppy up – this should be an absolute must in the UK. **NOTE:** Some American breeders do not allow the public on to their properties when they have unvaccinated pups. Also, when vast distances are involved, personal visits are not always possible.

In these cases speak at length on the phone to the breeder, video call, ask lots of questions and ask to see photos and videos of the pups from birth to present day. Reputable breeders will be happy to answer all your questions - and will have lots for you too.

Corgi puppies should be **at least eight weeks old** before they leave the breeder. Puppies need this time to physically develop and learn the rules of the pack from their mothers and littermates. In the UK and some US states it is illegal to sell a puppy younger than eight weeks.

Some Corgi breeders keep their puppies up to 12 weeks old to allow them to develop in the litter.

....

Buyer Beware

Good breeders do not sell their dogs on general purpose websites, Gumtree, Craig's List or Freeads, in car parks or somebody else's house. In 2020, the UK Government passed *Lucy's Law* saying:

"Lucy's Law' means that anyone wanting to get a new puppy or kitten in England, Scotland or Wales must now buy direct from a breeder, or consider adopting from a rescue centre instead.

"Licensed dog breeders are required to show puppies interacting with their mothers in their place of birth. If a business sells puppies or kittens without a licence, they could receive an unlimited fine or be sent to prison for up to six months. The law is named after Lucy, a Cavalier King Charles Spaniel who was rescued from a puppy farm."

Unfortunately, in practice, there are lots and lots of people breeding for profit in the UK who are not licensed, and there is no such law in the US.

And if you are looking at dogs on Pets4Homes in the UK, follow their guidelines carefully, see the pup with the mother and check what health testing has been carried out.

There is a difference between *a hobby breeder* and a *backyard or backstreet breeder*. Both may breed just one or two litters a year and keep the puppies in their homes, but that's where the similarity ends.

In the UK there are many good **hobby breeders.** They often don't have a website and you will probably find out about them via word of mouth. Good hobby breeders are usually breed enthusiasts or experts; sometimes they show their pedigree dogs. They carry out health tests and lavish care and love on their dogs. They are not professional dog breeders.

NOTE: While it is often a good sign in the UK, the term *"hobby breeder"* can have negative implications in the USA.

Backyard breeders are often breeding their own pets. They have less knowledge about the breed, pay little attention to the health and welfare of their dogs and are doing it primarily for extra cash. They may be very nice people, but avoid buying a dog from them.

FACT ❯ All GOOD breeders, professional or hobby, have in-depth knowledge of the Corgi. They take measures to prevent potential health issues being passed on to puppies, and are passionate about the breed.

Here are four reasons for buying from a good breeder:

1. **HEALTH:** Like all breeds, Corgis have potentially inheritable health issues. The way to improve breed health is for breeders to health test their breeding dogs and NOT mate two dogs whose combined results mean there's a significant risk of passing on inherited disorders.

2. **SOCIALISATION:** Scientists and dog experts now realise that the critical socialisation period for dogs is up to the age of four months. An unstimulated puppy is likely to be less well-adjusted and more likely to have fear or behaviour issues as an adult. Good breeders start this process, they don't just leave the puppies in an outbuilding for two or three months. Socialisation is important for all dogs.

3. **TEMPERAMENT:** Good breeders select their breeding stock based not only on sound structure and health, but also on temperament. They will not breed from an aggressive or overly timid dog.

4. **PEACE OF MIND:** Most good breeders agree to take the dog back at any time in her life or rehome her if things don't work out - although you may find it too hard to part with your beloved Corgi by then.

Avoiding Bad Breeders

Getting a puppy is such an emotional decision - and one that should have a wonderfully positive impact on you and your family's life for a decade or longer. Unfortunately, the high price of puppies has resulted in unscrupulous people producing litters primarily for the money.

This section helps you avoid the pitfalls of getting a puppy from a puppy mill or farm, a puppy importer, dealer or broker (somebody who makes money from buying and selling puppies) or a backyard breeder.

You can't buy a Rolls Royce or a Corvette for a couple of thousand pounds or dollars - you'd immediately suspect that the *"bargain"* on offer wasn't the real deal. No matter how lovely it looked, you'd be right – well, the same applies to Corgis.

Become Breeder Savvy

❖ Websites have become far more sophisticated and it's getting harder to spot the good, ethical breeders from those who are driven by the cash. Avoid websites where there are no pictures of the owner's home or kennels or the dogs in the home

❖ If the website shows lots of photos of cute puppies with little information about the family, breeding dogs, health tests or environment, click the X button

❖ Don't buy a website puppy with a shopping cart symbol next to them

❖ **See the puppies with their mother face-to-face.** You should always do this in the UK. If this is not possible in the US due to distances, speak at length on the phone with the breeder, ask lots of questions and ask to see videos of the puppies in their surroundings and beds

❖ Be wary if the mother is not with the puppies, but brought in to meet you

❖ Is the pup interacting with the "mother" or do the two dogs appear to have no connection? If the pups are really hers, she will interact with them

❖ You hear: "You can't see the parent dogs because......" ALWAYS ask to see the parents or, as a minimum, the mother

❖ Be wary if the puppies look small for their stated age

❖ At the breeder's, ask to see where the puppy is living. If the breeding dogs are not housed in the family home, they should be in clean kennels, not too hot or cold, with access to grass and time spent with humans, and ask to see the other puppies from the litter

❖ Good breeders are happy to provide lots of information. If the breeder is reluctant to answer your questions, look elsewhere

❖ **Check all paperwork with the puppy,** and if the breeder says that the dam and sire are Kennel Club or AKC registered, ask to see the registration papers

❖ Ask for at least one reference from another puppy owner before you commit

- Pressure selling: on the phone, the breeder doesn't ask you many questions and then says: "There are only X many puppies left and I have several other buyers interested." Walk away

- You hear "Our Corgi puppies are cheaper because…." Walk away

- Photographs of so-called "champion ancestors" do not guarantee the health of the puppy

 Look beyond the cute, fluffy exterior. The way to look INSIDE the puppy is to see the parents – or at least the mother - and check what health tests have been carried out. NOTE: *"Vet checked"* **does NOT mean the pup or parents have passed any health test**

- The person you are buying the puppy from did not breed the dog themselves. Deal with the breeder, not an intermediary

- The only place you meet the puppy seller is a car park, somebody else's house or place other than the puppies' home – Walk away

- The seller tells you that the puppy comes from top, caring breeders from your own or another country. It is now illegal in the UK to buy a puppy from a third party - i.e. anyone other than the breeder

- Ask to see photos of the puppy from birth to present day

- Beware of "rare colours" or "rare markings" as it probably means that the puppy you are looking at is not pure Corgi

Photo: A beautiful merle Cardigan Welsh Corgi. Merle is an acceptable colour for Cardigans, but not Pembrokes.

- Price – if you are offered a very cheap puppy, there is usually a reason

- Familiarise yourself with the Breed Standard and what an eight to 12-week-old Corgi should look like. Make sure the puppy you are interested in looks and acts like a Corgi

- Google the name of the breeder and prefix (kennel name), see if any comments come up

- Go on to Corgi Facebook groups and ask if anybody has had a puppy from this breeder and if so, ask is the dog still healthy and would they recommend buying from the breeder

- NEVER buy a puppy because you feel sorry for it; you are condemning other dogs to a life of misery

- If you have any doubt, go with your gut instinct and WALK AWAY - even if this means losing your deposit. It will be worth it in the long run

- If you get a rescue Corgi, make sure it is from a recognised rescue group and not a "puppy flipper" who may be posing as a do-gooder, but is in fact getting dogs (including stolen ones) from unscrupulous sources

 Bad breeders do not have two horns coming out of their heads! Most will be friendly when you phone or visit - after all, they want to make the sale. It's only later that problems develop.

Licences and Imports

Licences

If your potential breeder is licensed, DO YOUR RESEARCH. Holders of dog breeding licences range from very good, responsible breeders to puppy farms.

Minimum requirements vary from state to state in the US; it can be anything from five to 30 breeding dogs - and legal minimum standards of care vary wildly. Many of them just cover the basics, such as adequate food, water and paperwork. This does not make for a good puppy. Responsible licensed breeders put a great deal more time and effort into their puppies than this.

In some states, licence holders are not even visited by an inspector. Personally, I would not consider buying a dog from anybody who has more than about half a dozen breeding dogs – unless they are all living in the house with the owner.

Establishments with 20 or 30 breeding dogs are, in my book, puppy farms. The licence holders cannot possibly know so many individual dogs and then properly socialise, stimulate and interact with many hundreds of puppies every year.

In the UK, anybody breeding three or more litters a year or who is "breeding puppies and advertising a business of selling them" should be licensed. This latter part is abused as there are many unlicensed people regularly breeding puppies for five-figure profits.

There is something to help UK buyers navigate this minefield and that is the licensing star system: **One Star** - Minor Failings, **Two or Three Stars** - Minimum Standards have been met, **Three or Four Stars** - Higher Standards have been met**Look for a breeder who meets the higher standards.**

One such is the licensed five-star Creslow Corgis in Somerset run by Kennel Club Assured Breeders Piotr and Johnathan Mazur-Jones who have been producing healthy, happy Pembrokes for 15 years.

They said: "Any licensed star rating gives a buyer confidence that the breeder has been inspected and assessed by the local authority. The more stars a breeder has, the more of the higher standards they have had to meet to achieve that rating."

Photo: A good start in life. Creslow puppies raised in the home with lots of activities and attention.

"Already being KC Assured Breeders, we knew it was the right thing to do for us, to know we are doing all we can for our dogs and for our prospective forever families, providing them with a level of assurance and transparency of who they are buying from.

"For us we are proud of our five stars. It was hard work at first pulling it all together, but then raising a litter and finding the right families is hard work."

Imports

Occasionally Corgis are imported, usually by experienced breeders to improve their bloodlines. Another scenario is that a top exhibitor might import a Corgi with an excellent track record in the show ring **or** show potential.

If a Corgi is imported, these are the official documents required: UK - a pet passport with all the inoculations listed; Rabies done 21 days prior to importing. If the puppy travels with a courier he or she will need paperwork from DEFRA. USA: if the puppy travels as excess luggage, he or she will need a pet passport and paperwork to be filled in by the courier.

FACT ❯ Pet Corgis are not normally imported. Be aware there are puppy factories in some Eastern European countries and other places producing poorly-bred puppies and exporting them

Be very wary if offered a Corgi from another country. Only buy if you are 100% sure the dog's home and ancestry are genuine and if all the above paperwork is in order, with the relevant certificates accompanying the puppy.

Cowboy Corgis and American Corgis

If you live in North America and are looking for a purebred Corgi puppy, steer clear of so-called 'Cowboy Corgis' and 'American Corgis.' Neither are purebred. A Cowboy Corgi is a cross between a Pembroke Welsh Corgi and an Australian Cattle Dog or Heeler, and an American Corgi is a cross between a Pembroke and a Cardigan. Neither is accepted as a breed by the AKC.

Puppy Farms and Mills

Unscrupulous breeders are everywhere. That's not to say there aren't some excellent Corgi breeders out there; there certainly are. You just have to do your research.

While new owners might think they have bagged a cheap or a quick puppy, it often turns out to be false economy and emotionally disastrous when the puppy develops health problems or behavioural problems due to poor temperament or lack of socialisation.

The UK's Kennel Club says as many as one in four puppies bought in the UK may come from puppy farms - and the situation is no better in North America.

The KC Press release states: "As the popularity of online pups continues to soar:

* Almost one in five pups bought (unseen) on websites or social media die within six months

* One in three buys online, in pet stores and via newspaper adverts - outlets often used by puppy farmers - this is an increase from one in five in the previous year

* The problem is likely to grow as the younger generation favour mail order pups, and breeders of fashionable breeds flout responsible steps

"We are sleepwalking into a dog welfare and consumer crisis as new research shows that more and more people are buying their pups online or through pet shops, outlets often used by cruel puppy farmers, and are paying the price with their pups requiring long-term veterinary treatment or dying before six months old."

The KC research found that:

* One third of people who bought their puppy online or over social media failed to experience "overall good health"

* Some 12% of puppies bought online or on social media end up with serious health problems that require expensive on-going veterinary treatment from a young age

The Kennel Club said: "Whilst there is nothing wrong with initially finding a puppy online, it is essential to then see the breeder and ensure that they are doing all of the right things. This research clearly shows that too many people are failing to do this, and the consequences can be seen in the shocking number of puppies that are becoming sick or dying."

Marc Abraham, TV vet and founder of Pup Aid, added: "Sadly, if the *"buy it now"* culture persists, then this horrific situation will only get worse. There is nothing wrong with sourcing a puppy online, but people need to be aware of what they should then expect from the breeder.

"For example, you should not buy a car without getting its service history and seeing it at its registered address, so you certainly shouldn't buy a puppy without the correct paperwork and health certificates and without seeing where it was bred."

"However, too many people are opting to buy directly from third parties, such as the internet, pet shops, or from puppy dealers, where you cannot possibly know how or where the puppy was raised.

"Not only are people buying sickly puppies, but many people are being scammed into paying money for puppies that don't exist, as the research showed that 7% of those who buy online were scammed in this way."

As a canine author, I hear these stories all the time. In fact a good friend of mine was scammed out of a £350 ($460) deposit on a puppy internet scam earlier this year. Then there are people breeding puppies who are not fraudsters, but who have absolutely no idea how to do it properly, resulting in third-rate puppies.

An intelligent, well-educated friend and her husband recently lost their beloved dog of 13 years and shortly afterwards answered an advert for a puppy on Pets4Homes – rather than contacting a good breeder and waiting.

They visited the "breeder's" house, which had five different dogs of different ages and breeds, none of them interacting with the family. They asked to see the puppy's mother, who was allowed into the room and promptly ran around like crazy before pooping on the sofa. She had not been out of the house all day.

All puppies are cute and it's virtually impossible to walk away from one once you've seen them. So my friends bought the attractive puppy. She was 13 weeks old and had only been out of the house twice in her life - once to the vet's and once into the garden!

Now she's home, the puppy is very timid, especially with people. She is suffering from a lack of socialisation and, at the moment, the jury is out on whether, temperament-wise, she will ever overcome this – no matter how hard my friends try. They regret their hasty decision and have months of hard work ahead of them if the puppy is to have a chance of meeting their expectations.

 If you really care about Corgis, avoid buying from a breeder-for-profit. Ultimately, they are damaging the breed by introducing dogs that are not fit for purpose into the Corgi gene pool.

Visit the UK Kennel Club's *Buying a Dog* section for more tips: www.thekennelclub.org.uk or type *UK Kennel Club buying a dog* into a search engine. In the US, search for *AKC Tips for Finding and Working With a Responsible Breeder.*

Where to Find a Good Breeder

1. The Kennel Club in your country.

    In the US look for an AKC Breeder of Merit or a Bred with H.E.A.R.T. breeder:
    Pembrokes - https://marketplace.akc.org/puppies/pembroke-welsh-corgi
    Cardigans - https://marketplace.akc.org/puppies/cardigan-welsh-corgi

    And Assured Breeders in the UK at:
    www.thekennelclub.org.uk/search/find-an-assured-breeder

2. In the US, the Pembroke Welsh Corgi Club of America (PWCCA) has a full list of regional clubs at https://pembrokecorgi.org/about-the-pwcca/membership-directory - contact a local breeder.

3. The Cardigan Welsh Corgi Club of America (CWCCA) https://cardigancorgis.com has a list of regional clubs under **Events.**

4. The UK's national breed club for the Pembroke is the Welsh Corgi League. Visit the website at www.welshcorgileague.org and fill in the form at the **Find a Puppy** section, which will be forwarded to the Puppy Co-ordinator.

5. UK Cardigans, visit The Cardigan Welsh Corgi Association (CWCA) website at: www.cardiganwelshcorgiassoc.co.uk and search **Current Litters and Available Dogs**. If none are available, fill in the Contact form.

A healthy litter of Cardigans bred by Fran Fricker.

6. Visit dog shows or canine events where Corgis are participating and talk to owners and breeders.

7. Get a recommendation from somebody who has a Corgi that you like - check the breeder health screens her dogs.

8. Ask your vet for details of local, ethical Corgi breeders.

9. Search the internet - there are lots of breeders out there; use the advice in this chapter to find the right one.

10. If you are in the UK, visit the Pembroke or Cardigan breed stand at **Discover Dogs** during the annual Crufts dog show in early March or Discover Dogs at Excel in London, normally held during November. See the Events and Activities section on the Kennel Club website for dates.

Questions to Ask a Breeder

Here's a list of the questions you should be asking:

1. **Can I see the litter with the parents** - or at least the mother? It's important to see the pup in his or her normal surroundings, not brought out of a building and shown to you.

2. **Have the parents been health tested?** Ask to see certificates and what guarantees the breeder is offering in terms of genetic illnesses.

3. **What veterinary care have the pups had so far?** Puppies should have had their first wormings by eight weeks old and usually at least their first vaccinations.

4. **Are you an Assured Breeder (UK), Breeder of Merit or Bred With Heart breeder (US) or a member of a Corgi breed club?** Not all good Corgi breeders are, but these are good places to start.

5. **How long have you been breeding Corgis?** You are looking for someone with a good track record with the breed.

6. **Can you put me in touch with someone who already has one of your puppies?** ALWAYS contact at least one owner.

7. **How many litters has the mother had?** Females should be 18 months or two years old before their first litter. The UK Kennel Club will not register puppies from a dam under one year old, had more than four litters or is over the age of eight.

8. **What happens to the mother once she has finished breeding?** Are they kept as part of the family, rehomed in loving homes, sent to animal shelters or auctioned off? Do you see any old Corgis at the breeder's home?

9. **Do you breed any other types of dog?** Buy from a specialist, preferably one who does not have lots of other breeds.

10. **What is so special about this litter?** You are looking for a breeder who has used good breeding stock and his or her knowledge to produce handsome, healthy dogs with good temperaments.

11. **What is the average lifespan of your dogs?** Generally, pups bred from healthy stock tend to live longer.

12. **How socialised and housetrained is the puppy?** Good breeders usually start the socialisation and housetraining process before they leave.

13. **How would you describe the temperament of the parents?** Temperament is extremely important; try to interact with both parents, or at least the mother.

14. **What do you feed your adults and puppies**? A reputable breeder will feed top quality food and advise you to do the same.

15. **Do you provide a written Sale or Puppy Contract?**

16. **Why aren't you asking me any questions?** A good breeder is committed to making a good match between the new owners and their puppies. If (s)he doesn't, then walk away.

Choosing a Healthy Corgi

Once you've selected your breeder and a litter is available, you then have to decide WHICH puppy to pick, unless the breeder has already earmarked one for you after asking lots of questions. Here are some pointers on puppy health:

1. Your chosen Corgi puppy should have **a well-fed appearance.** She should not, however, have a distended abdomen (pot belly) as this can be a sign of worms or other illnesses. The ideal puppy should not be too thin either - you should be able to feel, but not see, her ribs.

2. **The pup's eyes should be bright and clear** with no discharge or tear stain. Steer clear of a puppy that blinks a lot. (Bordetella and Kennel Cough vaccines can sometimes cause runny eyes and nose for up to 10 days – ask when the litter was vaccinated for these).

3. **Her nose should be cool, damp and clean** with no discharge.

4. **The pup's ears should be clean** with no sign of discharge, soreness or redness and no unpleasant smell.

5. **Check the puppy's rear end** to make sure it is clean and there are no signs of watery poo(p).

6. **The pup's coat should look clean,** feel soft, not matted - and puppies should smell good! The coat should have no signs of ticks or fleas. Red or irritated skin or bald spots could be a sign of infestation or a skin condition. Also, check between the toes of the paws for signs of redness or swelling.

7. **Corgis are friendly and alert dogs and puppies should be the same.** Pembroke puppies may be naturally more outgoing than Cardigans. They should all be relaxed, not timid or frightened by your presence. Be wary if the breeder makes excuses for the puppies' behaviour.

8. **Gums should be clean and pink.**

9. **Choose a puppy that moves freely** without any sign of injury or lameness. It should be a fluid movement, not jerky or stiff, and the pup should have a straight back.

10. When the puppy is distracted, clap or make a noise behind her - not so loud as to frighten her - to **make sure she is not deaf.**

11. Finally, **ask to see veterinary records** to confirm your puppy has been wormed, possibly had her first vaccinations and a vet check.

If you get the puppy home and things don't work out for whatever reason, good breeders will either take the puppy back or find them a suitable home.

 Take your puppy to a vet to have a thorough check-up within 48 hours of purchase. If your vet is not happy with the pup's condition, return her - no matter how painful it may be. Keeping an unhealthy puppy will only lead to further distress and expense.

Puppy Contracts

Most good breeders provide their puppy parents with an official Puppy Contract, also called a Sale Contract. This protects both buyer and seller by providing information on the puppy until he or she leaves the breeder. A Puppy Contract will answer such questions as whether the puppy:

- Is covered by breeder's insurance and can be returned if there is a health issue within a certain time period
- Has been micro-chipped (compulsory in the UK) and/or vaccinated and details of worming treatments
- Has been partially or wholly toilet-trained
- Has been socialised and where he or she was kept
- What health conditions the pup and parents have been screened for
- What the puppy is currently being fed and if any food is being supplied
- Was born by Caesarean section (C-section)
- And details of the dam and sire

It's not easy for caring breeders to part with their puppies after they have lovingly bred and raised them, and so many supply extensive care notes for new owners, which may include details of:

- The puppy's daily routine
- Feeding schedule
- Vet and vaccination schedule
- General puppy care
- Toilet training
- Socialisation

The Royal Society for the Prevention of Cruelty to Animals (RSPCA) has a free downloadable puppy contract, *pictured,* endorsed by vets and animal welfare organisations; you should be looking for something similar from a breeder. Visit https://puppycontract.org.uk/about-us or type *"AKC Preparing a Puppy Contract"* if you're in the US.

Advice from Corgi Experts

Kennel Club Assured Breeder Fran Fricker describes what to expect: "A breeder should always welcome prospective puppy owners into their home. It is a chance to get to know them and for the breeder to see how they are with his or her dogs; you have an instinct of how they will react to a puppy.

"A healthy well-bred puppy will be outgoing, healthy, chunky and playful. You will see the pups with their siblings and also mum. The environment they are in will be clean with fresh water and fresh food available and toys.

"A bad breeder will be reluctant to have a meeting at their home address. Puppies may be seen separately and not always with mum. Pups may be lethargic and dirty and may have distended tummies, which can indicate worms; they may also be in a dirty environment. Pups may be advertised in shops and on *Pets for sale* web sites.

"There are many stories about unscrupulous breeders and prospective owners who, having made contact through adverts, may not get the puppy they believe they are buying. Or there is no follow-up once they have purchased the puppy. It's as if once they have paid, that's it."

Fellow Assured Breeders Piotr and Johnathan Mazur-Jones, Creslow Corgis, have plenty of advice for prospective owners and describe their own methods: "A well-bred puppy is one that is alert, energetic, playful with siblings and has bright eyes. The puppy should be chunky (not skinny) in appearance and raised in the home environment, not kennels.

"It is getting incredibly hard to spot a bad breeder, so the key for us as breeders is **transparency and engagement.** A good breeder should want to engage with potential buyers, provide all the required background information and be happy to answer any questions. They should be focused on finding good homes, not just the financial transaction.

"From the outset we provide a lot of information, at the point of enquiry laying out what the process involves, what they get and can expect by buying a puppy from us, cost, endorsements, puppy kit, etc. and the steps or the process we will take to find our puppies their forever families. We also give weekly updates and live video calls prior to the all-important 'M**eet the Gang'** visit."

Pictured are Piotr and Johnathan's Anja (Creslow Quantock Belle) and Maia (Creslow la Vie en Rose).

"We actively encourage our prospective families to ask as many questions of us as they wish, there is no such thing as a silly question. Prospective owners should ask about the temperament of the parents, ask to meet them or see a video of the sire; ask to speak to the sire's breeders if the sire isn't resident with the litter. Never buy a puppy without seeing the mum and puppies together.

"We encourage prospective families to do their research about us as breeders and request that they reach out to past forever families for their experience about us and buying a puppy from us.

"Personally, we do not take deposits or payment before the pup is delivered to their forever family at a minimum age of 10 weeks (which is two weeks older than the minimum age a pup can be placed in their home). If you are asked to pay in advance or even a deposit, I would be very cautious and ask why. There are so many stories of bad breeders, they crop up time and time again."

Kevin Dover echoes some of those points: "When anyone visits a breeder, I would always ask for the dam (mother) of the litter to be clearly visible and preferably interacting with the puppies. It has been known for 'false' mothers to be presented due to the condition of an actual mother - especially from puppy farmers.

"A puppy should be bright and active and be seeking attention from a prospective buyer. Anything sitting in a corner and not wanting to be social should be avoided. There are many unscrupulous breeders who use various internet sites to sell puppies. Unfortunately, it doesn't matter how much people are told to seek reputable breeders, many will always want a puppy here and now rather than waiting for something that has been planned for the right reasons.

"Potential buyers should also have access to vaccination records and the veterinary surgeon who has vaccinated them, along with the microchip registration (which is compulsory in the UK). No puppy should be available for sale under eight weeks of age – preferably 10."

Assured Breeder Jo Evans: "It's important to speak to the breeder with as many questions as possible. The Corgi is a rare breed (in the UK) and breeding can be difficult. I met a breeder who told me she had difficulty getting her bitch in pup and was only going to the closest one she could find. I suspect they were being inbred, hence the difficulty. I avoided buying one from this litter."

Photo: Lottie, bred by Jo, with her monkey, which has been her favourite toy since she was a tiny puppy.

AKC Bred With Heart Breeder Lisa Thompson: "Look for pups with clear eyes who run up to meet you and don't hide. Check their environment and their cleanliness. Ask to see the puppy's parents. Signs of bad breeders are pups in a dirty condition, pups scared of you, or goopy eyes, or the breeder won't show you where the pups were raised or show you the parents."

Lucy Badham-Thornhill: "I would advise anyone to go via their local breed club network or reliable word of mouth - not to get one online. Corgis used to have a reputation for being snappy, a trait that has largely been bred out by responsible breeders. Sadly there are those breeding who do not concentrate on temperament..."

Linda Roberts, experienced breeder and Breed Health Co-ordinator for the Welsh Corgi League: "When looking for a puppy, potential owners should expect to have lots of conversations with the breeder before they even are invited to visit the litter.

"It is likely that a reputable breeder will have a waiting list, including people returning for their second or third dog. The breeder will want to know how suitable they are for the breed, whether their lifestyle will suit the breed and whether they can reasonably be expected to give a puppy the best life.

"Speaking personally, I generally invite prospective owners to visit the litter when the puppies are around four to five weeks old and that visit is a good opportunity for everybody to get to know each other; for the prospective owner to see not only the litter, but also the mum (and possibly the dad if I have him) and other relatives. We can all get a good feel as to whether the breed is going to be a good fit for these people. I have no problem saying a clear **No** if I'm not 100% happy.

"I am unlikely to encourage picking of a particular puppy at this stage, but this visit will give me a good idea of what type of personality of puppy would suit the potential owners. Some puppies are obviously much more outgoing and energetic and are perhaps going to suit people who like lots of hiking or who might want to take part in Agility or Obedience.

"Other puppies might be a little bit steadier (though still outgoing and typical) and might suit, say, retired people who may not be quite so energetic but still might be able to provide the exercise and stimulation that the breed needs. It's very much a fact-finding visit on both sides.

"There are many points to look out for when looking at a litter. You would want to see healthy, active, lively, alert and typical puppies, solid to pick up with clean, clear eyes, good bone and well-covered bodies and a clean coat. There should be no signs of parasites, worms or sickness in any puppy. You should expect to see at least the puppies' mother (save for the very unfortunate and thankfully very rare circumstances where she has died or is very ill after whelping) and she will give you a good indication of how the puppy will turn out, both in terms of type and temperament. She may look a little ragged around the edges because rearing a litter is hard work, but she should still look healthy, alert and have a kind, outgoing temperament."

Photo: Sadie, UK. Ch. Cherastayne Snow Bride JW, twice Best of Breed at Crufts, bred by Linda

"Look at the surroundings... does the breeder maintain a clean organised operation? Is all the paperwork in order? Do they give you every indication that if there are any problems they will be there to support you once you have bought the puppy?

"Will the puppy have been vet checked? Will the puppy have been microchipped (a legal requirement before sale) and will the puppy have received at least one set of vaccinations before you collect it? Is the puppy KC registered (or AKC in the US) and will you receive the documents and pedigree at the time of collection?

"These are all essentials that a puppy purchaser should expect. Will you be given a contract of sale and will you be given food to see the puppy through the first few days? Will you be given dietary and general care information concerning exercise (including the need for sufficient rest as the puppy grows), grooming tips and ongoing healthcare advice, such as worming and future vaccinations?

"These are all signs that the breeder is doing their very best for their puppies and is as concerned as you that they will be as happy in their new home. If you have any doubts at all, please do not hand over any money without, at least, making a second visit to reassure yourself. Never send a deposit without visiting. Any breeder asking for money without meeting prospective owners is likely to be more interested in the bank balance than the quality of life on offer for the puppy.

"A carefully bred well-reared puppy will not be cheap, but the quality of life on offer should be the overriding consideration of the breeder. Unfortunately in our breed, as in many others, there are breeders who fall short of the high standards expected."

....

A good course of action would be something like this:

1. Decide to get a Welsh Corgi.
2. Decide whether a Pembroke or Cardigan would best suit you.
3. Decide on a male or female.
4. Do your research and find a good breeder with healthy Corgis.
5. Register your interest, keep in touch with the breeder for updates - and WAIT until a litter becomes available.
6. Pick a puppy with a suitable temperament - a good breeder will help you choose one that will fit in with your family and lifestyle.
7. Enjoy a decade or longer with a beautiful, healthy Corgi.

Some people pick a puppy based on how the dog looks. If coat colour or size, for example, are very important to you, make sure the other boxes are ticked as well.

5. Bringing Puppy Home

Getting a new puppy is so exciting; you can't wait to bring him home. Before that happens, you probably dream of all the things you are going to do together: going for long walks, playing games, travelling, snuggling down at home together, and maybe even taking part in Agility, Obedience or shows.

Your pup has, of course, no idea of your big plans, and the reality when he arrives can be a BIG shock! Corgi puppies are determined little critters with minds of their own and sharp teeth. They leak at both ends, chew anything in sight, constantly demand your attention, herd the kids, cry and don't pay a blind bit of notice to your commands... There is a lot of work ahead before the two of you develop that unique bond!

Your pup has to learn what you require from him before he can start to meet some of your expectations - and you have to learn what your pup needs from you.

....

Once your puppy lands in your home, your time won't be your own, but you can get off to a good start by preparing things before the big day. Here's a list of things to think about getting beforehand - your breeder may supply some of these:

Puppy Checklist

- ✓ A dog bed or basket
- ✓ Bedding – a Vetbed or Vetfleece is a good choice
- ✓ A piece of cloth (remove buttons, etc.) that has been rubbed on the puppy's mother to put in the pup's bed
- ✓ A puppy gate or pen
- ✓ A crate if you decide to use one
- ✓ A collar or puppy harness with ID tag and a lead (leash)
- ✓ Food and water bowls, preferably stainless steel
- ✓ Puppy food – find out what the breeder is feeding and stick to that to start with
- ✓ Puppy treats - healthy ones, carrot and apple pieces are good, no rawhide
- ✓ Newspapers or pellet litter and a bell if you decide to use them for housetraining
- ✓ Poo(p) bags
- ✓ Toys and chews suitable for puppies
- ✓ Old blanket for cleaning and drying and partially covering the crate

AND PLENTY OF TIME!

Later, you'll also need grooming brushes, flea and worming products and maybe a car grille or travel crate. Many good breeders provide Puppy Packs, which contain some or all of these items:

- ✓ Pedigree certificate
- ✓ Puppy contract
- ✓ Information pack with details of vet's visits, vaccinations and wormings, parents' health certificates, diet, breed clubs, etc.
- ✓ Puppy food
- ✓ ID tag/microchip info
- ✓ Blanket that smells of the mother and litter
- ✓ Soft toy that your puppy has grown up with, possibly a chew toy as well
- ✓ A month's free insurance

FACT ❯ By law, all UK puppies have to be microchipped and registered BEFORE they leave the breeder. New owners are legally bound to ensure their puppy's microchip registration is updated with their own details and also to register any change of address or ownership.

Puppy Proofing Your Home

Some adjustments will be needed to make your home safe and suitable. Corgi puppies are small bundles of curiosity, instinct and energy when they are awake, with little common sense and even less self-control. They have bursts of energy before running out of steam and spending much of the rest of the day sleeping. As one breeder says: "They have two speeds – ON and OFF!"

They also have an incredible sense of smell and love to investigate with their noses and mouths. Fence off or remove all poisonous or low plants with sharp leaves or thorns, such as roses, that could cause eye injuries.

There are literally dozens of plants harmful to a puppy if ingested, including azalea, daffodil bulbs, lily, foxglove, hyacinth, hydrangea, lupin, rhododendron, sweet pea, tulip and yew.

The Kennel Club has a list of some of the most common ones, type "*Kennel Club poisons in your garden*" into Google. The ASPCA has an extensive list for the USA if you Google *"ASPCA poisonous plants."*

Make sure any fencing planks are extremely close together and that EVERY LITTLE GAP has been plugged; Corgi puppies can get through almost anything and they have no road sense whatsoever. Don't leave your puppy unattended in the garden or yard in the beginning.

FACT ❯ Dognapping is on the increase. Over 2,000 dogs are now being stolen each year in the UK. The figures are much higher for the US, where the AKC reports increasing dog thefts and warns owners against leaving dogs unattended.

Puppies are little chew machines and puppy-proofing your home involves moving anything sharp, breakable or chewable - including your shoes.

Lift electrical cords, mobile phones and chargers, remote controls, etc. out of reach and block off any off-limits areas of the house with a child gate or barrier, especially as he may be shadowing you for the first few days.

Create an area where your puppy is allowed to go, perhaps one or two rooms, preferably with a hard floor that is easy to clean. Keep the rest of the house off-limits, at least until the pair of you have mastered potty training.

This area should be near the door to the garden or yard for toileting. Restricting the puppy's space also helps him to settle in. He probably had a den and small space at the breeder's home. Suddenly having the freedom of the whole house can be quite daunting - not to mention messy!

You can buy a purpose-made dog barrier or use a sturdy baby gate, which may be cheaper, to confine a puppy to a room or prevent him from going upstairs.

 Corgi puppies' heads are tiny, choose a gate with narrow vertical gaps or mesh, and check that your puppy can't get his head stuck between the bars - or put a mesh over the bottom of the gate initially.

You can also make your own barrier, but bear in mind that cardboard, fabric and other soft materials will definitely get chewed. Don't underestimate your puppy! Young Corgis are lively and determined.

You'll then need a bed and/or a crate. A rigid moulded bed that's more difficult for a puppy to damage is a good option initially, with Vetbed or blankets inside for comfort. A luxury soft bed could prove to be an expensive mistake while puppies are still at the chewing stage! Some owners also like to create a penned area for their pup.

....

Collecting Your Puppy

* Let the breeder know what time you will arrive and ask her not to feed the pup for a couple of hours beforehand - unless you have a very long journey, in which case the puppy will need to eat something. He will be less likely to be car sick and should be hungry when he lands in his new home. The same applies to an adult dog moving to a new home

* Ask for an old blanket or toy that has been with the pup's mother – you can leave one on an earlier visit to collect with the pup. Or take one with you and rub the mother with it to collect her scent and put this with the puppy for the first few days. It will help him to settle

* Get copies of any health certificates relating to the parents and a Contract of Sale or Puppy Contract – see **Chapter 4. Finding Your Puppy** for details. It should also state that you can return the puppy if there are health issues within a certain time frame. The breeder should also give you details of worming, vaccinations and microchip registration (UK), as well as an information sheet

❖ Find out exactly what the breeder is feeding and how much; dogs' digestive systems cannot cope with sudden changes in diet - unless the breeder has deliberately been feeding several different foods to her puppies to get them used to different foods. In the beginning, stick to whatever the pup is used to; good breeders send some food home with the puppy

The Journey Home

Bringing a new puppy home in a car can be a stressful experience. Your puppy will be sad at leaving his mother, brothers and sisters and a familiar environment. Everything will be strange and frightening and he may whimper and whine or even bark on the way home.

If you can, take somebody with you on that first journey – some breeders insist on having someone there to hold and cuddle the pup to make the journey less stressful for the pup.

Under no circumstances have the puppy on your lap while driving. It is simply too dangerous - a Corgi puppy is extremely cute, wriggly and far too distracting. Have an old towel between your travel companion and the pup as he may quite possibly pee, drool or be sick - the puppy, not the passenger! Kitchen towel is also useful, as is a large plastic bag for putting any soiled items in.

If you have to travel any distance, take a crate – a canvas or plastic travel crate with holes in for air flow, or a wire crate he'll use at home. Cover the bottom of the crate with a waterproof material and then put a comfortable blanket on top. You can put newspapers in half of the crate if the pup is partly housetrained.

Don't forget to allow the pup to relieve himself beforehand, and if your journey is more than a couple of hours, take water to give him en route. He may need the toilet, but don't let him outside on to the ground as he is not yet fully vaccinated. As soon as you arrive home, let your puppy into the garden or yard, and when he "performs," praise him for his efforts.

These first few days are critical in getting your puppy to feel safe and confident in his new surroundings. Spend time with the latest addition to your family, talk to him often in a reassuring manner. Introduce him to his den and toys, slowly allow him to explore and show him around the house – once you have puppy-proofed it.

If you've got other animals, introduce them to each other slowly and in supervised sessions on neutral territory - or outdoors where there is space so neither feels threatened - preferably once the pup has got used to his new surroundings, not as soon as you walk through the door.

Gentleness and patience are the keys to these first few days, so don't overwhelm your pup.

Tip Have a special, gentle puppy voice and use his new name frequently - and in a pleasant, encouraging manner. <u>Never use his name to scold</u> or he will associate it with bad things. The sound of his name should always make him want to pay attention to you as something good is going to happen - praise, food, playtime, and so on.

Settling In

We receive emails from worried new owners. Here are some of their most common concerns:

- 🐾 My puppy won't stop crying or whining
- 🐾 My puppy is shivering
- 🐾 My puppy won't eat
- 🐾 My puppy is very timid
- 🐾 My puppy follows me everywhere, he won't let me out of his sight
- 🐾 My puppy sleeps all the time, is this normal?

These behaviours are quite common at the beginning. They are just a young pup's reaction to leaving his mother and littermates and entering into a strange new world. It is normal for puppies to sleep most of the time, just like babies. It is also normal for some puppies to whine during the first couple of days.

Tip If you constantly pick up a crying pup, he will learn that your attention is the reward for his crying. Wait until your puppy STOPS crying before giving him your attention.

If he's on the same food as he was at the breeder's and won't eat, then it is probably just nerves. If he leaves his food, take it away and try it later, don't leave it down all of the time or he may get used to turning his nose up at it. Corgis have a thick double coat, so if your puppy is shivering, it's probably nerves again - but check that he's warm enough as he's used to the warmth of his siblings.

Make your new pup as comfortable as possible, ensuring he has a warm (but not too hot), quiet den away from draughts, where he is not pestered by children or other pets. Handle him gently, while giving him plenty of time to sleep. Avoid placing him under stress by making too many demands. If your puppy whines or cries, it is usually due to one of the following reasons:

- 🐾 He is lonely
- 🐾 He is hungry
- 🐾 He is cold
- 🐾 He needs to relieve himself
- 🐾 He wants attention from you

If it is none of these, then physically check him over to make sure he hasn't picked up an injury. Try not to fuss too much! If he whimpers, reassure with a quiet word. If he cries and tries to get out of his allotted area, he may need to go to the toilet. Take him outside and praise him if he performs.

FACT Corgi puppies from breeders who have already started socialisation and training are often more confident and less fazed by new things. They often settle in quicker than those reared with less human contact and new experiences.

A puppy will think of you as his new mother, and if you haven't decided what to call him yet, "Shadow" might be apt as he will follow you everywhere! But after a few days start to leave your pup for periods of a few minutes, gradually building up the time. A puppy unused to being left alone can grow up to have Separation Anxiety - see **Chapter 8. Typical Corgi Traits** for more information.

Helping a new pup to settle in is virtually a full-time job. If your routine means you are normally out of the house for a few hours during the day, get your puppy on a Friday or Saturday so he has at least a couple of days to adjust to his new surroundings.

A far better idea is to book time off work to help your puppy to settle in, if you can. (Easier to do in the UK than the US). If you don't work, leave your diary free for the first couple of weeks.

 **Your puppy's arrival at your home coincides with his most important life stage for bonding, so the first few weeks are very important.**

The most important factors in bonding with your puppy are TIME and PATIENCE, even if he makes a mess in the house or chews something. Spend time with your Corgi pup and you will have the most loyal lifelong friend. This emotional attachment may grow to become one of the most important aspects of your life – and certainly his.

Where Should the Puppy Sleep?

Just as you need a home, so a puppy needs a den; a haven where your pup feels safe. One of the most important things you can do for your young Corgi puppy is to ALLOW HIM LOTS AND LOTS OF SLEEP – as much as 18 or 20 hours a day!

Your puppy doesn't know this and will play until he drops, so make sure you put him in his quiet place regularly during the day - even if he doesn't want to go, he will fall asleep and get the rest he needs.

 The importance of pups getting enough sleep cannot be overemphasised. Lack of sleep can lead to over-excitement and naughtiness, which will make him harder to train.

Where do you want your new puppy to sleep? In the beginning, you cannot simply allow a pup to wander freely around the house. Ideally, he will be in a contained area at night, such as a pen or a crate. While it is not acceptable to shut a dog in a cage all day, you can keep your puppy in a crate at night until housetrained, and some adult Corgis prefer to sleep in a crate - with the door open.

Some breeders recommend putting the puppy in a crate (or similar) next to your bed for the first two or three nights before moving him to the permanent sleeping place. Knowing you are close and being able to smell you may help overcome initial fears.

Others recommend biting the bullet and starting the puppy off in his permanent sleeping place; he will quieten down after a few nights. Ask your own breeder's advice on this one.

 It's normal for most puppies to cry for the first night or two. Resist the urge to get up to hold and comfort your pup, who learns that crying equals attention. Invest in a pair of silicone earplugs; they soon settle down.

Young puppies can't go through the night without needing to pee (and sometimes poo); their bodies simply aren't up to it.

Many breeders recommend putting newspapers or pellets in the pup's confined area — but away from his bedding — so he can relieve himself during the night, until he can last for six or seven hours. Set your alarm for an early morning wake-up call and take him out first thing, even before you are dressed. As soon as he wakes, he will want to pee.

Alternatively, we set our alarm and get up with a puppy once in the middle of the night for the first week - lights off, no fuss, quick trip outside - to speed up housetraining. Again, ask your breeder what she recommends for your puppy.

We don't advise letting new puppies sleep on the bed. They are not housetrained. They need to learn their place in the household and have their own quiet place for resting.

It's up to you whether to let yours on the bed or not once housetrained. Corgis can sleep anywhere and anyhow; they don't need your comfy bed - and jumping on or off furniture can damage their joints.

And be aware that dogs snuffle, snore, fart and - if not in a crate - pad around the bedroom in the middle of the night and come up to the bed to check you are still there - or see if you want to play! None of this is conducive to a good night's sleep.

 A Corgi puppy used to being on his own every night (i.e. not in your bedroom) is less likely to develop Separation Anxiety, so consider this when deciding where he should sleep.

While it is not good to leave a dog alone all day, it is also not healthy to spend 24 hours a day together, as a dog can become too dependent. Although this is very flattering for you, it actually means that the dog is nervous and less sure of himself when you are not there. The last thing you want on your hands is an anxious Corgi.

The puppy's designated sleeping area should not be too hot, cold or damp and should be free from draughts. Little puppies can be sensitive to temperature fluctuations; if you live in a hot climate, your new pup may need air conditioning in the summertime.

It may surprise American readers to learn that it's not uncommon practice in the UK to contain the puppy in the kitchen or utility room until he's housetrained, and then to allow him to roam around the house at will. There are owners who do not allow their dogs upstairs, but many do.

When deciding whether to let your pup upstairs, remember that while he is still growing, his bones are not yet fully developed.

Studies have shown that pups who run up and down stairs regularly or jump on and off furniture before their growth plates are fully formed, may be more likely to develop joint problems later in life.

The time any young children spend with the puppy should be limited to a few short sessions a day and supervised. You wouldn't wake a baby every hour or so to play, and the same goes for puppies.

Wait a day or two before inviting friends round to see your handsome new puppy... and even then, don't inundate the puppy with constant visitors. However excited you are, your new arrival needs a few days to get over the stress of leaving mother and siblings and start bonding with you.

While confident, well-socialised puppies may settle in right away, other puppies may feel sad and a little afraid. Make the transition as gentle and unalarming as possible.

After a few sleep-deprived nights followed by days filled with entertaining your little puppy and dealing with chewed shoes, nipping and a few housetraining "accidents," your nerves might be a tiny bit frayed! Try to remain calm and patient... your puppy is doing his best... it just takes a little time for you both to get on the same wavelength.

 How you react and interact with each other during these first few days and weeks will help to shape your relationship and your Corgi's character for the rest of his life.

Treats and Toys

Puppies explore the world with their noses. Once they have found something interesting, they usually want to put it in their mouths, so chew treats and toys are a must. Don't scold a pup for chewing; it's natural.

Instead, put objects you don't want chewed out of reach and replace them with chew toys. There are some things you can't move out of puppy's way, like kitchen cupboards, doors, sofas, fixtures and fittings, so try not to leave your pup unattended for any length of time where he can chew something that is hard or expensive to replace.

 Avoid giving old socks, shoes or slippers, or your pup will naturally come to think of your footwear as fair game!

You can give a Corgi puppy a raw bone to gnaw on - NEVER cooked bones as these can splinter.

Avoid poultry and pork bones. Ribs - especially pork ribs - are too high in fat. Knuckle bones are a good choice and the bone should be too big for the puppy to swallow.

Photo: A "Fluffy" puppy eating a raw bone under supervision. More on Fluffies in Chapter 15. Grooming.

Puppies should ALWAYS BE SUPERVISED and the bone removed after an hour or so. Don't feed a puppy a bone if there are other dogs around, it could lead to food aggression.

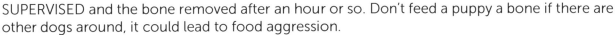 Raw bones contain bacteria, and families with babies or very young children shouldn't feed them indoors. Keep any bones in a fridge or freezer and always wash your hands after handling them.

Alternatives to real bones or plastic chew bones include natural ***reindeer antler*** chew toys which have the added advantage of calcium, although they are hard and have been known to crack teeth.

Natural chews preferred by some breeders include ears, dried rabbit pelt and tripe sticks – all excellent for teething puppies - once you have got over the smell!

Rawhide chews are not recommended as they can get stuck in a dog's throat or stomach, but bully sticks *(pictured)* are a good alternative.

Made from a bull's penis(!) they can be a good distraction from chewing furniture, etc. and help to promote healthy teeth and gums.

Bully sticks are highly digestible, break down easily in the stomach and are generally considered safe for all dogs. They are made from 100% beef, normally contain no additives or preservatives, come in different sizes and dogs love 'em.

NOTE: Puppies should be supervised while eating bully sticks or any other treats.

Dental sticks are good for cleaning your dog's teeth, but many contain preservatives and don't last very long with a determined chewer. One that does last is the **Nylabone Dura Chew Wishbone, pictured,** made of a type of plastic infused with flavours appealing to dogs. Get the right size and throw it away if it starts to splinter with sharp edges.

Another long-lasting treat option is the *Lickimat (pictured),* which you smear with a favourite food. This inexpensive mat will keep your puppy occupied for some time – although they can leave a bit of a mess.

Other choices include *Kong toys,* which are pretty indestructible, and you can put treats - frozen or fresh - or smear peanut butter inside (one without Xylitol, which is highly toxic to dogs) to keep your dog occupied while you are out. All of these are widely available online, if not in your local pet store.

As far as toys go, the *Zogoflex Hurley* and the *Goughnut (pictured)* are both strong and float – and you'll get your money back on both if your Corgi destroys them!

For safety, the Goughnut has a green exterior and red interior, so you can tell if your dog has penetrated the surface - as long as the green is showing, you can let your dog "goughnuts!"

A *natural hemp* or cotton tug rope is another option, as the cotton rope acts like dental floss and helps with teeth cleaning. It is versatile and can be used for fetch games as well as chewing.

FACT ⟩ Puppies' stomachs are sensitive, so be careful what goes in. Even non-poisonous garden plants can cause intestinal blockages and/or vomiting. Like babies, pups can quickly dehydrate, so if your puppy is sick or has watery poop for a day or two, seek veterinary advice.

Vaccinations and Worming

We recommend having your Corgi checked out by a vet soon after picking him up. In fact, some Puppy Contracts stipulate that the dog should be examined by a vet within a couple of days. This is to everyone's benefit and, all being well, you are safe in the knowledge that your puppy is healthy, at least at the time of purchase.

 Keep your pup on your lap away from other dogs in the waiting room as he will not yet be fully protected against infectious diseases.

Vaccinations

Puppies are covered by immunity from their mum until around eight weeks. Then all puppies need immunisation, and currently the most common way of doing this is by vaccination. They receive their first dose at around eight weeks old - although it can be any time from six to nine weeks old.

When you collect your puppy from the breeder, check if he has had his first round of vaccinations.

The second vaccination is done two to four weeks later, typically at 11 to 13 weeks.

UK veterinarian Dr Vicky Payne says: "Puppies are considered to be fully protected one to two weeks after their second vaccination (depending on brand). If intranasal Kennel Cough vaccine is given, this provides protection after three weeks.

"The WSAVA suggests an additional DHP vaccine at or after 16 weeks, but this is rarely offered by UK vets unless there is a disease outbreak (except Rottweilers who have weirdly long-acting maternal antibodies!).

"It is not advisable to delay the first vaccine so the second can be after 16 weeks as this severely impacts socialisation and habituation (getting used to new things).

"Speak to your vet to discuss a vaccine protocol which best suits local disease risks and the lifestyle of your puppy."

A booster is then required at six to 12 months.

One UK Corgi breeder added: "There are several different makers of

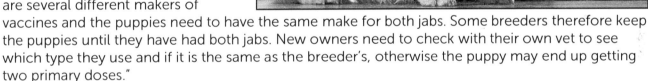

vaccines and the puppies need to have the same make for both jabs. Some breeders therefore keep the puppies until they have had both jabs. New owners need to check with their own vet to see which type they use and if it is the same as the breeder's, otherwise the puppy may end up getting two primary doses."

Good breeders provide new owners with full details of which vaccinations their pups have had and on what dates.

 An unimmunised puppy is at risk every time he meets other dogs as he has no protection against potentially fatal infectious diseases – and it is unlikely a pet insurer will cover an unvaccinated pup.

It should be stressed that vaccinations are generally safe and side effects are uncommon. If your Corgi is unlucky enough to be one of the *very few* that suffers an adverse reaction, here are some signs to look out for; a pup may exhibit one or more of these:

MILD REACTION - Sleepiness, irritability and not wanting to be touched. Sore or a small lump at the place where he was injected. Nasal discharge or sneezing. Puffy face and ears.

SEVERE REACTION - Anaphylactic shock. A sudden and quick reaction, usually before leaving the vet's, which causes breathing difficulties. Vomiting, diarrhoea, staggering and seizures.

A severe reaction is rare. There is a far greater risk of your Corgi either being ill or spreading disease if he does not have the injections.

BSAVA (British Small Animal Veterinary Association) recommends the following core vaccinations in the UK:

- ❖ CDV (Distemper)
- ❖ CPV (Parvo)
- ❖ CAV (Adenovirus or Infectious Canine Hepatitis)
- ❖ Leptospirosis (often called **Lepto**)

The Leptospira vaccine is not always considered to be a core vaccination as its use depends on veterinary advice within different parts of the UK and on the environmental and lifestyle risks of individual dogs.

Risk factors include exposure to (or drinking from) rivers, lakes or streams, roaming on rural properties (because of potentially infected wildlife, farm animals or water), exposure to wild or farm animals, and contact with rodents.

Owners should discuss the best course of action with their vet.

Many vets also recommend vaccinating against Kennel Cough (Bordetella). Rabies is very rare in the UK; it's more commonly seen in some US states and Europe. When deemed necessary, Rabies vaccines start at 12 weeks.

UK veterinarian Dr Sam Goldberg told us: "I also recommend puppies have at least one course of Fenbendazole (marketed in the UK as Panacur) as it also covers Giardia, which we see commonly in puppies with diarrhoea."

Google **"AKC puppy shots"** for a list of recommended vaccinations in the US. In-depth information on core vaccinations for America can be found on the World Small Animal Veterinary Association website, search online for **"WSAVA dog vaccinations"** or visit: https://wsava.org/wp-content/uploads/2020/01/WSAVA-Vaccination-Guidelines-2015.pdf (skip to Page 17).

WSAVA states: "Core vaccines for dogs are those that protect against canine distemper virus (CDV), canine adenovirus (CAV) and the variants of canine parvovirus type 2 (CPV-2)...with the final dose of these being delivered at 16 weeks or older and followed by a booster at six or 12 months of age."

Puppies in the US also need vaccinating separately against Rabies after 16 weeks, but this varies by state. There are optional vaccinations for Coronavirus (C) and - depending on where you live and if your dog is regularly around woods or forests - Lyme Disease.

Bordetella (Kennel Cough) is another non-core vaccine. It can be given intranasally, by tablet or injection, with boosters recommended for dogs deemed to be at high risk, e.g. when boarding or showing.

- ❖ Boosters for Distemper, Parvo and Canine Hepatitis are recommended no more often than every three years
- ❖ Boosters for Leptospirosis are every year

The current Lepto vaccine only protects against certain types of the many different variants of the Leptospira bacteria. However, having your dog vaccinated does decrease their risk of becoming sick with Lepto. The Lepto vaccination should not be given at the same time as Rabies.

NOTE: Some dogs have been known to have bad reactions to the Lepto 4 vaccine, although Corgis are not thought to be a particularly susceptible breed. A 2005 study of one million dogs found that only Dachshunds, Pugs, Miniature Pinschers, Boxers, Boston Terriers and Chihuahuas had a higher than average risk of vaccine reaction.

One UK breeder said: "Mine have one Lepto only along with the usual DHPP combo; I personally don't like to overload the immune system more than necessary. My pups will leave with at least the first round of vaccines completed at 10 weeks. In an ideal world they would not leave until 12 to 13 weeks plus... but there is good reason for suggesting that they adapt better to their new homes at a slightly younger age."

Diseases such as Parvo and Kennel Cough are highly contagious and you should not let your new arrival mix with other dogs - unless they are your own and have already been vaccinated - until a week after his last vaccination, otherwise he will not be fully immunised.

Parvovirus can also be transmitted by the faeces of many animals, including foxes.

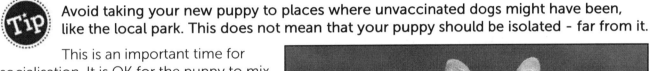 **Avoid taking your new puppy to places where unvaccinated dogs might have been, like the local park. This does not mean that your puppy should be isolated - far from it.**

This is an important time for socialisation. It is OK for the puppy to mix with other dogs that you absolutely know are up-to-date with their vaccinations and appropriate boosters.

Perhaps invite a friend's dog round to play in your garden or yard to begin the socialisation process.

The vet should give you a record card or send you a reminder when a booster is due, but it's also a good idea to keep a note of the date in your diary.

Tests have shown that the Parvovirus vaccination gives most animals at least seven years of immunity, while the Distemper jab provides immunity for five to seven years. In the US, many vets now recommend that you take your dog for a titre test once he has had his initial puppy vaccinations and six or 12-month booster.

··

The Diseases

Vaccinations protect your puppy and adult dog against some nasty diseases, so it's important to keep your Corgi up to date with protection.

Canine Distemper (CDV) is a contagious disease that affects different parts of the body, including the gastrointestinal and respiratory tracts, spinal cord and brain.

Common symptoms include a high fever, eye inflammation, eye and/or nose discharge, struggling for breath, coughing, vomiting, diarrhoea, loss of appetite and lethargy, and hardening of nose and footpads. It can also result in bacterial infections and serious neurological problems.

Canine Parvovirus (CPV) is a highly contagious viral disease that causes acute gastrointestinal illness in puppies commonly aged six to 20 weeks old, although older dogs are sometimes also affected. Symptoms include lethargy, depression and loss or lack of appetite, followed by a sudden onset of high fever, vomiting, and diarrhoea. Sadly, it is often fatal.

Infectious Canine Hepatitis (ICH), also called Canine Adenovirus or CAV, is an acute liver infection. The virus is spread in the poop, urine, blood, saliva, and nasal discharge of infected dogs, and other dogs pick it up through their mouth or nose.

The virus then infects the liver and kidneys. Symptoms include fever, depression, loss of appetite, coughing and a tender abdomen. Dogs can recover from mild cases, but more serious ones can be fatal.

Rabies is a fatal virus that attacks the brain and spinal cord. All mammals, including dogs and humans, can catch rabies, which is most often contracted through a bite from an infected animal.

Rabies usually comes from exposure to wild animals like foxes, bats and raccoons.

Leptospirosis (Lepto) is a bacterial disease that causes serious illness by damaging vital organs such as the liver and kidneys. Leptospirosis bacteria can spread in urine and can enter the body through the mouth, nose or open wounds.

Symptoms vary but include fever, jaundice (yellow gums and eyes), muscle pain and limping, weakness, reduced appetite, drinking more, vomiting, bloody diarrhoea, mouth ulcers and difficulty breathing.

An infected dog may quickly become restless and irritable, even showing aggression, or be excessively affectionate. One of the most well-known symptoms is foaming at the mouth, a sign that the disease is progressing.

Bordetella (Kennel Cough) - Dogs catch Kennel Cough when they breathe in bacteria or virus particles. The classic symptom is a persistent, forceful cough that often sounds like a goose honk.

Some dogs may show other symptoms, including sneezing, a runny nose or eye discharge, but appetite and energy levels usually remain the same. It is not often a serious condition and most dogs recover without treatment.

Lyme Disease gets into a dog's or human's bloodstream via a tick bite. Once there, the bacteria travel to different parts of the body and cause problems in organs or specific locations such as joints. These ticks are often founds in woods, tall grasses, thick brush and marshes – all places that Corgis love.

Lyme Disease can usually be treated if caught early enough. It can be life-threatening or shortening if left untreated.

Giardia is an infection caused by a microscopic parasite that attaches itself to a dog's intestinal wall causing a sudden onset of foul-smelling diarrhoea. It may lead to weight loss, chronic intermittent diarrhoea, and fatty poop.

The disease is not usually life threatening unless the dog's immune system is immature or compromised. Treated dogs usually recover, although very old dogs and those with compromised immune systems have a higher risk for complications.

Titres (Titers in the USA)

Some breeders and owners feel strongly that constantly vaccinating our dogs is having a detrimental effect on our pets' health, especially as some vaccinations are now effective for several years.

Vets recommend boosters every three years for the core vaccines; however, one alternative is titres. The thinking behind them is to avoid a dog having to have unnecessary repeat vaccinations for certain diseases as he already has enough antibodies present. Known as a *VacciCheck* in the UK, they are still relatively uncommon here; they are more widespread in the USA.

Not everybody agrees with titres. One vet I spoke to said that the titre results were only good for the day on which the test was taken, and it is true that many boarding kennels do NOT accept titres.

To *"titre"* is to take a blood sample from a dog (or cat) to determine whether he has enough antibodies to provide immunity against a particular disease, particularly Parvovirus, Distemper and Adenovirus (Canine Hepatitis).

If so, then a booster injection is not needed. Titering is NOT recommended for Leptospirosis, Bordetella or Lyme Disease, as these vaccines provide only short-term protection. Many US states also require proof of a Rabies vaccination.

The vet can test the blood at the clinic without sending off the sample, thereby keeping costs down for the owner. A titre for Parvovirus and Distemper currently costs around $100 in the US, sometimes more for Rabies, and a titre test in the UK costs as little as £40.

Titre levels are given as ratios and show how many times blood can be diluted before no antibodies are detected. So, if blood can be diluted 1,000 times and still show antibodies, the ratio would be 1:1000, which is a strong titre, while a titre of 1:2 would be "weak."

A *strong (high) titre* means that your dog has enough antibodies to fight off that specific disease and is immune from infection. A *weak titre* means that you and your vet should discuss revaccination - even then your dog might have some reserve forces known as *"memory cells"* that will provide antibodies when needed.

If you are going on holiday and taking your dog to kennels, check whether the kennel accepts titre records; many don't as yet.

In the UK, not many dog breeders use titres as yet, it is far more common in the US. But here's what some who do titre said: "I titre test periodically rather than do automatic boosters. They have all still had a full level of immunity on the tests - that's after their initial puppy vaccinations."

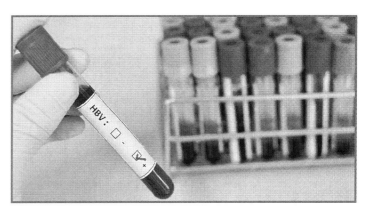

Another said: "When my puppies go to their new homes, I tell all my owners to follow their vet's advice about worming and vaccinating, as the last thing new owners require is to be at odds with their vets. All dogs must have their puppy vaccinations; it is now thought that the minimum duration of immunity is between seven and 15 years.

"However, a few owners do express concern about all the chemicals we are introducing into our puppies' lives and if they do, I explain how I try to give my dogs a chemical-free life, if possible, as adult dogs.

"Instead of giving my adult dogs their core vaccinations for Canine Distemper, Parvovirus and Adenovirus (Hepatitis) every three years, I just take my dogs down to the local vet and ask them to do something called a titre test, also known as a VacciCheck.

"They take a small amount of blood and check it for antibodies to the diseases. If they have antibodies to the diseases, there is no reason to give dogs a vaccination.

"However, you should note that there is a separate vaccination for Leptospirosis and Canine Parainfluenza, which is given annually. Leptospirosis is recommended by the BSAVA (British Small Animal Veterinary Association).

"Leptospirosis is more common in tropical areas of the world and not that common in England. In order to make a decision about whether to give this to your dog annually, you need to talk to your vet and do some research yourself so you can make an informed decision.

"We vaccinate our children up to about the age of 16. However, we don't vaccinate adults every one to three years, as it is deemed that the vaccinations they receive in childhood will cover them for a lifetime. This is what is being steadily proved for dogs and we are so lucky that we can titre test our dogs so we don't have to leave it to chance."

Another added: "I do not vaccinate my dogs beyond the age of four to five years, I now have them titre-tested. Every dog I have titre tested aged five to 10 years has been immune to the diseases vaccinated against when younger. I believe many vets over-vaccinate."

The (UK) Kennel Club now includes titre testing information in its Assured Breeder Pack, but has yet to include it under its general information on vaccines on its website. You dog may have to have the core vaccines before you can get insurance, Google *Pet vaccines: what owners need to know boughtbymany*" for more info.

···

Worming

All puppies need worming (technically, deworming). A good breeder will give the puppies their first dose of worming medication at around two weeks old, then probably again at five and eight weeks before they leave the litter – or even more often. Get the details and inform your vet exactly what treatment, if any, your pup has already had.

The main worms affecting puppies are roundworm and tapeworm. In certain areas of the US, the dreaded heartworm can also pose a risk. If you live in an affected area, discuss the right time to start heartworm medication when you visit your vet for puppy vaccinations – it's usually from a few months old.

The pill should be given every month when there is no heavy frost (frost kills mosquitos that carry the disease); giving it all year round gives the best protection. The heartworm pill is by prescription only and deworms the dog monthly for heartworm, round, hook, and whip worm.

Roundworm can be transmitted from a puppy to humans - often children - and can in severe cases cause blindness, or miscarriage in women, so it's important to keep up to date with worming.

Worms in puppies are quite common, usually picked up through their mother's milk. If you have children, get them into the habit of washing their hands after they have been in contact with the puppy – lack of hygiene is the reason why children are susceptible.

Most vets recommend worming a puppy once a month until he is six months old, and then around every two to three months. If your Corgi is regularly out and about running through woods and fields, it is important to stick to a regular worming schedule, as he is more likely to pick up worms than one that spends more time indoors.

Fleas can pass on tapeworms to dogs, but a puppy would not normally be treated unless it is known for certain he has fleas - and then only with caution. You need to know the weight of your puppy and then speak to your vet about the safest treatment to get rid of the parasites.

NOTE: Buy age-appropriate worming treatments.

It is necessary for breeders to worm their puppies. However, there are ways to reduce worming treatments for adult dogs.

Following anecdotal reports of some dogs experiencing side effects with chemical wormers, more owners are looking to use natural wormers on their dogs. If you go down this route, check exactly which worms your chosen herbal preparation deals with – it may not be all of them.

A method of reducing worming medication by testing your dog's stools is becoming more popular. You send a small sample of your dog's poo(p) off in an envelope every two to three months. If the result is positive, your dog needs worming, but if negative, no treatment is necessary.

In the UK this is done by veterinary labs like Wormcount www.wormcount.com and similar options are available in the USA – there is even a *"fecal worm test"* available from Amazon.com.

6. Crate and Housetraining

Crates are becoming more popular year on year. Used correctly, they speed up housetraining (potty training), give you and your puppy short breaks from each other and keep him safe at night or when you are out.

Most breeders involved in this book use crates with their puppies and young dogs. They may put them in for an hour or two during the day to give everyone a break, and then overnight until housetrained. Several also find that their adult Corgis like to take themselves off to their crates for a nap or to sleep overnight, normally with the door open. Trainers, behaviourists and people who show, compete or train dogs all use crates.

....

Using A Crate

A crate should always be used in a humane manner. If you decide to use one, spend time getting your puppy or adult dog used to it, so he comes to regard the crate as his own safe haven and not a punishment cell or prison.

Crates may not be suitable for every dog – or owner. Corgis are social animals; they thrive on interaction. Being caged for long periods is a miserable existence for any dog, but particularly for breeds with working heritage like the Welsh Corgi.

They are, however, very useful for puppies. We prefer a wire crate that allows air to pass through, although some breeders like the plastic ones.

A crate should NEVER be used as a means of confinement while you are out of the house for six, eight or more hours every day.

1. Always remove your dog's collar before leaving him inside when you are not there. Sadly, dogs have been known to die after panicking when their collars or tags got caught.

2. If the door is closed, your dog must have access to water while inside during the day. Non-spill water bowls are available from pet shops and online, as are bowls to attach to the bars.

Crates are ideal for giving you or the puppy some down time. You cannot watch a puppy 24/7 and a crate is a safe place for him while you get on with doing other things. Corgi puppies need LOTS OF SLEEP - but they don't know this, so a crate (or puppy pen) is an excellent place for resting without distractions. Your puppy first has to get used to the crate so he looks forward to going in there - some breeders may have already started the process.

NOTE: An eight-week-old puppy should not be in a crate for longer than two hours at a time during the day.

Not every owner wishes to use a crate, but used correctly they:

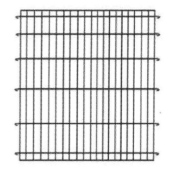

- ❖ **Are a useful housetraining tool**
- ❖ **Create a canine den**
- ❖ **Give you a break**
- ❖ **Limit access to the rest of the house until potty trained**
- ❖ **Are a safe place for the dog to nap or sleep at night**
- ❖ **Provide a safe way to transport your dog in a car**

Another very good reason to crate-train is that if your dog has to visit the vet or be confined for an illness, he will not have the added stress of getting used to a crate. Confining a Corgi NOT used to a crate is very stressful for both dog and owner.

Which Crate and Where?

The crate should be large enough to allow your dog to stretch out flat on his side without being cramped, and he should be able to turn around easily and sit up without hitting his head on the top.

Male corgis are generally larger than females and Cardigans are bigger than Pembrokes, so the size of crate will depend on the size of your dog. There should be room for him to stand up, turn around, and stretch out to sleep as well as a small water bowl. A general guideline is that a 36" (91.5cm) crate is a good size for most adult Welsh Corgis – although larger Corgis may require a bigger crate.

If the crate is too big for your pup, it can slow down housetraining. Some owners use a crate divider *(pictured, top right)* or block off a part of the crate while the pup is growing. A smaller area also helps him to feel more secure.

 Partially covering the crate with an old blanket creates a den for your new puppy at night. Only cover on three sides - leave the front uncovered and a gap around the bottom on all sides for air to flow. You can also just cover half or part of the crate to make it cosier for the pup.

Place the crate in the kitchen or another room where there are people during the day, preferably one with a hard, easy-to-clean floor. Puppies are curious pack animals and like to see and smell what is going on. If you have children, strike the balance between putting the crate in a place where the pup won't feel isolated, yet allowing him some peace and quiet.

Avoid putting the crate in a closed utility room or garage away from everybody, or he will feel lonely and sad. If you are using a room off the kitchen, allow the pup free run of the room and use a pet gate or baby gate with narrowly-spaced bars so his head can't get stuck but he can still see what's going on.

If you've got the space, a playpen, *pictured*, is great to use in addition – or as an alternative – to a crate.

The chosen location should be draught-free, not too hot and not in bright sunshine.

Opinions vary, but some owners put the crate right next to the bed for the first night or two - even raised up next to the bed - to help the puppy settle in quicker. A few have even been known to sleep downstairs on the sofa or an air mattress next to the crate for the first one or two nights! Others believe in putting the crate in its permanent place from day one.

Put the following items inside the crate during the day:

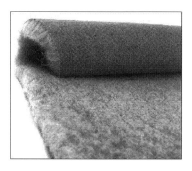

- ❧ Bedding – Vet Bed *(pictured)* or other bedding your puppy won't chew in a few days
- ❧ A blanket or item that has been rubbed with the mother's scent
- ❧ A non-spill water bowl
- ❧ A healthy chew to stop him gnawing the crate and bedding
- ❧ Possibly a toy to keep him occupied

At night, remove the water and chew. Add an extra blanket if you think he might get cold overnight; he has been used to the warmth of his littermates and mother. Puppies are little chew machines so, at this stage, don't spend a lot of money on a fluffy floor covering for the crate, as it is likely to get destroyed.

The widely available and washable *"Vet Bed"* is a good choice for bedding. Made from double-strength polyester, they retain extra heat, allow air to flow through and are widely used in vets' clinics to make dogs feel warm and secure. They also have drainage properties, so your pup will stay dry if he has an accident.

Vet Beds are also a good option for older dogs, as the added heat is soothing for aging muscles and joints. You can buy "Vet Bedding" by the roll, which keeps costs down. One breeder added: "Don't use beds with stuffing at this age, as once they learn to de-stuff a bed, it may become a lifelong habit and possibly graduate into de-stuffing furniture or pillows later!"

 Consider putting a Snuggle Puppy in the crate with the new puppy. The Snuggle Puppy *(pictured)* is a safe soft toy with a heartbeat. (Remove it if your dog chews it and exposes the internal mechanism).

Whining

If your puppy is whining, whimpering or howling in the crate, make sure:

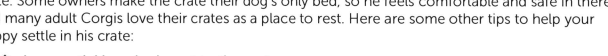

A. **He doesn't need the toilet.**

B. **He is warm.**

C. **He is physically unharmed.**

Then the reason is because he doesn't want to be alone. He has come from the warmth and security of his mother and litter, and the Brave New World can be a very daunting place for a two- or three-month-old puppy all alone in a new home.

He is not crying because he is in a cage. He would cry if he had the freedom of the room - he is crying because he is separated. Dogs are pack animals and being alone is not a natural state for them.

However, with patience and the right training, he will get used to being alone and being in the crate. Some owners make the crate their dog's only bed, so he feels comfortable and safe in there, and many adult Corgis love their crates as a place to rest. Here are some other tips to help your puppy settle in his crate:

- ❧ **Leave a ticking clock next to the crate, or**

- ❖ Leave a radio on softly nearby
- ❖ Lightly spray DAP on a cloth or small towel and place in the crate

FACT ❯ DAP, or Dog Appeasing Pheromone, is a synthetic form of the pheromone that nursing Corgis (and other breeds) give off after giving birth and then again after weaning to reassure their puppies that everything is fine.

DAP has been found to help reduce fear in young puppies, as well as Separation Anxiety, phobias and aggression caused by anxiety in adult dogs. According to one French study: "DAP has no toxicities or side effects and is particularly beneficial for sick and geriatric dogs." Google *"Canadian Veterinary Journal Dog Appeasing Pheromone"* for more details of the study.

NOTE: There is also an ADAPTIL collar with slow-release DAP, which is designed to reduce fear in anxious adult dogs. It gets good reports from many, not all, owners.

Travel Crates

Special travel crates are useful for the car, or for taking your dog to the vet's, a show or on holiday. Choose one with holes or mesh in the side to allow free movement of air rather than a solid one, in which a dog can soon overheat.

Put the crate on the shady side of the interior and make sure it can't move around; put the seatbelt around it. If it's very sunny and the top of the crate is wire mesh, cover part of it so your dog has some shade and put the windows up and the air conditioning on.

Photo: Margaret E. Leighton's Owain (Brnayr Over the Hills and Far Away) and Bubbles (Pemcader Black Glamour) securely crated in the car.

Alternatively, you can buy a metal grille/dog guard to keep your dogs confined to the back of the car.

One breeder adds: "Crate training applies to travel too. Often, people get frustrated if a dog has an "accident" in the car, but forget to let them out before they set off. I also use a Ventlock, *pictured,* on the car boot to keep it open slightly, allowing air to flow, if they have to be in there."

NOTE: Dogs can also be safely transported using a seat belt harness – make sure it's the right size and fitted properly. Some owners feel it is safer for their dogs if they fasten the crates on the back seat, as modern cars are designed to crumple in a crash; another alternative is a crush-proof crate.

By law, dogs have to be *"suitably restrained"* inside a car. Allowing your dog to roam freely inside the car is not safe, particularly if you - like me – are a bit of a "lead foot" on the brake and accelerator!

And avoid letting your Corgi ride with his head out of the window - even if he does look like Easy Rider! Wind pressure can cause ear infections or bits of dust, insects, etc. to fly into unprotected eyes. Your dog will also fly forward if you suddenly hit the brakes.

Tip Corgis have thick double coats. If it's a hot or even warm day, don't leave yours unattended in a vehicle, they can overheat alarmingly quickly - within minutes.

Getting your Puppy Used to a Crate

Once you've got your crate, you'll need to learn how to use it properly so that it becomes a safe, comfortable den for your dog. Many breeders will have already started the process but, if not, here's a tried-and-tested method of getting your dog firstly to accept a crate, and then to actually want to spend time in there.

These are the first steps:

1. Drop a few puppy treats around and then inside the crate.

2. Put your pup's favourite toy in there.

3. Keep the door open.

4. Feed your puppy's meals inside the crate. Again, keep the door open.

 Place a chew or treat INSIDE the crate and close the door while your puppy is OUTSIDE the crate. He will be desperate to get in there! Open the door, let him in and praise him for going in. Fasten a long-lasting chew inside the crate and leave the door open. Let your puppy wander inside to spend some time eating the chew.

5. **After a while, close the crate door and feed him some treats through the mesh.** At first just do it for a few seconds at a time, then gradually increase the time. If you do it too fast, he may become distressed.

6. **Slowly build up the amount of time he's in the crate.** For the first few days, stay in the room, then gradually leave first one minute, then three, then 10, 30 and so on.

Next Steps

7. Put your dog in his crate at regular intervals during the day - maximum two hours.

8. **If your pup is not yet housetrained, make sure he has relieved himself BEFORE you put him in the crate.** Putting him in when he needs to eliminate will slow down training.

9. **Don't crate only when you are leaving the house.** Put him in the crate while you are home as well. Use it as a *"sleep zone"* or *"safe zone."* By using the crate both when you are home and while you are gone, your dog becomes comfortable there and not worried that you won't come back, or that you are leaving him alone. This helps to prevent Separation Anxiety.

10. **If you are leaving your dog unattended,** give him a chew and remove his collar, tags and anything else that could become caught in an opening or between the bars.

11. **Make it very clear to any children that the crate is NOT a den for them,** but a *"special room"* for the dog.

12. **Although the crate is your dog's haven and safe place, it must not be off-limits to humans.** You should be able to reach inside at any time.

13. **Try and wait until your dog is calm before putting him in the crate.** If he is behaving badly and you grab him and shove him in the crate straight away, he will associate the crate with punishment. Try not to use the crate if you can't calm him down, instead either leave the room or put the dog in another room until he calms down.

14. **The crate should ALWAYS be associated with a positive experience in your dog's mind.**

15. **Don't let your dog out of the crate when he is barking or whining,** or he'll think that this is the key to opening the door. Wait until he has stopped whining for at least 10 or 20 seconds before letting him out.

Reminder:

❖ During the day the crate door should not be closed until your pup is happy with being inside

❖ At night-time it is OK to close the door

❖ If you don't want to use a crate, use a pet gate, section off an area inside one room, or use a puppy pen to confine your pup at night

---

Housetraining

You have four major factors in your favour when it comes to toilet training a Corgi:

1. **They are intelligent.**
2. **They are biddable (willing to accept instruction).**
3. **They respond very well to rewards - praise, treats, games or toys.**
4. **They enjoy pleasing you.**

Puppies naturally want to keep their space clean; it's instinctive. From when he can first walk, a pup will move away from his mother and sleeping area to eliminate.

The aim of housetraining is to teach the puppy exactly WHERE this space starts and finishes.

When a puppy arrives at your home, he may think that a corner of the crate, the kitchen, your favourite rug or anywhere else in the house is an OK place for him to relieve himself.

Through training and vigilance, you will teach him that the house is part of his and your "space" and therefore it's not OK for him to pee or poop indoors.

Many good breeders will have already started the process, so when you pick up your puppy, all you have to do is carry on the good work!

 The speed and success of housetraining depends to some degree on the individual dog and how much effort the breeder has already put in. However, the single most important factor in success is undoubtedly the owner.

The more vigilant you are during the early days, the quicker your Corgi will be housetrained. It's as simple as that.

How much time and effort are YOU prepared to put in at the beginning to speed up housetraining? Taking the advice in this chapter and being consistent with your routines and repetitions is the quickest way to get results. Clear your schedule for a week or so and make housetraining your No.1 priority – it'll be worth it.

I get complaints from some American readers when I write: "Book a week or two off work and housetrain your dog!" I know Americans get much shorter vacation time than most Europeans, but honestly, if you can take a few days off work to monitor housetraining at the beginning, it will speed the process up no end.

If you're starting from scratch, your new arrival thinks that the whole house is away from his sleeping quarters, and therefore a great place for a pee or a poop! And, if yours is a rescue Corgi, he may well have picked up some bad habits before arriving at your home. In these cases, time, patience and vigilance are essential to teach your dog the new ways.

Corgis, like all dogs, are creatures of routine - not only do they like the same things happening at the same times every day, but establishing a regular routine with your dog also helps to speed up obedience and toilet training.

 To keep things simple in a pup's mind, have a designated area in your garden or yard that the pup can use as a toilet. Dogs are tactile creatures, so they pick a toilet area that feels good under their paws.

Dogs often like to go on grass - but this will do nothing to improve your lawn, so think carefully about what area to encourage your puppy to use.

Perhaps consider a small patch of crushed gravel in your garden – but don't let your puppy eat it - or a particular corner of the garden or yard away from any attractive or spiky plants. *Photo courtesy of Lisa Thompson.*

Opinion is divided on puppy pads. Some breeders advise against using them as they can slow down potty training, and some say that newspapers can also encourage a pup to soil inside the house. Because dogs are tactile and puppy pads are soft and comfy, dogs like going on them! When you remove the pads, the puppy may be tempted to find a similar surface, like a carpet or rug.

A general rule of thumb is that puppies can last for one hour per month of age without urinating, sometimes longer. So:

- 🐾 An eight-week pup can last for two hours
- 🐾 A 12-week-old pup can last for three hours
- 🐾 A 16-week pup can last for four hours
- 🐾 A six-month-old can last for six hours

NOTE: This only applies when the puppy is calm and relaxed.

 If a puppy is active or excited, he will urinate more often, and if he is excited to see you, he may urinate at will.

To speed up the process even more, consider setting your alarm clock to get up in the night to let the pup out to relieve himself for the first week. Don't switch the lights on or make a fuss of the pup, just take him outside. You might hate it, but it can shorten the overall time spent housetraining.

Housetraining Tips

Follow these tips to speed up housetraining:

1. Constant supervision is essential for the first week or two if you are to housetrain your puppy quickly. If nobody is there, he will learn to pee or poop inside the house.

2. Take your pup outside at the following times:
   a) As soon as he wakes – every time
   b) Shortly after each feed
   c) After a drink
   d) When he gets excited
   e) After exercise or play
   f) Last thing at night
   g) Initially every hour or two - whether or not he looks like he wants to go

You may think that the above list is an exaggeration, but it isn't! Housetraining a pup is almost a full-time job in the beginning. If you are serious about toilet training your puppy quickly, then clear your diary for a week or two and keep your eyes firmly glued on your pup...learn to spot that expression or circling motion just before he makes a mess on your floor.

1. Take your pup to **the same place** every time, you may need to use a lead (leash) in the beginning - or tempt him there with a treat. Some say it is better to only pick him up and dump him there in an emergency, as it is better if he learns to take himself to the chosen toilet spot.

   Dogs naturally develop a preference for going in the same place or on the same surface. Take or lead him to the same patch every time so he learns this is his toilet area.

2. **No pressure – be patient. Welsh Corgis do not perform well under pressure.** You must allow your distracted little darling time to wander around and have a good sniff before performing his duties – but do not leave him, stay around a short distance away. Unfortunately, puppies are not known for their powers of concentration, so it may take a while for him to select the perfect bathroom spot!

3. **Housetraining a Corgi should ALWAYS be reward-based, never negative or aggressive.** Give praise and/or a treat IMMEDIATELY after he has performed his duties in the chosen spot. Persistence, praise and rewards are best for quick results.

4. **Share the responsibility.** It doesn't have to be the same person who takes the dog outside all the time. In fact, it's easier if there are a couple of you, as this is a very time-demanding business. Just make sure you stick to the same principles, command and patch of ground.

5. **Stick to the same routine.** Sticking to the same times for meals, exercise, playtime, sleeping and toilet breaks will help settle him into his new home and housetrain him quicker.

6. **Use the same word** or command when telling your puppy to go to the toilet – or while he is in the act. He will gradually associate this phrase or word with toileting.

7. **Use your voice ONLY if you catch him in the act indoors.** A short sharp sound is best - **ACK! EH!** It doesn't matter, as long as it is loud enough to make him stop.

    Then either pick him up or run enthusiastically towards your door, calling him to the chosen place and wait until he has finished what he started indoors. Only use the ACK! sound if you actually catch him MID-ACT.

8. **No punishment, no scolding, no smacking or rubbing his nose in it.** Your Corgi will hate it. He will become either more stubborn or afraid to do the business in your presence, so may start going secretly behind the couch or under the bed.

    Accidents will happen. He is a baby with a tiny bladder and bowels and little self-control. Housetraining takes time - remain calm, ignore him (unless you catch him in the act) and clean up the mess.

FACT ❭ Corgis have a highly developed sense of smell. If there's an "accident" indoors, use a special spray from your vet or a hot washing powder solution to completely eliminate the smell, which will discourage him from going there again.

9. **Look for the signs.** These may be:
    a. Whining
    b. Sniffing the floor in a determined manner
    c. Circling and looking for a place to go
    d. Walking uncomfortably - particularly at the rear end!

    Take him outside straight away, and try not to pick him up all the time. He has to learn to walk to the door himself when he needs to go outside.

10. **Use a crate at night-time.**

Corgis love being with you and young puppies certainly won't pee or poop outside on their own when it's pouring down. One breeder advises new owners to invest in a good umbrella and be prepared for lots of early mornings in the first few weeks!

Troubleshooting

Don't let one or two little accidents derail your potty training - accidents WILL happen! Here is a list of some possible scenarios and action to take:

* **Puppy peed when your back was turned -** Don't let him out of his crate or living space unless you are prepared to watch his every move

* **Puppy peed or pooped in the crate -** Make sure the crate isn't too big; it should be just enough for him to stand up and turn around, or divided. Also, make sure he is not left in the crate for too long

- ❖ **Puppy pooped without warning** - Observe what he does immediately beforehand. Next time you'll be able to scoop him up and take him outside before an accident happens

- ❖ **Puppy pees on the same indoor spot daily** - Make sure you get rid of the smell completely and don't give puppy too much indoor freedom too soon. Some breeders use *"tethering"* and fasten the pup to them on a lead indoors so they can watch the puppy like a hawk and monitor his behaviour. They only do this for perhaps a week - but it can speed up housetraining no end

- ❖ **Puppy not responding well** - Increase the value of your treats for housetraining and nothing else. Give a tiny piece of meat, chicken etc. ONLY when your Corgi eliminates outdoors in the chosen spot.

Even after all your hard work, occasionally some dogs continue to eliminate indoors, often males, even though they understand housetraining perfectly well. This is called "marking" and they do it to leave a scent and establish your home as their territory. This can take time to cure - although neutering generally reduces the urge to mark indoors.

Apartment Living

Although Corgis were bred for a life in the Great Outdoors, they are adaptable dogs. Provided the dog's exercise needs are met and his brain is challenged, there is no reason why a Corgi can't live in an apartment. If you do live in an apartment, access to outdoors is often not so easy and you may wish to indoor housetrain.

Most dogs can be indoor housetrained fairly easily, especially if you start early. Stick to the same principles already outlined, the only difference is that you will be placing your Corgi on puppy pads or newspaper instead of taking him outdoors.

Start by blocking off a section of the apartment for your pup. Use a baby gate or make your own barrier.

You will be able to keep a better eye on him than if he has free run of the whole place, and it will be easier to monitor his "accidents."

Select a corner away from his eating and sleeping area that will become his permanent bathroom area – a carpeted area is to be avoided if possible.

At first, cover a larger area than is actually needed - about 3x3 or 4x4 feet - with puppy pads or newspapers and gradually reduce the area as training progresses.

Take your puppy there as indicated in the **Housetraining Tips** section.

Praise him enthusiastically when he eliminates on the puppy pad or newspaper. If you catch him doing his business out of the toilet area, pick him up and take him back there. Correct with a firm voice - never a hand.

With positive reinforcement and close monitoring, he will learn to walk to the toilet area on his own.

Owners attempting indoor housetraining should be aware that it does generally take longer than outdoor training. Some dogs will resist. Also, once a dog learns to go indoors, it can be difficult to train them to go outdoors on their walks. If you don't monitor your puppy carefully enough in the beginning, indoor housetraining will be difficult.

Tip **Whether you are indoor or outdoor housetraining, the first week or two is crucial to your puppy learning what is expected of him.**

Bell Training

Bell Training is a method that works well with some dogs. There are different types of bells, the simplest are inexpensive and widely available, consisting of a series of adjustable bells that hang on a nylon strap from the door handle.

Another option is a small metal bell attached to a metal hanger that fixes low down on the wall next to the door with two screws. As with all puppy training, do bell training in short bursts of five to 10 minutes or your easily-distracted little student will switch off!

1. Show your dog the bell, either on the floor, before it is fixed anywhere or by holding it up. Point to it and give the command *"Touch," "Ring,"* or whatever word you decide.

2. Every time he touches it with his nose, reward with praise.

3. When he rings the bell with his nose, give him a treat. You can rub on something tasty, like peanut butter, to make it more interesting.

4. Take the bell away between practice sessions.

5. Once he rings the bell every time you show it to him, move on to the next step.

6. Take the bell to the door you use for housetraining. Place a treat just outside the door while he is watching. Then close the door, point to the bell and give the command.

7. When he rings the bell, open the door and let him get the treat outside.

8. When he rings the bell as soon as you place a treat outside, fix the bell to the door or wall.

9. The next time you think he needs to relieve himself, walk to the door, point to the bell and give the command. Give him a treat or praise if he rings it, let him out immediately and reward him again with enthusiastic praise when he performs his duty.

Tip **In between training sessions, ring the bell yourself EVERY time you open the door to let him outside.**

Some dogs can get carried away by their own success and ring the bell any time they want your attention, fancy a wander outdoors or see a passing squirrel!

Make sure that you ring the bell every time your puppy goes out through the door to relieve himself, but DON'T ring the bell if he is going out to play. And if he starts playing or dawdling around the garden or yard, bring him in!

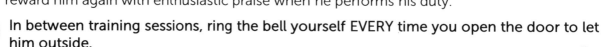

Expert Opinion

Fran Fricker, Kennel Club Assured Breeder of Kerman Cardigan Welsh Corgis and multiple prizewinner at Crufts: "When it leaves me a puppy will have its own snuggle blanket that will have the smell of mum and siblings on. I always recommend a crate to sleep in - you can make this cosy and include a toilet area; it also becomes their own space in the future. A clock ticking or the radio on low and a low light are also reassuring in the beginning.

"Place the crate in a room where it will stay, probably the kitchen as when you lock up for the night you can form a routine of out for toileting then into bed, and when you come down in the morning straight out to toilet.

"I know it's tempting to let the puppy sleep in the crate in your bedroom, but they soon get wise to this - and the attention - and will not like being put downstairs at a later date. Also stairs are a no-no, there's a lot of weight in an adult Cardigan."

Fran and her Kerman show team.
Photo by Will Harris.

"When a puppy leaves me, I always recommend a crate. As a breeder I am happy to advise and even purchase a suitable crate on a new owner's behalf. I have a crate in all my rooms and when at work I have a crate in my office.

"My van is custom-fitted with crates for travelling and showing, but before I had this, I would assemble crates and secure them in my car before setting off.

"From a young age my pups are used to going in and out of a crate; it holds no fear for them and is looked upon as a safe haven - their own space - and not as a punishment. It allows a puppy to have rest time and yet still see what's going on around them.

"They can be fed in a crate and also may sleep in a crate. Water should always be available and can be supplied by a feeder bottle, which is great for travelling, or a bowl.

"A crate should be large enough for an adult to stand up in with *"ear room"* and long enough to stretch out and turn around in. It's important that puppies do not over-exercise, and a crate is ideal to ensure this. Also, it's regarded as the puppy's space so when the children are around, they respect this and will leave the puppy to rest; remembering that puppies are NOT playthings.

"Having two crates is ideal and I recommend a larger living crate for the house where a puppy will have a bedding and a toilet area, and a smaller crate for travelling. Many hotels will accept dogs in crates in the bedrooms, so they can be easily accommodated on holidays.

"How long in a crate? For a puppy, short spells when resting, but if the crate is open they will often go in for a sleep at whatever age. Overnight, after toileting and before breakfast is part of the crate training routine, and a puppy owner is advised accordingly."

Here's what some experienced Pembroke breeders and owners have to say, starting with Carole Turner, of Cottonfields Pembrokes, who has been involved with Corgis for over 50 years and is Secretary of the South West Welsh Corgi Club: "Crates are a really good safety device as it's not always possible to watch a puppy - the average home has so many potential hazards for a mischievous puppy. Also, a crate is a good place for a puppy to relax and have a nap before they get overtired.

"With a new puppy, I recommend putting newspaper in part of the crate overnight, but then getting up after about three or four hours to take the puppy outside for the first few nights. It really pays off by speeding up housetraining. Corgis are intelligent and I think you can get a puppy trained within a week or so if you are very vigilant. I don't normally recommend the use of puppy pads unless you live in an apartment.

"In the beginning, I teach them to like the crate by putting their food in there and biscuits at bedtime. Mine love their crates; I can hardly open the door before they dash inside."

SMILE LADIES! Pictured left to right are Carole's Cottonfields gals: M (The Bond Girl, aged 3), Jessie (Black Eye'd Pea, 12) and Violet (Antipodean, 5). Photo by Lucy Badham-Thornhill.

"Getting your puppy used to a crate is very useful if you travel, if they have to go to the vet's or if you show them. It's their safe place. I have my crates on the back seat of my car and always lift my Corgis out of the car - you don't want them jumping out."

Bred With Heart Breeder Lisa Thompson, Thompson's Corgis, Wisconsin: "I do use a crate, but not for long stretches of time. They don't like to potty in their beds, so they learn really fast with a crate. The second the pup wakes up, take it outside.

"All my dogs have crates, the adults usually don't have the door closed, but they go in there anyway to get away from kids or other dogs that are annoying them!"

Linda Roberts, Cherastayne Pembroke and Welsh Corgi League Breed Health Co-Ordinator: "I would encourage puppy buyers to invest in a suitably-sized crate that can be used both in the car for travelling and in the house as a safe, secure environment for the puppy. Providing there is a warm bed, suitable toys, and fresh water at all times, then they make a perfect bed for both puppies and adults.

"You will need a larger crate as your puppy grows up. It should be big enough to allow the dog to lie flat out without touching the sides. It goes without saying that the puppy should receive adequate exercise, mental and physical stimulation and the opportunity to go outside to be clean as often as possible."

Kevin Dover, breeder of 45 years with Pemcader Pembrokes: "The biggest mistake any new owner can make is to take the puppy to bed. Puppies have to learn parameters, so I always recommend that they are kept downstairs, preferably in a large crate or a pen with a bed and somewhere to pee if required (pads are great for this).

"Some will make a meal of the first night or two - usually howling for some time - and others will just settle down and sleep. It's always a good idea to feed as late as you possibly can as this will help to settle them. Some people recommend a clock close by as the ticking tends to soothe but I've never personally used this method.

"Over time they should be let out to relieve themselves and then go onto their bedding for the night. I've always slept mine in crates as they feel this is "their" space and feel secure."

Lucy Badham-Thornhill has owned Corgis for 30 years: "I bred Lettice and was able to get her used to a crate right from the beginning, in a pen with her littermate. They slept in the crate day and night, but at night I shut the door. I then separated them, crates side by side. By the time her brother left, they were both very used to - and quite happy in - the crate.

"At that point I moved Lettice to a room with her mother and grandmother at night. They were in their beds, Lettice in her crate. She was happy with this, but after a few months and when she could last the night, she swapped into her own bed with no problem."

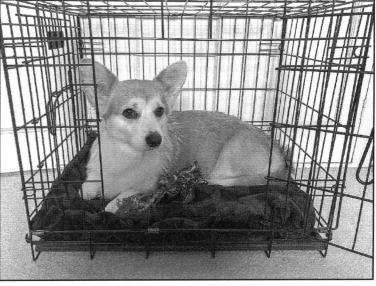

Home Sweet Home! Lettice in her crate. Photo by Lucy.

"A new puppy can be a small lost being, which is where I think a crate is useful. It needs to be made a safe cosy *'own'* sanctuary. Safe toys, bedding and, initially, meals in the crate are useful.

"Shut in for short times at first, but gradually lengthen the time, e.g. when you can see the puppy is getting sleepy, put him or her in for a nap, (s)he will probably then choose it as a place to sleep in. I also think it is important for the owner to be around, not to leave a new puppy by itself too soon.

"Crates can be useful protection from other boisterous dogs, children etc. and for a sick or injured dog. Nervous dogs can sometimes be better if the crate is covered. In the car I just put them in their crates, which becomes a normal part of any car journey.

"When they are at home they sleep in beds, but sometimes elsewhere they sleep in crates and do not seem to mind at all. I do not leave them in crates in the daytime because we are lucky with space here."

Alexandra Trefán-Török, Born To Be Corgis, Hungary: "We don't use crates, we have a special dog room, and five to six hours is the maximum time they are in there. We always do plenty of outside activity beforehand, so they just sleep through these hours."

Kennel Club Assured Breeder Jo Evans, Cerdinen Pembrokes: "I have always used a crate for my dogs to sleep in to start with and do suggest this to other people. It needs to be made comfortable with a few toys, but from the dog's point of view it is a safe place to be away from the bustle of life. They can relax in there in peace.

"From an owner's point of view, you know where your dog is and that it isn't up to mischief chewing anything! It also makes housetraining easier as a dog doesn't want to wee in its bed. But I wouldn't suggest it is shut in all day. They do need periods of playtime.

"My puppies tend to be in their crates with the door closed from 10.30pm until about 6am; I do this as long as is necessary when they are young, or keep them in a safe room. I have found my Corgis like to go in their crate even when the door is open."

Experienced owner Kevin Egan: "The crate is used only at shows so the dogs can settle during proceedings. We did use crates when the dogs were puppies; they were placed in there at bedtime so they could get used to their own place and sleep peacefully.

"The crate can, of course, work as car transport. But I have now found a waterproof throw with individual harness attachments that I think is more suited to a regular saloon car."

Assured Breeders Piotr and Johnathan Mazur-Jones, Creslow Corgis: "We always tell our new puppy families they should think long term and set the rules early, so start off where you want the pup or adult dog to sleep.

"Our pups go crate-trained to their new homes and we always advise families to keep this up until at least one year of age as it gives pups sense of security and safety. And owners know the pup cannot come to harm while they may be out or distracted."

Photo: Hello World! Moose (Creslow River Exe), bred by Piotr and Johnathan.

"Long term we give our adult dogs choices where they sleep, and most select inside their crate - even if they start off somewhere else; it's their safe space."

Experienced owner Vicky Methuen, Pembrokeshire: "We travel a lot, both in Wales and the rest of the UK, and I put Billie Corgi in the crate, usually for about two to three hours before we stop for a break; she is content.

"Corgis are very good forward planners. On longer journeys they seem to know where we are going before we get there - I am assuming they can even understand Satnav instructions!"

7. Feeding a Corgi

Providing the right nutritional fuel helps keep your dog's biological machine in excellent working order. It is important for Corgis of all ages to have a healthy diet because:

1. They can become overweight if they get too many calories.

2. They are active dogs that need the right fuel.

3. The right food can help reduce or eliminate food sensitivities and skin issues.

4. Good nutrition can have a beneficial effect on joints and other potential health issues.

While the good news is that the vast majority of Corgis thrive on a fairly straightforward diet of high-quality kibble, some owners prefer a more natural diet for their dogs. And a handful of Corgis can have sensitive stomachs or occasional bouts of colitis, so this chapter aims to cover all the bases.

The topic of feeding can be a minefield; owners are bombarded with advertisements and numerous choices. There is not one food that gives every single dog the strongest bones, the most energy, the best coat, the easiest digestion, the least gas and the longest life.

The question is: *"Which food is best for MY Corgi?"* Fortunately, Corgis are not a breed known for having many food problems – the main issue is how to stop them eating everything! Food only becomes an issue if:

❖ You are feeding too much, or

❖ Your dog has a reaction to a certain type of food

Veterinarian Dr Marianne Dorn, The Rehab Vet, says:

"There are three really important points to make about feeding dogs:

1. Feed a *"complete"* adult diet - and puppies need "complete puppy food." For commercial food, whether kibble, tinned, raw, etc., the label "complete diet" is a legal term.

    "Complementary diets" and many home-made diets fail to meet the dog's basic nutritional needs. In order to make a home-made diet, the owner must look up full details on how to do this, and then measure the quantities each day.

2. Measure the daily ration of food and stick to this. Otherwise the dog is likely to become overweight.

3. Limit treats and extras. Otherwise they can easily become the main source of calories each day.

Feeding Puppies

Corgi puppies should stay with the litter until at least eight to 10 weeks old to give the mother enough time to teach her offspring important rules about life.

Initially, pups get all their nutrients from their mother's milk and then are gradually weaned (put on to a different food by the breeder) from three or four weeks of age. Unless the puppy has had an extremely varied diet at the breeder's, continue feeding the same puppy food and at the same times as the breeder when you bring your puppy home.

It is always a good idea to find out what the breeder feeds, as she knows what her bloodlines do well on.

If you decide to switch foods, do so gradually, as dogs' digestive systems cannot handle sudden changes of diet. (By the way, if you stick to the identical brand, you can change flavours in one go). These ratios are recommended by Doctors Foster & Smith Inc:

- Days 1-3 add 25% of the new food

- Days 4-6 add 50%

- Days 7-9 add 75%

- Day 10 feed 100% of the new food

If at any time your puppy starts being sick, has loose stools or is constipated, slow the rate at which you are switching the food. Puppies soon dehydrate, so seek veterinary advice if vomiting or loose or watery poop continues for more than a day.

Some breeders purposely feed their pups lots of different foods over the first few weeks of life to reduce the risk of them developing sensitive stomachs or becoming fussy eaters – although Corgis who turn their nose up at food are very few and far between!

As a general rule of thumb, feed puppies:

- Four meals a day up to the age of 18 weeks

- Three meals a day at regular intervals from 18 weeks to 9 months

- Two meals a day from 9 to 18 months

Theoretically you can then put your dog on one meal a day, although most vets and breeders now recommend feeding adult dogs two meals a day at the same times, one in the morning and one in the late afternoon/early evening. Corgis are small to medium-sized dogs, so twice a day suits them.

During the first six months, puppies grow quickly and it is important that they grow at **a controlled rate.** Giving your puppy more or less food will not affect his adult size, it will only affect his weight and rate of growth.

Regardless of what you may have read, do NOT let your puppy free feed - i.e. eat as much as he wants.

It's very important during the first weeks and months that body weight is monitored, and most Corgis - young and old - will eat until they pop!

FACT ❯ Corgi puppies should look well-covered, not skinny and not have a pot belly. Overfeeding a pup leads to excess weight, which can make them vulnerable to health issues in later life.

There are three **Life Stages** to consider when feeding: **Puppy, Adult and Senior**, also called **Veteran**.

Some manufacturers also produce a **Junior** feed for adolescent dogs. If you decide on a commercially-prepared food, choose one approved either for **Puppies** or for **All Life Stages**.

An **Adult** feed won't have enough protein, and the balance of calcium and other nutrients will not be right for a pup. Puppy food is very high in calories and nutritional supplements. Look at switching to an **Adult** food when your pup is around 10 to 14 months old.

NOTE: Feeding elderly dogs is covered in **Chapter 18. Caring for Older Corgis.**

....

Reading Dog Food Labels

A NASA scientist would have a hard job understanding some manufacturers' labels, so it's no easy task for us lowly dog owners. Here are some things to look out for on the manufacturers' labels:

- 🐾 **The ingredients are listed by weight and the top one should always be the main content,** such as chicken or lamb. Don't pick one where grain is the first ingredient; it is a poor-quality feed. If your Corgi has a food allergy or intolerance to wheat, check whether a food is gluten free; all wheat contains gluten

- 🐾 **Chicken meal (dehydrated chicken) has more protein than fresh chicken, which is 80% water.** The same goes for beef, fish and lamb. So, if any of these "meals" are No. 1 on the ingredient list, the food should contain enough protein

- 🐾 Anything labelled *"human-grade"* is higher quality than normal dog food ingredients. E.g. human-grade chicken includes the breast, thighs and other parts of the chicken suitable for human consumption. Human-grade chicken complies with United States Department of Agriculture (USDA) welfare standards

- 🐾 A certain amount of flavouring can make a food more appetising for your dog. **Choose a food with a specific flavouring,** like *"beef flavouring"* rather than a general *"meat flavouring,"* where the origins are not so clear

- 🐾 **Find a food suitable for the breed and your dog's age and activity level.** Talk to your breeder or vet, or visit an online Corgi forum to ask other owners' advice

- 🐾 **Natural is best.** Food labelled *'natural'* means that the ingredients have not been chemically altered, according to the FDA in the USA. However, there are no such guidelines governing foods labelled *"holistic"* – so check ingredients and how they have been prepared

❖ In the USA, dog food that meets American Feed Control Officials' (AAFCO) minimum nutrition requirements has a label that states: *"[food name] is formulated to meet the nutritional levels established by the AAFCO Dog Food Nutrient Profiles for [life stage(s)]"*

 If you live in the USA, we recommend looking for a food *"as fed"* to real pets in an AAFCO-defined feeding trial. The AAFCO label is the gold standard, and brands that do costly feeding trials indicate so on the package.

Dog food labelled *'supplemental'* isn't complete and balanced. Unless you have a specific, vet-approved need for it, it's not something you want to feed your dog long term. The *Guaranteed Analysis* listed on a sack or tin legally guarantees:

GUARANTEED ANALYSIS	
Crude protein (min.)	28.00 %
Crude fat (min.)	12.00 %
Crude fiber (max.)	4.50 %
Moisture (max.)	11.00 %
Docosahexaenoic acid (DHA) (min.)	0.05 %
Calcium (min.)	1.20 %
Phosphorus (min.)	1.00 %
Omega-6 fatty acids* (min.)	2.20 %
Omega-3 fatty acids* (min.)	0.30 %
Glucosamine* (min.)	500 mg/kg
Chondroitin sulfate* (min.)	500 mg/kg

* Not recognized as an essential nutrient by the AAFCO Dog Food Nutrient Profiles.

❖ Minimum percentages of crude protein and crude fat, and

❖ Maximum percentages of crude fibre and moisture

While it is a start, don't rely on it too much. One pet food manufacturer made a mock product with a guaranteed analysis of 10% protein, 6.5% fat, 2.4% fibre, and 68% moisture (similar to what's on some canned pet food labels) – the ingredients were old leather boots, used motor oil, crushed coal and water!

❖ **Protein** – found in meat and poultry, protein should be the first ingredient and is very important. It helps build muscle, repair tissue and contributes to healthy hair and skin. According to AAFCO, a growing puppy requires a diet with minimum 22% **protein,** while an adult requires 18% minimum

❖ **Fats** – these are a concentrated form of energy that give your dog more than twice the amount of energy that carbohydrates and proteins do. Common fats include chicken or pork fat, cottonseed oil, vegetable oil, soybean oil, fish oil, safflower oil, and many more.

They are highly digestible and are the first nutrients to be used by the body as energy. AAFCO recommends minimum 8% fat for puppies and 5% for adults

❖ **Fibre** – found in vegetables and grains. It aids digestion and helps prevent anal glands from becoming impacted. The average dry dog food has 2.5%-4.5% crude fibre, but reduced-calorie feeds may be as high as 9%-10%

❖ **Carbohydrates** typically make up anywhere from 30%-70% of a dry dog food. They come mainly from plants and grains, and provide energy in the form of sugars

❖ **Vitamins and Minerals** – have a similar effect on dogs as humans. Glucosamine and chondroitin are good for joints

❖ **Omegas 3 and 6** – fatty acids that help keep Corgis' skin and coat healthy. Also good for inflammation control, arthritic pain, heart and kidneys

Well-formulated dog foods have the right balance of protein, fat, carbohydrates, vitamins, minerals and fatty acids. Check out these websites for lots of information on individual brands (we have no vested interest in any websites):

www.dogfoodadvisor.com run by Mike Sagman in the USA, and

www.allaboutdogfood.co.uk run by UK canine nutritionist David Jackson (ignore the adverts).

How Much Food?

Keeping your Corgi at a healthy weight can be a challenge. You may have a nervous dog who is a fussy eater, making it hard to put the weight on. Far more likely, however, is a permanently hungry one who'd eat the entire contents of the kitchen given half a chance! Or your dog may be in between the two extremes.

Maintaining a healthy body weight is all about balancing calories taken in with calories burned. If a dog gets plenty of exercise or takes part in an activity, he'll need more calories than a less active or older dog. There are many factors governing weight:

- Calories consumed
- Amount of daily exercise
- Quality of the food
- Breed
- Gender and age
- Natural energy levels
- Metabolism
- Temperament
- Health
- Environment
- Number of dogs in the house
- Whether your Corgi is a pet or takes part in canine competitions

Energy levels vary from one dog to the next. Dogs that have been spayed may be more likely to put on weight; their calorie requirements often reduce, so the food needs to be reduced accordingly.

Certain health conditions, e.g. underactive thyroid, diabetes, arthritis or heart disease, can lead to dogs putting on weight. And just like us, a dog kept in a very cold environment will need more calories to keep warm than a dog in a warm climate, as extra calories are burned to keep warm.

 A Corgi kept on his own is more likely to be overweight than one kept with other dogs, as he receives all of the food-based attention.

Manufacturers of cheap foods may recommend feeding more than necessary as a major ingredient is cereal, which doesn't add much in terms of nutrition, but increases the weight of the food – and possibly triggers allergies.

Look for a *"complete"* food and feed the amount for the **ideal adult weight**, not for the weight your Corgi is now.

Type *Belpatt Pembroke (or Cardigan) Welsh Corgi Weight* into a search engine to get a rough idea of what yours should weigh as he or she grows. Bear in mind that puppies tend to grow in spurts, so anything 10% either side of the ideal weight is acceptable for young dogs.

 There is also an excellent leaflet that clearly explains each component of a dog's diet and how much to feed your dog based on weight and activity level. Search for *National Academies Your Dog's Nutritional Needs* online.

Feeding Options

We are what we eat. The right food is a very important part of a healthy lifestyle for dogs as well as humans. Here are the main options explained:

Dry dog food - or kibble, is a popular and relatively inexpensive way of providing a balanced diet. Millions of dogs, including most Corgis, thrive on high quality kibble.

It comes in a variety of flavours and with differing ingredients to suit the different stages of a dog's life. Quality has improved a lot over the years, but cheap kibble is still false economy.

Canned food - dogs love the taste and it generally comes in a variety of flavours. Some owners feed kibble mixed with some canned food. These days there are hundreds of options, some are high quality made from natural, organic ingredients with herbs.

Read the label closely, the origins of cheap canned food can be somewhat dubious. Some dogs can suffer from stomach upsets with too much soft food. Avoid fillers and preservatives and brands with lots of grain, or recalls.

Semi-Moist - this food typically has a water content of around 60%-65%, compared to 10% in dry food, making it easier to digest. It also has more sugar and salt, so not suitable for all dogs. Semi-moist treats are shaped like pork chops, bacon *(pictured),* salamis, burgers, etc. They are the least nutritional of all dog foods, full of sugars, artificial flavourings and colourings, so avoid giving them regularly.

Home-Cooked - some owners want the ability to be in complete control of their dog's diet. Feeding a home-cooked diet can be time-consuming and expensive.

The difficult thing (as with the raw diet) is sticking to it once you have started out with the best of intentions, but your dog will love it and he won't be eating preservatives or fillers. Some high-end dog food companies now provide boxes of freshly-prepared meals with natural ingredients.

Dehydrated - this dried food, *pictured,* is becoming increasingly popular. It looks similar to kibble, but is only minimally processed. It offers many of the benefits of raw feeding, including lots of nutrients, but with none of the mess or bacteria.

Gentle heating slowly cooks proteins and helps start the digestive process, making it easier on the digestive tract of older dogs, or those with sensitive stomachs. Owners just add water and let it stand for a minute or two to reconstitute the meal.

Freeze-Dried - this is usually raw, fresh food that has been freeze-dried by frozen food manufacturers. It's a more convenient, hygienic and less messy option than raw, and handy if you're going on a trip.

It contains healthy enzymes but no preservatives, is highly palatable and keeps for six months to a year. It says *"freeze-dried"* on the packet, but the process bumps up the cost. A good option for owners who can afford it.

The Raw Diet

Opinions are divided on a raw diet. There is anecdotal evidence that some dogs thrive on it, particularly those with food intolerances or allergies, although scientific proof is lagging behind. Claims made by fans of the raw diet include:

- ❧ Reduced symptoms of - or less likelihood of - allergies, and less scratching

- Better skin and coats
- Easier weight management
- Improved digestion
- Less doggie odour and flatulence
- Higher energy levels
- Helps fussy eaters
- Fresher breath and improved dental health
- Drier and less smelly stools, more like pellets
- Overall improvement in general health and less disease
- Most dogs love a raw diet

If your Corgi is not doing well on a dry dog food or has skin issues, you might consider a raw diet. Some commercial dog foods contain artificial preservatives, grains and excessive protein and fillers, causing a reaction in some dogs. Dry, canned and other styles of processed food were mainly created as a means of convenience – for humans, not dogs!

Some nutritionists believe there are inherent beneficial enzymes, vitamins, minerals and other qualities in meats, fruits, vegetables and grains in their natural, uncooked state.

However, critics of a raw diet say that the risks of nutritional imbalance, intestinal problems and food-borne illnesses caused by handling and feeding raw meat outweigh any benefits.

It is true that owners must pay strict attention to hygiene when preparing a raw diet and it may not be a suitable option if you have small children. The dog may also be more likely to ingest bacteria or parasites such as Salmonella, E. Coli and Ecchinococcus - although freeze-dried meals greatly reduce the risk.

If you do switch your dog over to raw feeding, do so over a period of at least a week.

 Raw is not for every dog; it can cause loose stools, upset stomach and even vomiting in some, and there are other dogs who simply don't like the taste.

There are two main types of raw diet, one involves feeding raw, meaty bones (*pictured above*) and the other is known as the BARF diet (Biologically Appropriate Raw Food or Bones And Raw Food), created by Dr Ian Billinghurst.

Raw Meaty Bones

- Raw meaty bones or carcasses form the bulk of the diet. **Cooked bones should NOT be fed, as they can splinter**
- Table scraps both cooked and raw, such as vegetables
- Australian veterinarian Dr Tom Lonsdale is a leading proponent of the raw meaty bones diet. He believes the following foods are suitable:
- Chicken and turkey carcasses, after the meat has been removed for human consumption
- Poultry by-products, e.g. heads, feet, necks and wings
- Whole fish and fish heads
- Sheep, calf, goat, and deer carcasses sawn into big pieces of meat and bone
- Pigs' trotters and heads, sheep heads, brisket, tail and rib bones

- ❖ A certain amount of offal can be included in the diet, e.g. liver, lungs, trachea, hearts, tripe
- ❖ Table scraps and some fruit and vegetable peelings, but should not make up more than one-third of the diet

Low-fat game animals, fish and poultry are the best source of food. If you feed meat from farm animals (cattle, sheep and pigs), avoid excessive fat and bones too large to be eaten. It depends on price and what's available locally - start with your local butcher or farm shop.

 **Dogs are more likely to break their teeth eating large knuckle bones and bones sawn lengthwise than when eating meat and bone together.**

You'll also need to think about WHERE and WHEN you are going to feed. A dog takes some time to eat a raw bone and will push it around the floor, so the kitchen may not be the most hygienic place.

Outside is one option, but what do you do when it's raining? If you live in a hot climate, evening feeding may be best to avoid flies.

Photo of Mole tucking into a juicy marrow bone courtesy of Lucy Badham-Thornhill.

Establishing the right quantity is based on your dog's activity levels, appetite and body condition. A very general guide of raw meaty bones for the average dog is:

15%-20% of body weight per week, or 2%-3% a day.

Dr Lonsdale says: "Wherever possible, feed the meat and bone ration in one large piece requiring much ripping, tearing and gnawing. This makes for contented pets with clean teeth." More information is available from www.rawmeatybones.com

NOTES: Pregnant or lactating females and growing puppies need more food. This diet may not be suitable for old dogs used to a processed diet or those with dental issues, or in households with children, due to the risk of bacterial infection from raw meat.

Monitor your dog while he eats, especially in the beginning. Don't feed bones with sharp points, and remove any bone before it becomes small enough to swallow.

Raw meaty bones should be kept separate from human food and any surface the uncooked meat or bones have touched should be thoroughly cleaned afterwards.

Tip **Puppies can and do eat diets of raw meaty bones, but consult your breeder or vet before embarking on raw with a young dog.**

The BARF diet - A variation of the raw meaty bones diet. A typical BARF diet is made up of 60%-75% of raw meaty bones - with about 50% meat, such as chicken neck, back and wings - and 25%-40% of fruit and vegetables, offal, meat, eggs or dairy foods. There is lots of information on the BARF diet online.

What the Experts Feed

Pembroke breeder and Welsh Corgi League Breed Health Co-ordinator Linda Roberts says: "The breed does seem pre-disposed to gastrointestinal upsets, but feeding a consistent sensible diet with the appropriate amount of exercise and stimulation seems to keep these issues under control.

"In my opinion, the biggest health issue facing the breed is obesity. Unfortunately, many Pembrokes are overfed and under-exercised. This is a tough, hardy breed developed for hard work on a basic farmyard diet. They certainly weren't bred to sit on sofas all day and eat themselves square!

"Aim to have a well-covered dog with a defined waist and ribs, and a spine just capable of being felt beneath the coat. Obesity obviously has many implications for the overall health and lifespan of a dog and almost certainly contributes to the development of heart issues, cancers, diabetes, etc. as a dog ages.

"Personally, I have fed James Wellbeloved complete food (not grain-free) for over 20 years. I find it ideal for the dogs, they enjoy the four flavour varieties; I alternate and it doesn't cause any digestive upsets. I add in herring, chicken, sausages, scrambled egg and raw vegetables for variety. Fresh, cool water is always readily available."

As Linda has said, most Corgis thrive on a straightforward diet. The majority of breeders and experienced owners involved in this book feed a complete dry food to their Corgis. A surprising number of them feed the same brand - Royal Canin - and find that their dogs do well on it.

Here's what some said, starting with Kevin Egan: "All of ours have Royal Canin dry kibble. It is the type and brand first recommended back in 2011 and so we have kept with it ever since."

Looking the picture of health on his diet is young Barney. Photo courtesy of Kevin.

Fran Fricker: "I have always fed Royal Canin from birth onwards, the nutritional content and size of kibble suits the Cardigan Corgis well. I will feed raw on top, such as tripe or beef, but I do not feed just raw.

"I also use nutritional supplements from Aniforte: Salmon Oil Capsules, and Wheatgerm and Seaweed Powder. These compliment the food and are of nutritional benefit to the dogs."

Lucy Badham-Thornhill: "I feed complete dried food and stick to one brand - Royal Canin - and they seem well on it. I give them raw marrow bones (which I freeze first) periodically."

Carole Turner: "I feed Royal Canin Medium Breed. I switch the puppies from the Puppy to the Adult formula at around 11 months to one year old. When a puppy leaves me, I tell the new owner to give them a bit less food that night and the following morning. Their tummies can be a bit tight from being nervous, and with a bit less food they are unlikely to have an upset stomach.

"If you are giving treats, take them out of the food ration. Also, I reduce the food the day my dogs are spayed - I monitor their weight by eye and then adjust their food accordingly. Similarly, if it's raining and we do a bit less exercise one day, I give them a bit less food later."

Alexandra Trefán-Török, Hungary: "I feed dry dog food; we use a no-grain salmon formula. Every month they also get a big beef bone or ostrich leg bone to chew on."

Margaret E. Leighton: "I have fed all my dogs on high quality kibble mixed with wet canned food. I think plain kibble is very boring and unappetising, so I add the canned meat to it. I sometimes cook chicken and vegetables for them, blend it and mix that with the kibble."

Johnathan and Piotr Mazur-Jones: "We feed different food to different dogs, including raw. We always see how the individual does on different foods; some, just like humans, are better on a different diet. It's important to use manufacturers' guidelines. Body Condition Scoring is the best way to know how your dog is doing. Get your hands on your dog every day and you will know."

Jo Evans: "I have fed completely raw - raw meat, veg and fruit and bones - but find the vet doesn't agree with this, particularly when pregnant or nursing. I do find choosing dog food a minefield as there is so much out there. Raw meat also takes a lot of room up in the freezer.

"The Corgi will eat masses given half the chance, and hence many are obese. Now I feed a lightweight, quality, dry food. I randomly add to this puréed fruit and veg, raw chicken bones, leftover cooked veg or meat, salmon oil, and Plaque Off seaweed supplement to help with teeth."

Lisa Thompson adds that she feeds her dogs Fromm Family pet food, which has been produced in Wisconsin by the same family for five generations.

Breeder Eileen Eby feeds all of her Corgis a raw diet. She has owned both types of Corgi for over 30 years and is a committee member of the Cardigan Welsh Corgi Association.

Eileen has bred Kilvroch Cardigans since 2001 and says: "I've been feeding raw since the mid-1990s. I tried it because lots of people were starting to feed that way, and I liked the results - healthy teeth, gleaming coats, etc. I have rarely needed to scrape a dog's teeth for plaque."

Photo: In the pink of condition aged 10, Fang (Kilvroch Rackett), bred by Eileen.

"I used to mince my own meat and veg, but since Natures Menu started their nuggets, I have bought from them. I also used to get chicken carcasses from a local processing plant, bag and freeze them, but find the Natures Menu bags of chicken wings much simpler to use.

"I introduce raw food to my pups as soon as they begin to wean and feed it right throughout my dogs' lives."

Sue Hardy has owned Pembrokes since 1989 and does Scentwork with Mambo. She is another fan of the raw diet and says: "I feed raw; it was recommended by my trainers and I've never looked back."

"We buy it from the training school; they buy it in bulk from a company in Somerset and it comes in 400g (14oz) minced frozen packs. You just take a pack out of the freezer the day before and put it in the fridge. I have found sandwich containers with clip-on airtight lids of exactly the right size; I do not have to handle the meat at all, so no problems with cross-contamination or hygiene."

Photo: Mambo (right) relaxing at home with Rosie. Photo courtesy of Sue.

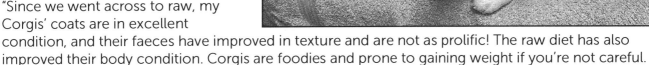

"All of the instructors' dogs are raw fed. They say that it is a species-appropriate diet that has less processing and fillers to cause allergens, but they do NOT 'force' it on owners. The owners make their own decisions, taking into account their circumstances and the welfare of their dogs.

"Since we went across to raw, my Corgis' coats are in excellent condition, and their faeces have improved in texture and are not as prolific! The raw diet has also improved their body condition. Corgis are foodies and prone to gaining weight if you're not careful.

"Bear in mind raw is not for everyone. Some dogs I know have an allergic reaction to chicken and their owners have to be careful what they feed them. I have heard and read that raw feeding can be a contentious issue, but it works for us.

"Raw provides approximately 70% of their daily food intake. The remainder comprises sausage segments and low fat/calorie kibble during training sessions."

Breeder and Crufts prizewinner Kevin Dover: "I feed a raw diet and have done for many years. Having been brought up in the days before all the "completes" we see advertised these days, I find a diet of tripe and tripe mixes, along with a plain wholemeal biscuit, gives my dogs all they require.

"They also have fresh vegetables and love raw carrots as a treat. Everyone has their own reasons to feed what they feel works for them but a raw or BARF diet I feel gives the condition and body I want to see on my dogs."

Corgi Feeding Tips

1. If you choose a manufactured food, pick one where meat or poultry (or meat or poultry meal) is the **first** item listed. Many dogs do not do well on cheap cereals or sugar, so choose a high quality one.

2. If a Corgi has sensitive skin, "hot spots" or allergies, a cheap food bulked up with grain will only make this worse. A dry food described as *"hypoallergenic"* on the sack means *"less likely to cause allergies."*

3. Consider feeding a probiotic - such as a spoonful of natural, live yoghurt - to each meal to help maintain healthy gut bacteria.

4. Feed your adults twice a day, rather than once. Smaller feeds are easier to digest, and reduce the risk of *Bloat* as well as gas.

5. Establish a feeding regime and stick to it. Dogs like routine. Stick to the same times, morning and late afternoon/early evening. Feeding too late won't give your dog's body time to process the food before bed. Feeding at the same times also helps your dog establish a toilet regime.

6. Take away uneaten food between meals. Most Corgis LOVE their food, but any dog can become fussy if food is constantly available. Remove the bowl after half an hour – even if there is some left. A healthy, hungry dog will look forward to the next meal. If he's off his food for a couple of days or more, it could be a sign of illness.

7. Feeding time is a great training opportunity - particularly for the commands **SIT** and **STAY** and the release.

8. Use stainless steel or ceramic bowls. Plastic bowls don't last as long and can trigger an allergic reaction around the muzzle in some sensitive dogs.

9. Use apple or carrot slices, or other healthy alternatives, as training treats for puppies.

10. If you feed dried animal product treats, check the country of origin. Some use toxic chemicals that can damage kidneys. Dried jerky-type treats can be very good for teeth, but read the labels carefully.

11. Don't feed too many tidbits or treats between meals as they throw a balanced diet out of the window and cause obesity. Feed leftovers in the bowl as part of a meal, rather than from the table, as this encourages attention-seeking behaviour, begging and drooling.

12. Don't feed cooked bones, as these can splinter and cause choking or intestinal problems. And avoid rawhide, as a dog can gulp it without chewing, causing an internal blockage.

13. Obesity leads to all sorts of health issues, such as joint problems, diabetes, high blood pressure and organ disease. Your Corgi's tummy should be higher than his rib cage - if his belly is level or hangs down below it, reduce his food.

14. Check your dog's faeces (aka stools, poo or poop)! If the diet is suitable, the food should be easily digested and produce dark brown, firm stools. If your dog is producing light or sloppy poo or lots of gas, his diet may well need changing. Consult your vet or breeder for advice.

15. These are poisonous to dogs: grapes, raisins, chocolate, onions, Macadamia nuts, any fruits with seeds or stones, tomatoes, avocados, rhubarb, tea, coffee, alcohol and Xylitol artificial sweetener.

16. And finally, always make sure that your dog has access to clean, fresh water. Change the water and clean the bowl every day or so – it gets slimy!

17. If your dog is not responding well to a particular family member, get him or her to give the feeds.

Bloat

Although rare in Corgis, Bloat can affect any individual dog, so it's as well to understand the causes and try to avoid them.

Bloat occurs when there is too much gas in the stomach. It is known by several different names: *twisted stomach, gastric torsion* or *Gastric Dilatation-Volvulus (GDV)* and occurs mainly in larger breeds with deep chests, such as the Dobermann. Bloat is statistically more common in males than in females and in dogs over seven years old.

As the stomach swells with gas, it can rotate 90° to 360°. The twisting stomach traps air, food and water inside and the bloated organ stops blood flowing properly to veins in the abdomen, leading to low blood pressure, shock and even damage to internal organs.

The causes are not fully understood, but there are some well-known risk factors. One is the dog taking in a lot of air while eating - either because he is greedy and gulping the food too fast - or stressed, e.g. food competition.

A dog that is fed once a day and gorges himself could be at higher risk; another reason why most owners feed twice a day. Exercising straight after eating or after a big drink also increases the risk - like colic in horses. Another potential cause is diet. Fermentable foodstuffs that produce a lot of gas can cause problems for the stomach if the gas is not burped or passed into the intestines.

Symptoms are: swollen belly, standing awkwardly, restlessness, rapid panting, dry retching, or excessive saliva or foam, excessive drinking, licking the air and general weakness or collapse.

Tips to Avoid Canine Bloat:

❧ Avoid dog food with high fats or those using citric acid as a preservative, also avoid tiny pieces of kibble

❧ If your Corgi is a guzzler, invest in an anti-gulp bowl, *pictured*, to slow him down

❧ Feed twice a day rather than once

❧ Don't let your dog drink too much water just before, during or after eating

❧ Stress can possibly be a trigger, with nervous and aggressive dogs being more susceptible. Maintain a peaceful environment, particularly around mealtimes

❧ Avoid vigorous exercise before or after eating, allow one hour either side of mealtimes before strenuous exercise

FACT 》 Bloat can kill a dog in less than one hour. If you suspect your Corgi has it, get them into the car and off to the vet IMMEDIATELY. Bloat is one of the leading killers of dogs after cancer.

Food Allergies

Dog food allergies are a reaction to food that involves the body's immune system and affect about one in 10 dogs. They are the third most common canine allergy after atopy (inhaled or contact allergies) and flea bite allergies.

Food allergies affect males and females in equal measure as well as neutered and intact pets. They can start when your dog is five months or 12 years old - although the vast majority start when the dog is between two and six years old.

It is not uncommon for dogs with food allergies to also have other types of allergies. Here are some common symptoms of problems with food:

❧ Itchy skin - your dog may lick or chew his paws or legs and rub his face with his paws or on the furniture, carpet, etc.

❧ Excessive scratching

❧ Recurring ear or skin infections that clear up with antibiotics but recur when the antibiotics run out

- ❀ Hair loss
- ❀ Hot patches of skin – *"hot spots"*
- ❀ Redness and inflammation on the chin and face
- ❀ Increased bowel movements (maybe twice as often as usual)

The problem with food allergies is that the symptoms are similar to symptoms of other issues, such as environmental or flea bite allergies, intestinal problems, mange and yeast or bacterial infections.

There's also a difference between dog food *allergies* and dog food *intolerance*:

ALLERGIES = SKIN PROBLEMS AND/OR ITCHING

INTOLERANCE = DIARRHOEA AND/OR VOMITING

Dog food intolerance can be compared to people who get an upset stomach from eating spicy curries. Symptoms can be cured by changing to a milder diet. With dogs, certain ingredients are more likely to cause a reaction than others. Unfortunately, these are also the most common ingredients in dog foods! In order of the most common triggers in dogs in general, they are:

Beef - Dairy Products - Chicken - Wheat - Eggs - Corn - Soya (Soy in the US)

Veterinarian Dr Samantha Goldberg told us: "Many meats are triggers. However, cooked meats may trigger differently than raw due to protein denaturing at cooking. Not all diets are equal!

"Always aim for the highest quality diet you can afford with a high meat content. Also look at the process of production - some can appear good in theory, but if they have been processed within an inch of their life, they won't have many nutrients left. Grains per se are not all "bad," but finely-milled grains tend to produce glucose spikes when digested. Rolled or whole grains are digested more slowly.

"The balance of Omega 3 and 6 oils can also be very important for health. Omega 6 can be good for the skin and Omega 3 for joints, but too much or an imbalance is not good."

 A dog is allergic or sensitive to an <u>ingredient</u>, not to a particular brand, so it's important to read the label. If your Corgi reacts to beef, for example, he'll react to any food containing beef, regardless of how expensive it is or how well it has been prepared.

AVOID corn, corn meal, corn gluten meal, artificial preservatives (BHA, BHT, Propyl Gallate, Ethoxyquin, Sodium Nitrite/Nitrate and TBHQBHA), artificial colours, sugars and sweeteners, e.g. corn syrup, sucrose and ammoniated glycyrrhizin, powdered cellulose, propylene glycol.

Grain Intolerance

Although beef is the food most likely to cause allergies in the general dog population, there is anecdotal evidence to suggest that GRAIN can also cause issues for some dogs.

"Grain" is wheat or any other cultivated cereal crop. Some dogs also react to starch, which is found in grains and potatoes, as well as bread, pasta, rice, etc.

Dogs don't process grains as well as humans. Foods high in grains and sugar can cause increases in unhealthy bacteria and yeast in the stomach, which crowds out the good bacteria and allows toxins to affect the immune system. They also cause lots of GAS!

The itchiness related to food allergies can then cause secondary bacterial and yeast infections, which may show as hot spots, ear or bladder infections, excessive shedding, reddish or dark brown tear stains. You may also notice a musty smell.

 Drugs like antihistamines and steroids will help temporarily, but they do not address the root cause.

Before you automatically switch to a grain-free diet, veterinarian Dr Marianne Dorn has these words of caution: "A true *'grain intolerance'* is rare.

"Owners should at least try cutting out rich treats, cheese, milk, buttered toast and other *'extras'* from the kitchen before considering a grain-free diet."

Latest studies show that a grain-free diet may also predispose some breeds to getting a potentially fatal heart condition known as Dilated Cardiomyopathy (DCM) - although the Welsh Corgi is not considered a high-risk breed.

Some food allergy symptoms - particularly the scratching, licking, chewing and redness - can also be a sign of environmental allergies or flea bites. See **Chapter 14. Skin and Allergies** for more details.

 If you've switched diet to little effect, it's time to see a vet. Many vets promote specific dog food brands, which may or may not be the best option for your Corgi. Do your own research.

Food Trials

The only way to completely cure a food allergy or intolerance is complete avoidance, which is not as easy as it sounds. First you have to determine your dog DOES have an allergy to food - and not pollen, grass, etc. - and then you have to discover WHICH food is causing the reaction.

A **food trial or exclusion diet** involves feeding one specific food for 12 weeks, something the dog has never eaten before.

Before you embark on one, know that they are a real pain-in-the-you-know-what! You have to be incredibly vigilant and determined, so only start one if you are prepared to see it through to the end or you are wasting your time.

The chosen food must be the **only thing** eaten during the trial. During the trial, your dog shouldn't roam freely, as you can't control what he is eating or drinking when out of sight. Don't give:

- Treats
- Rawhide (not recommended anyway)
- Bones, pigs' ears, cows' hooves or other animal chews
- Flavoured medications (including heartworm treatments) or supplements
- Flavoured toothpastes
- Flavoured plastic toys

A more practical, less scientific approach is to eliminate ingredients one at a time by switching diets over a period of a week or so. If you switch to home-cooked or raw, you know exactly what your dog is eating; if you choose a commercial food, a hypoallergenic one is a good place to start.

They all have the word *"hypoallergenic"* in the name and do not include wheat protein or soya. They are often based around less common ingredients.

....

Overweight Corgis

Some Corgis are obsessive about food - which is great for training, but not so good for maintaining a healthy weight. According to VCA (Veterinary Centers of America):

"In North America, obesity is the most common preventable disease in dogs. Approximately 25-30% of the general canine population is obese, with 40-45% of dogs aged 5-11 years old weighing in higher than normal."

You may think you are being kind to your beloved Corgi by giving him extra treats and scraps, but the reality is that you are shortening his life.

The extra weight puts huge strain on his organs, often resulting in a reduced lifespan. It is far easier to regulate your dog's weight and keep it at a healthy level than to slim down a pleading Corgi once he becomes overweight. Overweight dogs are susceptible to:

Joint disease – excessive body weight increases joint stress, which then tends to lead to a vicious circle of less exercise and weight gain, further reducing exercise.

Heart and lung problems – fatty deposits within the chest cavity and too much circulating fat contribute to cardio-respiratory and cardiovascular disease.

Diabetes – a major risk factor for overweight dogs.

Tumours – obesity increases the risk of mammary tumours in females. (Study: "Effects of Obesity and Obesity-Related Molecules on Canine Mammary Gland Tumors," by H-Y Lim et al).

Liver disease – fat degeneration can result in liver insufficiency.

Reduced lifespan - one of the most serious proven findings in obesity studies is that obesity in both humans and dogs reduces lifespan.

Most Corgis are extremely loyal companions and very attached to their humans. They are a part of our family. However, beware of going too far.

FACT > Studies show that dogs regarded as "family members" by the owner (anthropomorphosis) are at greater risk of becoming overweight. This is because attention given to the dog often results in food being given as well.

If you have to put your dog on a diet, be aware that a reduced amount of food will also mean reduced nutrients, so he may need a supplement during this time.

 Don't despair if your Corgi is overweight. Many problems associated with being overweight are reversible with weight loss.

....

If your Corgi is happy and healthy, has lots of energy and is interested in life, is not too fat and not too thin, doesn't scratch a lot and has dark brown, firm stools, then... CONGRATULATIONS, you've got it right!

8. Typical Corgi Traits

Despite their short legs, you are getting a lot of dog with a Corgi. And if you've decided to share your life with one, it helps to have an insight into what is going on in that lively mind of theirs!

To get the best out of your Corgi, you first have to learn what makes them tick and what motivates them to learn. This chapter helps you to do just that.

....

Just as with humans, a dog's personality is made up of a combination of temperament and character – or **Nature and Nurture.**

Temperament is the nature - or inherited characteristics - a dog is born with; a predisposition to act or react to the world around him. Natural temperament is where good breeders come into their own. Not only do they produce puppies from physically healthy dams and sires, but they also look at temperament and only breed from Pembrokes or Cardigans with good traits.

Character is what develops through the dog's life and is formed by a combination of temperament and environment. How you treat your dog will have a huge effect on his personality and behaviour.

Start off on the right foot with your puppy by establishing the rules of the house and good routines. Treat him well and make lots of time for socialisation, training and, as his body matures, exercise.

FACT ❯ Socialisation means "learning to be part of society." With dogs, it means helping them learn to be comfortable living within a human society that includes many different people, environments, buildings, sights, noises, smells and other animals.

All dogs need different environments and experiences to help keep them socialised, stimulated and well-balanced.

....

What To Expect

- ❖ Corgis make great family dogs
- ❖ They are extremely loyal, affectionate and love being involved in the midst of the family, as well as snuggling up with their beloved owners
- ❖ They are good with children - provided both are taught respect for each other
- ❖ Photo: Two sisters with their 'fluffy.'
- ❖ They tend to love the whole family, rather than just one person
- ❖ This is an intelligent breed

- They were selectively bred to work alongside people and are 'biddable,' i.e. very trainable; they enjoy the challenge and, of course, getting a treat

- The same goes for housetraining; a Corgi can get the hang of it in a couple of weeks, provided you are vigilant in the beginning

- They can also be independent-minded and are very good at working out the best way to get what they want – so training is important for your Corgi to learn his place in the household

- Pembrokes generally want to be friends with everyone and will dash up to strangers for a pat, while Cardigans are initially more reserved and may take their time deciding about a person or situation

- Another difference between the two breeds is that Pems are often outgoing and adventurous, while Cardis are often a bit more laid-back, although both are plucky

- Both types are alert and usually make good watchdogs; they will bark if somebody approaches your home

- Some Corgis like the sound of their own voices a bit too much, so early socialisation is important to prevent nuisance barking

- But they are not guard dogs. They are likely to lick the intruders, or roll over for a tummy tickle - especially a Pembroke - while the robbers make off with the family jewels

- Most have a natural happy temperament

- They were originally bred as working dogs and thrive when their bodies and minds are regularly exercised through walks, playtime or canine activities

- They are adaptable and can thrive on farms and in apartments - provided their needs are met

- Like all dogs bred to work, Corgis like being with other animals and humans, and do not like being left alone for long periods

- Because they are friendly, trainable and not too big, they are suitable for first-time owners, but their thick, shedding coat makes them unsuitable for allergy sufferers

- A bored Corgi is a mischievous Corgi

- Some Pembrokes can be assertive - bossy even - if allowed to get their own way

- They are hardy and robust, bred to work outdoors over rough terrain in all weathers. Even if you don't want to go out in the rain, your Corgi probably will!

- They are lively dogs that love to be busy - physically and mentally. They thrive on an hour or more exercise a day and, once they've built up to it, can walk all day

- They have no road sense, so keep yours on a lead at all times near traffic

- They are surprisingly fast and can run at speeds of up to 23mph, which is faster than average for all breeds, so make sure you've instilled The Recall before you let yours loose in the park!

- Some love swimming and are surprisingly good at it, most enjoy a paddle, while a few dislike water

- Most enjoy being out in the snow

- They are social creatures, rarely aggressive when properly socialised, and usually do well with other dogs - especially Corgis

Left to right: Lettice, Mole and Topaz the cat. Photo by Lucy Badham-Thornhill.

- They get on with cats if introduced at an early age

- They are tenacious. They don't give up easily and enjoy problem-solving, so bolt down or move out of reach (which is higher than you think) anything you don't want yours to get into

- 'Hoover' or 'Dyson' is a nickname that has been given to Corgis – they are very food-focused! Keeping them at a healthy weight can be a challenge, but on the plus side, treats are highly effective motivation when training

- Many still retain a strong herding instinct and will round up the kids, cats, birds, etc. given half a chance

- Some also have a strong chase instinct, although they rarely catch anything. If the cat or small animal stands its ground, a Corgi will back off

- Some have a keen sense of smell and love to follow a scent with their nose to the ground. They can do well at the canine activity Scentwork

- They are playful and love games.... on their terms. If you throw a ball they may or may not fetch it back!

- Their intelligence means they can sometimes second-guess you - they know what's happening or where you are going before you get there!

- They require maintenance on the grooming front. Their thick double coat sheds twice a year - sometimes all year round - and their nails need trimming (which they usually hate)

- They are one of the longest-lived breeds, so taking on a Corgi is a long-term commitment

- The Corgi approaches life with happiness, enthusiasm and energy. He is a very honest, affectionate dog: WYSIWYG - what you see is what you get!

- There are very few, if any, bad temperament traits inherent in well-bred Corgis. If your dog starts showing signs of poor behaviour, it is often down to a lack of training, exercise, socialisation, or all three

- Corgis are honest dogs devoted to their owners; they will steal your heart. Be warned – Corgis are addictive!

Canine Emotions

As pet lovers, we are all too keen to ascribe human characteristics to our dogs; this is called **anthropomorphism** - "the attribution of human characteristics to anything other than a human being."

Most of us dog lovers are guilty of that, as we come to regard our pets as members of the family - and Corgis certainly regard themselves as members and guardians of the family.

An example of anthropomorphism might be that the owner of a male dog might not want to have him neutered because he will "miss sex," as a human might if he or she were no longer able to have sex. This is simply not true.

A male dog's impulse to mate is entirely governed by his hormones, not emotions. If he gets the scent of a bitch in heat, his hormones (which are just chemicals) tell him he has to mate with her. He does not stop to consider how attractive she is or whether she is *"the one"* to produce his puppies.

No, his reaction is entirely physical, he just wants to dive in there and get on with it!

It's the same with females. When they are in heat, a chemical impulse is triggered in their brain making them want to mate - with any male, they aren't at all fussy. So, don't expect your little princess to be all coy when she is in heat, she is not waiting for Prince Charming to come along - the tramp down the road or any other scruffy pooch will do! It is entirely physical, not emotional.

Food is another issue. A dog will not stop to count the calories of a delicious treat - you have to do that. No, he is driven by food and just thinks about getting the treat. Most Corgis will eat far too much, given the opportunity.

Corgis are incredibly loyal and loving. They are amusing characters and if yours doesn't make you smile from time to time, you must have had a humour by-pass. All of this adds up to one thing: a beloved family member that is all too easy to spoil.

 Corgis form deep bonds with their humans and respond well to the right motivation - usually treats. Teach yours to respect the authority figure, which is you - not him! In the beginning, think of yourself as a kindly but firm teacher with a slightly stubborn young student.

Learn to understand his mind, patiently train him to be comfortable with his place in the household.

Teach him some manners and household rules - like not constantly barking or nipping the kids on the back of the knees - and you'll be rewarded with a companion who is second to none and fits in beautifully with your family and lifestyle.

Photo: A black and a brindle Cardigan Welsh Corgi.

Dr Stanley Coren is well known for his work on canine psychology and behaviour. He and other researchers believe that in many ways a dog's emotional development is equivalent to that of a young child.

Dr Coren says: "Researchers have now come to believe that the mind of a dog is roughly equivalent to that of a human who is two to two-and-a-half years old. This conclusion holds for most mental abilities as well as emotions.

"Thus, we can look to human research to see what we might expect of our dogs. Just like a two-year-old child, our dogs clearly have emotions, but many fewer kinds of emotions than found in adult humans.

"At birth, a human infant only has an emotion that we might call excitement. This indicates how excited he is, ranging from very calm up to a state of frenzy. Within the first weeks of life the excitement state comes to take on a varying positive or a negative flavour, so we can now detect the general emotions of contentment and distress.

"In the next couple of months, disgust, fear, and anger become detectable in the infant. Joy often does not appear until the infant is nearly six months of age and it is followed by the emergence of shyness or suspicion. True affection, the sort that it makes sense to use the label "love" for, does not fully emerge until nine or ten months of age."

So, our Corgis can truly love us – but we knew that already!

According to Dr Coren, dogs can't feel shame. So, if you are housetraining your puppy, don't expect him to feel ashamed if he makes a mess in the house, he can't; he simply isn't capable of feeling shame. But he will not like it when you ignore him when he's behaving badly, and will love it when you praise or reward him for relieving himself outdoors.

Although Corgis can sometimes be stubborn, they can also be sensitive and show empathy – *'the ability to understand and share the feelings of another.'* They can pick up on the mood and emotions of their owner.

One emotion that all dogs can experience is jealousy. It may display itself by being overly-protective of humans, food or toys.

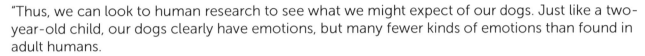

An interesting article was published in the PLOS (Public Library of Science) Journal in 2014 following an experiment into whether dogs get jealous.

Building on research that shows that six-month old infants display jealousy, the scientists studied 36 dogs in their homes and videoed their actions when their owners showed affection to a realistic-looking stuffed canine *(pictured)*.

Over three-quarters of the dogs pushed or touched the owner when they interacted with the decoy. The envious mutts were more than three times as likely to do this for interactions with the stuffed dog, compared to when their owners gave their attention to other objects, including a book.

Around a third tried to get between the owner and the plush toy, while a quarter of the put-upon pooches snapped at the dummy dog!

Professor Christine Harris from University of California in San Diego said: "Our study suggests not only that dogs do engage in what appear to be jealous behaviours, but also that they were seeking to break up the connection between the owner and a seeming rival."

The researchers believe that the dogs thought that the stuffed dog was real. The authors cite the fact that 86% of the dogs sniffed the toy's rear end during and after the experiment!

Professor Harris said: "We can't really speak of the dogs' subjective experiences, of course, but it looks as though they were motivated to protect an important social relationship. Many people have assumed that jealousy is a social construction of human beings - or that it's an emotion specifically tied to sexual and romantic relationships.

"Our results challenge these ideas, showing that animals besides ourselves display strong distress whenever a rival usurps a loved one's affection."

Expert Views on The Corgi Temperament

We asked our contributing experts how they first got involved with Corgis and about their dogs' typical temperaments traits. This is what they said:

Kevin Dover, breeder, international exhibitor and show judge: "I have been around the breed most of my life. I think most people initially had a Pembroke due to the Queen's involvement, but as they are so adaptable to town and country living, they seem to suit most households.

"I always say they are a big dog in a small package that is capable of most activities, including Herding, Obedience and, of course, Showing, as well as a loyal family pet.

"The Pembroke is a very intelligent dog and trains up extremely well. In the USA they have various championships for both Obedience and Herding, something that is only lightly covered here in the UK, but they do train very well. As with any dog, some take to it more readily - but perseverance is required as well as a pocket of treats!

"Knowing my own dogs over the years, I have found them to be a mixed bunch, some extremely one-person dogs and others who are happy to go to anyone with food. My current big show boy, Magnus, *pictured*, is totally devoted to me to the point of knowing what I want him to do without any command, something that was inbuilt right from a young puppy.

"In respect to chasing, the only one I have at present that chases is an import from Australia. He seems to like to chase vehicles, which does present a problem and something I have never encountered before. He also has a very short attention span, which makes it very difficult, so he has to be exercised on a leash for his own safety. They do like to chase things like squirrels and the occasional bird, but not to actually hunt, and they come back as soon as they have lost it or got bored.

"Corgis are good watchdogs. Living in the countryside, I know someone is coming down the track long before I can see a vehicle as the dogs start to bark. I've never personally had a dog that was protective of me or the household; they are usually just interested to see who has arrived.

"Barking has never been a problem; I have never stopped them for barking when they hear something different around the house. Being well-socialised, they tend not to bark at anyone out on walks - usually quite the opposite - they are just eager to say hello.

"As with any other training, I always use repetition commands on a young puppy and, if necessary, use distraction methods to stop any undue barking.

"Fortunately, I haven't seen any bad temperaments for some years and, when they do arise, these are due to the dogs not being given the socialisation they require and they usually come from puppy farms. It's very important to have a well-socialised puppy."

Alexandra Trefán-Török, of Born To Be Corgis, Hungary, also breeds both types, and shows her Pembrokes internationally:

"Corgis are very smart, passionate dogs with a high social level. They are ready for everything; true friends and soulmates and very funny... even when they are stubborn. In fact, their stubbornness has surprised me - but it also makes me laugh.

"Mine are really social with their own breed mates, but can form a group and power chase each other. This is their instinct that makes them ready to herd sheep and cows. More than 100 dogs from my kennel have successfully passed the FCI Herding Trial (FCI NHAT)."

Photos courtesy of Alexandra. Photographer Anna Szabo.

Alexandra added: "My Pembrokes played the roles of the Queen's Corgis in the Audience play at the Hungarian Pesti Theatre. The actors had no idea about Corgis, but the dogs soon made them their fans.

"The dogs would lay on their backs relaxing during waiting time - the cast said they were doing yoga before their performance! They very quickly learned the four acts and when it was their turn to go on stage, they were always ready for it. The signal was a piece of Scottish music in the 43rd minute. One day some time later we were watching TV at home and the same Scottish music came on in a film. My girls jumped up from their sleep straight away and looked up at me, waiting to go on stage! I told them no, but it clearly shows how extremely intelligent and always ready they are. I love them to bits; they make my life full."

Owner and Welsh Corgi League (WCL) committee member Kevin Egan: "As a child, my uncle owned a red-and-white male called Skippy. We would occasionally be invited to their home for Sunday lunch and Skippy immediately took ownership of all seating arrangements.

"While the adults were engaged in the kitchen, my brother and I were under strict instructions not to move from the settee so as not to get in the way. Skippy ensured that this condition was rigidly observed by blocking all possible exit movement from us.

"I recall being fascinated by Skippy's unblinking stare as he looked up at us with his dark eyes and pointy ears, his foxy muzzle resting on both front paws. If we tried to make a move, he briskly cut us off without a sound. We were being herded and were too young to realise it, so decided not to risk it - the first seed of Corgi interest had been sown!"

Kevin is now the proud owner of three Pembrokes, Edward, Mungo and Barney, aged 11, five and one. He said: "Without doubt, the Pembroke has an excellent temperament and a balanced nature and behaviour. They have a resolute character, which probably stems from their origins as a working dog, living mostly outside with an aptitude for herding livestock.

"Mine do not really have an overall powerful desire for pursuit, but they will retrieve items if they feel like it! The eldest ignores squirrels altogether but the middle boy is incensed at their presence and pulls hard on the lead as they scuttle past. The youngest does not react much.

"They are all very sociable around other animals and enjoy the presence of their fellow 'pack members' on their daily walks."

Photo of Barney courtesy of Kevin.

"One thing that's surprised me has been their jollity; I have never known such exuberance in an animal. Each time I return home after a journey, all three of them are lined up by the door jumping up and down and bundling each other out of the way to give me a 'hero's welcome!'

"This is the only time that they form a mob without demanding or expecting treats. They are genuinely pleased to see you. I make for the nearest available settee and let them clamber all over, it's glorious mayhem. Even if prior to that your day has been dreadful, the cure is immediate and your Corgi world is complete!"

Kennel Club Assured Breeder Jo Evans, Cerdinen Pembroke Welsh Corgis, New Quay, Wales: "Pembrokes are very loyal dogs, particularly with one member of a family. They want to be with you, even just sitting on or by your feet, and seem to know when you need a hug.

"They are Hoovers - not a patch of my kitchen floor seems to get missed. And on a walk they are still constantly looking to find anything they regard as food. They can be smart and crafty. On a walk I tell Cara to leave something behind that she has found to eat - but as soon as my back is turned, she goes back and gets what she found.

"The herding instinct is probably not as pronounced as it was when they were all working dogs, but mine will chase sheep, goats, squirrels, etc. They do like rounding me up, with a little nip behind my knee in excitement and play! My Corgis love children, but they have been known to grab small children around the bottom of their trousers and accidentally tip them up.

"My dogs have a strong instinct to chase, but often lose confidence when they reach their prey - but having more than one Corgi together makes them much more likely to bark and chase. They are good guard dogs and let you know when someone is about.

"They get on well with other dogs. They will always bark at them as well as people or anything else. On the beach they will bound up to other dogs enthusiastically, but then run away less confidently."

Sue Hardy has owned Pembrokes for over 30 years: "I have heard that people say the breed can be stubborn, I say they are determined, independent and intelligent. They are also sassy, funny, fun-loving, affectionate and adaptable.

"They all have their own personalities. My two boys thrive on being given a job to do, whereas Rosie, the only bitch we've had, was happy to have a quiet life at her own pace with all the home comforts.

"The only thing that got her fired up was squirrels - she used to give them a run for their money. She loved boating and caravanning, and articles about her travels appeared regularly in the Welsh Corgi League Newsletter!

"I remember one time when we were at a model aircraft get-together, Rosie decided to lie down and sun herself in the middle of the grassy area where all the models were being placed for a photoshoot, *pictured, aged 12.*

"The image of all the grown men walking round or over her to place their models in just the right place will make me smile for ever.

"Mambo, my current older guy, excels in Scentwork and is slightly wary of strangers. Samba, the youngster, will be a good Obedience dog; he is a snuggle bunny and loves everyone. However, they can both be reactive to sudden movement, e.g. postmen and bin men in orange jackets flashing past the window.

"I didn't expect Mambo to be so good at Scentwork. He also enjoys going round an Agility course, and we've started Mantrailing and competing in Scentwork UK Trials. My instructor says he is a natural."

Carole Turner has owned Corgis since the 1960s and went on to breed Cottonfields Pembrokes, she is also Secretary of the UK's South West Welsh Corgi Club: "Corgis are very intelligent with wonderful, expressive faces. They are adaptable and you can take them just about anywhere.

"Watch the way a Corgi subtly rounds up a group of people walking in the park, not necessarily together, and you will have no doubt the herding instinct is still there. They also love picking things up - like bits of food and cigarette ends!

"They watch and listen to your every move. They have a strong sense of timing so can predict when an owner is due home from work. One of mine, Sadie, was particularly close to me and seemed to anticipate my every move, it was so annoying!

"On car journeys to shows Jessie always knows when we are a couple of miles from the venue and starts chirruping - one of my friends says she is programmed like a sat nav! It also happens on visits to friends or the vet's. I enjoy the determination and impatience of the Pembroke, it seems to give them a zest for life."

Bred With Heart Breeder Lisa Thompson, of Thompson's Corgis, Wisconsin: "They are hardy. We get a lot of snow here in Wisconsin in the winters and my Corgis love to play in the snow, they will stay out for hours if you let them."

What me - shed?! Photo of Trixie (Thompson's Teach Me Trix), age 5, courtesy of Lisa.

"They are very sassy. Ours will talk back to you if they aren't happy; they have different sounds for different things.

"And they live to herd. When my kids are running around the yard, the Corgis will herd them and keep them all 'flocked' together - they nip ankles! They are also very loyal, they will lay by your side if you are sick and not feeling well, whether it is on the couch or on the bathroom floor."

Margaret E. Leighton: "I have owned Pembrokes for 30 years, prior to Corgis I owned three Siberian Huskies. I realised straight away just how smart Corgis are compared to Huskies, which are rather wilful and tough to train! The Corgi temperament is sweet, but they can also be stubborn at times.

"My female Bubbles has a fairly strong prey drive and is rather bossy around other dogs, but generally not interested in them, whereas Owain, my male, is friendly to all dogs and does not really chase. All my dogs went to Puppy Obedience classes and learned how to walk quietly on a leash.

"They are funny amusing scamps; people always comment on them when we are out walking. Because they are now a rare breed in the UK, people remark how lovely and well-behaved they are. I spent 40 years in California where they are extremely popular - I cannot understand why they are not more popular here in the UK. They are fabulous companions, loyal, smart and loveable."

Lucy Badham-Thornhill, who has also owned Pembrokes for 30 years, agrees: "Their loyalty is total. Pringle was watching my husband David playfighting with our four-year-old son. She was clearly miserable and eventually got up and bit David very gently! She could not have said more clearly: 'Please stop, I don't know what to do. My loyalties are split, my master is attacking my charge.'

"Corgis are intelligent working dogs who are happiest if their brains are occupied. They are very determined, have a lot of stamina and can be taught to do almost anything. They are anxious to please and very quick to learn. This, combined with a love of food, makes them easy to train.

"Some need firm handling initially. Boundaries need to be established from the start and unwanted behaviours, e.g. barking randomly, should be quashed before they become habits. They have neither the hound stubbornness nor the terrier hysteria.

"Mine understand the household and adored the children with whom they grew up, they played endlessly. We have had a lot of different animals around over the years and never had any problems with Corgis being aggressive towards anything.

"Corgis have wonderfully expressive faces. They watch every movement closely, they are experts in body language and understanding mood. I find them sensible; they know what matters and what doesn't. They both dislike going to the vet, but will comply with whatever is needed.

"We live in the country and mistakenly locked Lettice out on a cold night last week for about five hours. She sat on the doorstep the whole time completely unfazed and confident we would return.

"Corgis are wonderful, faithful companions and adaptable to all sorts of lifestyles. They are not lapdogs; they love attention and do sometimes need firm handling, but would go to any lengths for their families. I would not want any other breed."

Photo of Lucy's Mole living up to her name.

Karen Hewitt, of Cardhew Cardigan Corgis and Chairperson of the Cardigan Welsh Corgi Association: "Initially, I was looking for a smaller breed for my daughter to try to show; she was only four years old and I was showing German Shepherds at the time. We looked at several breeds, and as I had three very young children at the time, the dog had to be tough and steady of temperament. We settled on Cardigans and have never wanted any other breed since.

"Cardis are fantastic family dogs; mine have always been reared around children and grandchildren. Our current dogs are devoted to our grandchildren, never happier than when lying in a pile of kids having a tummy rub. Having said that, children must be taught to be kind and gentle, and respect the pup or dog's right to be left alone sometimes.

"Socialising and training are both incredibly important, Cardis are clever little souls, but they do need direction and exposure to as many experiences as possible. They need to know that their owner is in charge and that they must learn to follow the rules of the house and family.

"Getting them to see and hear as many different animals and people as possible during their early formative years is important so that they accept other animals and individuals without nervousness or aggression.

"Cardis are excellent watchdogs, they have super hearing and a range of barking tones - many people have commented that ours sound like much bigger dogs. They can be protective of home, family, car, etc, and this is why socialising is so vital. You must expand their world so that they are used to being with other people and having them on the family property."

Kennel Club Assured Breeder Fran Fricker, Kerman Cardigan Welsh Corgis: "They want to learn and to please; they love being rewarded and are very quick to learn new things. They have active minds and even doing puzzles or tackling filled Kongs holds their interest.

"There has always been one or more in our household from the early 1960s when my parents first became interested in the breed. I cannot imagine life without a Corgi - especially a Cardigan - that's not to say you will not see a Pembroke in my kennel in the future!"

9. Basic Training

Training a young dog is not unlike bringing up a child. Put in lots of time early on to work towards a good mutual understanding and you'll be rewarded with a well-adjusted, sociable member of the family you can proudly take anywhere!

The Corgi is a fairly active breed; however energy levels vary from one dog to the next. Originally bred to work, the Corgi may need more physical and mental exercise than, say, a dog bred purely for companionship. Many have retained an instinct to herd and some have a prey drive (desire to chase after critters), so training should always be tailored to meet the needs of the individual dog.

A well-trained Corgi doesn't magically appear overnight; it requires time and patience - especially in the beginning. Corgis make super family pets and companions, but let yours behave exactly as he wants and you could end up somewhere down the pecking order in your own home!

....

A Head Start

You already have a head start over many other breeds. Firstly, Corgis are intelligent and pick things up easily. Secondly, they have been selectively bred to work alongside Man (and Woman) and to follow their commands – so you have a dog who is:

1. Receptive to training (biddable)
2. Able to learn quickly
3. Willing to please you

Like all dogs from a working heritage, Corgis enjoy a challenge, such as games to keep them mentally occupied or playing with their owners or other dogs (provided they have been properly socialised). They can also do surprisingly well at organised activities and competitions, which all help to keep them stimulated.

 Most Corgis are food-focused and affectionate. Give yours a chance to shine; praise and reward often until the training task becomes ingrained.

Shouting, scolding or physical punishment will have the opposite effect. Your Corgi will switch off or otherwise respond poorly to rough or negative training methods. The secret of good training can be summed up in four words:

* ❧ Consistency
* ❧ Reward
* ❧ Praise
* ❧ Patience

 Police and service dogs are trained to a very high level with only a ball for reward. Corgis easily put weight on, so don't always use treats; praise or playtime can be enough sometimes. Also, get your pup used to a small piece of carrot or apple as a healthy alternative to calorie-laden treats.

The Intelligence of Dogs

Psychologist and canine expert Dr Stanley Coren has written a book called *The Intelligence of Dogs* in which he ranks the breeds. He surveyed dog trainers to compile the list and used *Understanding of New Commands* and *Obeying First Command* as his standards of intelligence. Dr Coren says there are three types of dog intelligence:

* Adaptive Intelligence (learning and problem-solving ability). Specific to the individual dog and is measured by canine IQ tests

* Instinctive Intelligence. Specific to the individual dog and is measured by canine IQ tests

* Working/Obedience Intelligence. This is breed-dependent

He divides dogs into six groups and the brainboxes of the canine world are the 10 breeds ranked in the 'Brightest Dogs' section of his list. It will come as no surprise to anyone who has ever been into the countryside and seen sheep being worked by a farmer and his right-hand man (his dog) to learn that the Border Collie is the most intelligent of all dogs.

No.2 is the Poodle, followed by the German Shepherd, Golden Retriever, Doberman Pinscher, Shetland Sheepdog, Papillon, Rottweiler and Australian Cattle Dog. All dogs in this class:

* Understand New Commands with Fewer than Five Repetitions

* Obey a First Command 95% of the Time or Better

The Pembroke Welsh Corgi is right behind, ranked 11 out of 138 breeds, followed by the Cardigan Welsh Corgi at 26. Both are in the second group, *Excellent Working Dogs*. They:

* Understand new commands with 5 to 15 repetitions

* Obey first command: 85% of the time or better

The full list can be seen on Wikipedia.

Five Golden Rules

1. Training must be reward-based, not punishment based.

2. Keep sessions short or your dog will get bored.

3. Never train when you are in a rush or a bad mood.

4. Training after exercise is fine, but never train when your dog is exhausted.

5. Keep sessions fun and finish on a high.

Tip **Establishing the natural order of things is not something forced on a dog through shouting or violence; it is brought about by mutual consent and good training.**

Dogs are happiest and behave best when they are familiar and comfortable with their place in the household. If you have adopted an older dog, you can still train him, but it will take a little longer to get rid of bad habits and instill good manners. Patience and persistence are the keys here.

Socialisation is a very important aspect of training. A good breeder will have already begun this process with the litter and then it's up to you to keep it going when puppy arrives home.

Puppies can absorb a great deal of information, but they are also vulnerable to bad experiences. They need exposing - in a positive manner - to different people, other animals and situations, otherwise they can find them very frightening when they do finally encounter them later.

FACT ⟩ If puppies have a variety of good experiences with other people, places, noises, situations and animals before four or five months old, they are less likely to either be timid or nervous or try to establish dominance later. See Chapter 11. Exercise and Socialisation for more information.

All pups are chewers and most, especially those with a lot of working instinct, are "mouthy" and will nip and play-bite, this is natural for them. Train your young pup to chew only the things you give – don't give him your old slippers, an old piece of carpet or anything that resembles something you DON'T want him to chew; he won't know the difference between the old and the new. Buy purpose-made long-lasting chew toys.

A puppy class is one of the best ways of getting a pup used to being socialised and trained. This should be backed up by short sessions of a few minutes of training a day back home. Corgis are great family dogs for anyone prepared to put in a fair bit of time to train one.

Some dogs, even well-trained ones, start to push the boundaries when they reach **adolescence** – any time between six months and two years old. Owners can't understand why their young dogs suddenly start behaving badly and unlearning some of their training; some males may "mark" or urinate in the house, even when they are housetrained.

In all cases, go back to basics and put the time in – sadly, there is no quick fix! You need to be firm with a strong-willed or high energy dog, but all training should still be carried out using positive techniques.

If you do need some professional one-on-one help (for you and the dog), choose a Corgi specialist and/or a trainer registered with the Association of Professional Dog Trainers (APDT) or other organisation using positive training methods. The old Alpha dominance theories have gone out the window.

Training Tips

1. **Start training and socialising straight away.** Like babies, puppies learn quickly and it's this learned behaviour that stays with them through adult life. Start with just a few minutes a day a couple of days after arriving home.

2. **Your voice is a very important training tool.** Your dog has to learn to understand your language and you have to understand him. Commands should be issued in a calm, authoritative voice - not shouted. Praise should be given in a happy, encouraging voice,

accompanied by stroking or patting. If your dog has done something wrong, use a stern voice (not a hysterical shriek).

3. **Avoid giving your dog commands you know you can't enforce** or he learns that commands are optional. Give only one command - twice maximum - then gently enforce it. Repeating commands will make him tune out; telling your dog to *"SIT, SIT, SIT, SIT!!!"* is neither efficient nor effective. Say a single *"SIT,"* gently place him in the Sit position and praise him.

4. **Train gently and humanely.** Corgis can be sensitive and do not respond well to being shouted at or hit. They also can get bored.

5. **Keep training sessions short and upbeat.** If obedience training is a bit of a bore, pep things up a bit by *"play training"* by using constructive, non-adversarial games.

6. **Do not try to dominate your dog.** Training should be mutual, i.e. your dog should do something because he WANTS to do it. Corgis are not interested in dominating you, they want to please you.

7. **Begin training at home around the house and garden/yard.** How well your dog responds at home affects his behaviour away from the home. If he doesn't respond well at home, he certainly won't respond any better out and about where there are 101 distractions, e.g. interesting scents, food scraps, other dogs, people, small animals or birds.

8. **Mealtimes are a great time to start training.** Teach Sit and Stay at breakfast and dinner, rather than just putting the dish down and letting him dash over immediately.

9. **Use his name often and in a positive manner** so he gets used to the sound of it. He won't know what it means at first, but it won't take long before he realises you're talking to him.

10. **DON'T use his name when reprimanding, warning or punishing.** He should trust that when he hears his name, good things happen. He should always respond to his name with enthusiasm, never hesitancy or fear. Use words such as *"No!"* *"Ack!"* or *"Bad Boy/Girl"* in a stern (not shouted) voice instead.

    NOTE: Some parents prefer not to use *"No!"* with their dog, as they use it so often around the kids that it can confuse the pup! You can use *"Ack!"* or *"Leave!"*

11. **In the beginning, give your dog attention when YOU want to – not when he wants it.** When you are training, give lots of positive attention when he is good. But if he starts jumping up, nudging you constantly or barking to demand your attention, ignore him. Wait a while and pat him when you are ready and always AFTER he has stopped demanding your attention.

12. **You can give Corgis TOO MUCH attention in the beginning.** This may create a rod for your own back when they grow into needy adults that are over-reliant on you. They may even develop Separation Anxiety, which is stressful for both dog AND owner.

13. **Don't give your dog lots of attention (even negative attention) when he misbehaves.** Corgis love your attention and if yours gets lots when he's naughty, you are inadvertently reinforcing bad behaviour.

14. **Timing is critical.** When your puppy does something right, praise him immediately. If you wait a while, he will have no idea what he has done right. Similarly, when he does something wrong, correct him straight away.

15. **If he has an "accident" in the house, don't shout or rub his nose in it; it will have the opposite effect.** He may start hiding and peeing or pooping behind the couch or other inappropriate places. **If you catch him in the act,** use your *"No!"* or *"Ack!"* sound and immediately carry him out of the house. Then back to basics with housetraining.

   If you find something but don't catch him in the act, ignore it. If your pup is constantly relieving himself indoors, he either has a medical or behaviour issue or - more likely - you are not keeping a close enough eye on him!

16. **Start as you mean to go on.** In terms of training, treat your cute little pup as though he were fully-grown. Introduce the rules you want him to live by as an adult.

17. **Make sure that everybody in the household sticks to the same set of rules.** If the kids allow him on to the couch or bed and you forbid it, your Corgi won't know what is allowed and what isn't.

....

Expert Opinion

We asked a number of breeders and long-time owners about training their Corgis and this is what they said, starting with experienced owner and Welsh Corgi League (WCL) committee member Kevin Egan: "The Welsh Corgi Pembroke, according to reliable research from the USA, has an IQ broadly equivalent to a five-year-old child.

"The breed is bright and quick to learn, and they are probably motivated by genuinely wanting to perform interesting tasks and go about their labours in a business-like way. The primary training tip for other owners is: Practice Makes Perfect.

"It is important to continuously reinforce the training tasks so that your dog does not decide to reassign what you think is important into their own personal change of plan and priorities. Because if you do not train your Corgi, your Corgi will train you!"

Kennel Club Assured Breeder of Cardigans, Fran Fricker: "The Cardigan is very intelligent and a quick learner. They are ideal for Obedience and Agility as they are eager to please and love the rewards. They have an inbuilt herding instinct and are steady.

"With their large well-padded feet, Cardigans are the drovers' dog and would drive the cattle over the rough terrain from the hills in Wales to the market towns in England with no problem."

Pictured are Fran's Rye (Multi Ch Kerman Catcher in the Rye) with his sister Eden (Kerman Field of Dreams) doing a spot of rock climbing. Photo by Will Harris.

Fellow Assured Breeder Jo Evans: "They are intelligent, and quick to learn – especially if food is involved. Although they are quick to learn, instructions may fall on deaf ears if they don't want to do something. In my experience they work better off the lead than on the lead. My Corgis love food, so always a good incentive when training. However, I do tend to make training fun."

Assured Breeders Piotr and Johnathan Mazur-Jones: "They are highly intelligent - almost as intelligent as the Poodle - and are very easy to obedience train. We have experienced Corgis being trained even as late as seven years of age. They just love to be intellectually challenged and getting praise makes it all the more worthwhile."

Breeder and WCL Breed Health Co-ordinator Linda Roberts: "Corgis are mostly motivated to learn by food and also, of course, by a willingness to please their owner. Training should be consistent, kind and age-appropriate, with no negative reinforcements."

Breeder and top show judge Kevin Dover: "The Pembroke is a very intelligent dog and trains up extremely well. In the USA they have various championships for both Obedience and Herding, something that is only lightly covered here in the UK, but they do train very well.

"As with any dog, some take to training more readily than others, but perseverance is required - as well as a pocket of treats!"

Bred With Heart Breeder Lisa Thompson: "Corgis are super smart; they can outsmart you if you let them. They are very treat-motivated, very trainable and love to please you."

Alexandra Trefán-Török, Born To Be Corgis, Hungary: "What motivates Corgis to learn? That's easy - Corgis have black holes instead of stomachs! With positive motivation and **small** treats, they will do anything for you.

"Always finish the training in good time; not too long, and never over-exercise a puppy. Mental and physical training are equally important."

Did somebody say "Treat?!" Photo courtesy of Alexandra.

Experienced owner Lucy Badham-Thornhill: "Corgis are anxious to please, quick to learn, and love food rewards. Be consistent with the training. They can be strong characters and some, especially dogs (as opposed to bitches) need a firm hand."

Sue Hardy, who has owned Corgis for over 30 years and who does Scentwork and Hide and Seek activities with her Corgis says: "Food, praise, consistency and repetition – and neither of my newbies like a grumpy owner/handler!"

Teaching Basic Commands

The Three Ds

The three Ds – **Distance, Duration** and **Distraction** – are the cornerstone of a good training technique.

Duration is the length of time your dog remains in the command.

Distance is how far you can walk away without your dog breaking the command.

Distraction is the number of external stimuli - such as noise, scents, people, other animals, etc. - your dog can tolerate before breaking the command.

Only increase one of the Three Ds at a time. For example, if your new pup has just learned to sit on command, gradually increase the time by a second or two as you go along.

Moving away from the dog or letting the kids or the cat into the room would increase the Distance or Distraction level and make the command too difficult for your pup to hold.

If you are teaching the Stay, gradually increase EITHER the distance OR the time he's in the Stay position; don't increase both at once.

 Start off by training your dog in your home before moving into the garden or yard where there are more distractions - even if it is quiet and you are alone, outdoor scents and sights will be a big distraction for a young dog. Once you have mastered the commands in a home environment, progress to the park or other safe open space.

Implement the Three Ds progressively and slowly, and don't expect too much too soon! Work within your dog's capabilities, move forward one tiny step at a time and set your Corgi up to consistently SUCCEED, not fail.

Treats

Different treats have different values and using them at the right time will help you to get the best out of your Corgi:

1. **High Value Food** is human food - usually animal-based - such as chicken, liver, cheese, ham and sausage — one owner we know refers to this as *"The S Word"* — her Corgis will do anything for it!

    All should be cooked and cut into pea-sized treats — you're looking to reward your dog, not fur up his arteries, so make sure you don't give too many!

 Place the tiny treats in a bag in the freezer to keep them fresh, then you can grab a handful when you go out training. There's not much water content and they quickly thaw.

When training, we want our dog to want more High Value Food. He smells and tastes it on his tongue but it is gone in a flash, leaving him wanting more. *So, all treats should be only as large as a pea - even if you're training a Great Dane!*

2. **Medium Value Food** such as moist pet shop treats or a healthy alternative like sliced apple or carrot.

3. **Low Value Food** such as kibble. Use your dog's own food if you feed dry or buy a small bag.

    Photo: A brindle Cardigan in the Sit position.

IMPORTANT: Whenever you are asking your dog **to do something new,** make it worth his while. Offer a High Value treat. Once your dog understands what you are asking, you can move down to Medium Value treat.

When he does it every time use Low Value... reducing the frequency after a while and then only give it every other time... then only occasionally until you have slowly stopped giving any treat when asking for that task.

The aim at this point is to start getting you in control of your dog. After all, you will be a better team if your dog is a willing partner and does what you tell him to do. Being in control brings good things.

··

The Sit

Teaching the Sit command to your Corgi is relatively easy. Teaching a young pup to sit still for any length of time is a bit more difficult. If your little protégé is very distracted or high energy, it may be easier to put him on a lead (leash) to hold his attention.

1. **Stand facing each other and hold a treat between your thumb and fingers or in your hand just an inch or so above his head** and let him sniff it. Don't let your fingers and the treat get much further away or you might have trouble getting him to move his body into a sitting position.

   In fact, if your dog jumps up when you try to guide him into the Sit, you're probably holding your hand too far away from his nose. If your dog backs up, you can practise with a wall behind him.

2. **As he reaches up to sniff it, move the treat upwards and back over the dog** towards his tail at the same time as saying *"Sit."* Most dogs will track the treat with their eyes and follow it with their noses, causing their noses to point straight up.

3. **As his head moves up toward the treat, his rear end should automatically go down towards the floor.** TaDa! (drum roll!).

4. **The second he sits, say "Yes!"** Give him the treat and tell your dog he's a good boy/girl. Stroke and praise him for as long as he stays in the sitting position.

5. **If he jumps up on his back legs** and paws you while you are moving the treat, be patient and start all over again. At this stage, don't expect your bouncy little pupil to sit for more than a nanosecond!

NOTE: For positive reinforcement, use the words *Yes!, Good Boy!* or *Good Girl!*

Another method is to put one hand on his chest and with your other hand, gently push down on his rear end until he is sitting, while saying *"Sit."* Give him a treat and praise; he will eventually associate the position with the word "sit."

Once your dog catches on, leave the treat in your pocket (or have it in your other hand). Repeat, but this time your dog will just follow your empty hand.

Say *"Sit"* and bring your empty hand in front of your dog's nose. Move your hand exactly as you did when you held the treat. When your dog sits, say *"Yes!"* and then give him a treat from your other hand or your pocket.

Gradually lessen the amount of movement with your hand. First, say *"Sit"* then hold your hand eight to 10 inches above your dog's face and wait a moment. Most likely, he will sit. If he doesn't, help him by moving your hand back over his head, like you did before, but make a smaller movement this time.

Then try again. Your goal is to eventually just say *"Sit"* without having to move or extend your hand at all.

Once your dog reliably sits on cue, you can ask him to sit whenever you meet people (it may not work straight away, but it should help to calm him down a bit). The key is anticipation. Give your dog the cue before he gets too excited to hear you and before he starts jumping up on the person just arrived. Generously reward him the instant he sits.

The Stay

This is a very useful command, but it's not so easy to teach a lively and distracted young Corgi pup - don't ask him to stay for more than a few seconds at the beginning.

Tip **This requires concentration from your dog, so pick a time when he's relaxed and well-exercised, or just after a game or mealtimes - but not too exhausted to concentrate.**

1. **Tell your dog to sit or lie down,** but instead of giving a treat as soon as he hits the floor, hold off for one second. Then say *"Yes!"* in an enthusiastic voice and give him a treat.

   If your dog bounces up again instantly, have two treats ready. Feed one right away, before he has time to move; then say *"Yes!"* and feed the second treat.

2. **You need a release word or phrase.** It might be *"Free!"* or *"Here!"* Once you've given the treat, immediately say the word and encourage your dog to get up.

   Repeat the exercise a few times, gradually waiting a tiny bit longer before releasing the treat. (You can delay the first treat for a moment if your dog bounces up).

3. **A common mistake is to hold the treat high and then give the reward slowly.** As your dog doesn't know the command yet, he sees the treat coming and gets up to meet the food.

   Instead, bring the treat toward your dog quickly - the best place to deliver it is right between his front paws. If you're working on a Sit-Stay, give the treat at chest height.

4. **When your dog can stay for several seconds, start to add a little distance.** At first, you'll walk backwards, because your dog is more likely to get up to follow you if you turn away from him. Take one single step away, then step back towards your dog and say *"Yes!"* and give the treat. Give him the signal to get up immediately, even if five seconds haven't passed.

5. **Remember DISTANCE, DURATION, DISTRACTION.** Work on one factor at a time. Whenever you make one factor more difficult, ease up on the others then build them back up. So, when you add distance, cut the duration of the stay.

6. Once he's mastered The Stay with you alone, **move the training on so that he learns to do the same with distractions.** Have someone walk into the room, or squeak a

toy or bounce a ball once. A rock-solid stay is mostly a matter of working slowly and patiently to start with. Don't go too fast. If he does get up, take a breather and then give him a short refresher, starting at a point easier than whatever you were working on when he cracked.

 If you think he's tired or had enough, leave it for the day and come back later - just finish off on a positive note by giving one very easy command you know he will obey, followed by a reward.

Don't use the Stay command in situations where it is unpleasant for your dog. For instance, avoid telling him to stay as you close the door behind you on your way to work. Finally, don't use Stay to keep a dog in a scary situation.

Down

There are a number of different ways to teach this command, which here means for the dog to lie down.

<u>NOTE:</u> If you are teaching this command, then use the **"Off"** command to teach your dog not to jump up. This does not come naturally to a young pup, so it may take a little while to master.

Don't make it a battle of wills and, although you may gently push him down, don't physically force him down against his will. This will be interpreted as you putting pressure on him and it won't get the reaction you were hoping for.

1. Give the Sit command.

2. **When your dog sits, don't give him the treat immediately**, but keep it in your closed hand. Slowly move your hand straight down toward the floor, between his front legs. As your Corgi's nose follows the treat, just like a magnet, his head will bend all the way down to the floor.

3. When the treat is on the floor between your dog's paws, start to move it away from him, like you're drawing a line along the floor. (The entire luring motion forms an L-shape).

4. At the same time say *"Down"* in a firm manner.

5. To continue to follow the treat, your dog will probably ease himself into the Down position. The instant his elbows touch the floor, say *"Yes!"* and immediately let him eat the treat. If your dog doesn't automatically stand up after eating the treat, just move a step or two away to encourage him to move out of the Down position.

Repeat the sequence above several times. Aim for two short sessions of five minutes per day.

If your dog's back end pops up, quickly snatch the treat away. Then immediately say *"Sit"* and try again. It may help to let him nibble on the treat as you move it toward the floor. If you've tried to lure your dog into a Down, but he still seems confused or reluctant, try this trick:

1. Sit down on the floor with your legs straight out in front of you. Your dog should be at your side. Keeping your legs together and your feet on the floor, bend your knees to make a 'tent' shape.

2. Hold a treat right in front of your dog's nose. As he licks and sniffs the treat, slowly move it down to the floor and then underneath your legs. Continue to lure him until he has to crouch down to keep following the treat.

3. The instant his belly touches the floor, say **"Yes!"** and let him eat the treat. If your dog seems nervous about following the treat under your legs, make a trail of treats for him to eat along the way.

Some dogs find it easier to follow a treat into the Down from a standing position.

- Hold the treat right in front of your dog's nose, and then slowly move it straight down to the floor, right between his front paws. His nose will follow the treat

- If you let him lick the treat as you continue to hold it still on the floor, your dog will probably plop into the Down position

- The moment he does, say **"Yes!"** and let him eat the treat (some dogs are reluctant to lie on a cold, hard surface. It may be easier to teach yours to lie down on a carpet). The next step is to introduce a hand signal. You'll still reward him with treats, though, so keep them nearby or hidden behind your back.

1. Start with your dog in a Sit.

2. Say **"Down."**

3. **Without** a treat in your fingers, use the same hand motion you did before. As soon as your dog's elbows touch the floor, say **"Yes!"** and immediately get a treat to give him.

 Important: Even though you're not using a treat to lure your dog into position, you must still give a reward when he lies down. You want him to learn that he doesn't have to see a treat to get one.

4. Clap your hands or take a few steps away to encourage him to stand up. Then repeat the sequence from the beginning several times for a week or two. When your dog readily lies down as soon as you say the cue and use your new hand signal, you're ready for the next step. To stop bending all the way down to the floor every time, you can gradually shrink the signal to a smaller movement. To make sure your dog continues to understand what you want him to do, progress slowly.

5. Repeat the hand signal, but instead of moving your hand all the way to the floor, move it ALMOST all the way down. Stop when it's an inch or two above the floor. Practise the Down for a day or two, using this slightly smaller hand signal. Then you can make your movement an inch or two smaller, stopping your hand three or four inches above the floor.

6. After practising for another couple of days, shrink the signal again. As you continue to gradually stop your hand signal farther and farther from the floor, you'll bend over less and less. Eventually, you won't have to bend over at all. You'll be able to stand up straight, say **"Down,"** and then just point to the floor.

Your next job is harder: practise your dog's new skill in different situations and locations. Start with calm places, like different rooms in your house or your garden/yard when there's no one around.

Then increase the distractions; so, do some sessions at home when family members are moving around, on walks and then at friends' houses, too.

....

The Recall

This basic command is the most important of all - and definitely one of the hardest with a lively and distracted English Corgi.

<u>It will require lots and lots of repetition and patience on your part,</u> but you are limiting both your lives if you can't let your Corgi do what he was born to do; run free.

A dog who obeys the Recall enjoys freedoms that other dogs cannot. Corgis love to run free, but don't allow yours off-lead beyond fenced areas until he has learned some Recall. If yours has strong hunting instincts, you will have your work cut out, but the reward is a dog you can take anywhere.

Whether you have a puppy or an older dog, the first step is always to establish that coming to you is the BEST thing he can do.

 Any time your dog comes to you - whether you've called him or not - acknowledge that you appreciate it with praise, affection, play or treats. This consistent reinforcement ensures that your dog will continue to "check in" with you frequently.

1. Start off a short distance away from your dog.

2. Say your dog's name followed by the command *"Come!"* in an enthusiastic voice. You'll usually be more successful if you walk or run away from him while you call. Dogs find it hard to resist chasing after a running person, especially their owner.

3. He should run towards you!

4. A young dog will often start running towards you but then get distracted and head off in another direction. Pre-empt this situation by praising your puppy and cheering him on when he starts to come to you and **before** he has a chance to get distracted.

   Your praise will keep him focused so that he'll be more likely to come all the way to you. If he stops or turns away, you can give him feedback by saying *"Oh-oh!"* or *"Hey!"* in a different tone of voice (displeased or unpleasantly surprised). When he looks at you again, smile, call him and praise him as he approaches you.

5. When your puppy comes to you, give him the treat BEFORE he sits down or he may think that the treat was earned for sitting, not coming to you.

6. Another method is to use two people. You hold the treats and let your dog sniff them while the accomplice holds on to the dog. When you are about 10 or 15 yards away, get your helper to let the dog go, and once he is running towards you, say *"COME!"* loudly and enthusiastically.

   When he reaches you, stop, bend down and make a fuss of him before giving a treat. Do this several times. The next step is to give the Come command just BEFORE you get your helper to release the dog, and by doing this repetitively, the dog begins to associate the command with the action.

NOTE: "Come" or a similar word is better than "Here" if you intend using the "Heel" command, as "Here" and "Heel" sound very similar.

Progress your dog's training in baby steps. If he's learned to come when called in your kitchen, you can't expect him to do it straight away at the park, in the woods or on the beach when surrounded by distractions. When you first use the Recall outdoors, make sure there's no one around to distract your dog.

 Try and do all the initial Recall training within a safe, fenced area. If you're having problems with his attention span, consider using a long training lead so he can't run off.

Only when your dog has mastered the Recall in a number of locations and in the face of various distractions can you expect him to come to you regularly.

Although not commonly used with Corgis, a couple of our contributors do use a whistle to recall their dogs. One said: "In the past I have used a whistle for a group of Corgis. While it worked OK, now I call them. I think a whistle is good if they are running in large open areas as the sound carries."

Collar and Lead (Leash) Training

You have to train your dog to get used to a collar and lead, then teach him to walk nicely beside you.

This can be challenging with young pups, who don't necessarily want to walk at the same pace as you - some puppies might even slump to the ground and refuse to move in the beginning!

All dogs will pull on a lead initially. It's not because they want to show you who's boss, it's simply that they are excited to be out and are forging ahead.

You will need a small collar to start off with. Some puppies don't mind collars, some will try to scratch or remove them, while others will lie on the floor.

You need to be patient and calm and proceed at a pace comfortable to him; don't fight your dog and don't force the collar on.

Photo: a tricolour Pembroke puppy with collar.

1. Start your puppy off with a lightweight collar and give praise or a treat once the collar is on, not after you have taken it off. Gradually increase the length of time you leave the collar on.

 If you leave your dog in a crate or leave him alone in the house, take OFF the collar and tags. They may get caught, causing panic or injury.

2. Put the collar on when there are other things that will occupy him, like when he is going outside to be with you, when you are interacting with him, at

mealtimes or when you are doing some basic training. Don't put it on too tight, you want him to forget it's there; **you should be able to get two fingers underneath.**

Some pups may react as if you've hung a two-ton weight around their necks, while others will be more compliant. If yours scratches the collar, get his attention by encouraging him to follow you or play with a toy to forget the irritation.

3. Once your puppy is happy wearing the collar, introduce the lead. Many owners prefer an extending or retractable lead, but consider a fixed-length one to start training him to walk close to you. Again, begin in the house or garden; don't try to go out and about straight away.

Think of the lead as a safety device to stop him running off, not something to drag him around with. You want a dog that doesn't pull, so don't start by pulling him around.

4. Attach the lead and give him a treat while you put it on. Use the treats (instead of pulling on the lead) to lure him beside you, so that he gets used to walking with the collar and lead on.

You can also make good use of toys to do exactly the same thing - especially if your dog has a favourite.

Walk around the house with the lead on and lure him forwards with the toy. It might feel a bit odd but it's a good way for your pup to develop a positive relationship with the collar and lead with the minimum of fuss.

Act as though it's the most natural thing in the world for you to walk around the house with your dog on a lead - and just hope the neighbours aren't watching!

Some dogs react the moment you attach the lead and they feel some tension on it - a bit like when a horse is being broken for the first time.

Drop the lead and allow him to run around the house or yard, dragging it behind, but be careful he doesn't get tangled and hurt himself.

Try to make him forget about it by playing or starting a short fun training routine with treats. While he is concentrating on the new task, occasionally pick up the lead and call him to you. Do it gently and in an encouraging tone.

5. **Don't yank on the lead.** If it gets tight, just lure him back beside you with a treat or a toy. Remember to keep the hand holding it down, so your dog doesn't get the habit of jumping up. If you feel he is getting stressed, try putting treats along the route you'll be taking to turn this into a rewarding game: good times are ahead... so he learns to focus on what's ahead of him with curiosity, not fear.

6. **Avoid taking your pup out on to the streets too soon.** Do some collar and lead training around the home first, or he will find everything too distracting.

Corgis have an innate desire to please their owner and like treats, so you have a head start – however, it may not all be plain sailing in the beginning...

Photo: Two different reactions to collar and leash training!

One method is to walk forward and when they pull, turn around in a circle to distract them. Then continue walking. Keep turning around until they learn to stop pulling. This method is described by dog trainer Victoria Stillwell as the *'Reverse Direction Technique.'*

When your dog pulls, say "Let's Go!" in an encouraging manner, then turn away from him and walk off in the other direction, without jerking on the lead. When he is following you and the lead is slack, turn back and continue on your original way.

It may take a few repetitions, but your words and body language will make it clear that pulling will not get your dog anywhere, whereas walking calmly by your side - or even slightly in front of you - on a loose lead will get him where he wants to go.

There is an excellent video (in front of her beautiful house!) which shows Victoria demonstrating this technique and highlights just how easy it is with a dog that's keen to please. It only lasts three minutes: https://positively.com/dog-behavior/basic-cues/loose-leash-walking

One breeder added: "I agree with starting collar and leash training in the house and yard, but I don't try to lead the puppy. I follow puppy and let him lead me at first. Then I start stopping and calling them to me for a treat.

"As the puppy becomes more comfortable coming to me standing still, I then start backing up as the puppy comes to me, so they learn to keep coming to me even with tension on the leash. This is the first step in teaching them to follow me. I am starting to "lead" them."

Some dogs are perfectly happy to walk alongside you off-lead but behave differently when they have one on. Others may become more excitable or aggressive on a lead once they gain their confidence when their *Fight-or-Flight* instinct kicks in.

 Take collar and lead training slowly. Let him gain confidence in you, the lead and himself. Some puppies sit or lie and refuse to move! If this happens, walk a few steps away, go down on one knee and encourage him to come to you, then walk off again.

Harnesses

Opinions on harnesses for Corgis vary, but it's fair to say that most Corgi experts are not in favour of them. This is what Carole Turner, Corgi breeder and owner for over 50 years, says: "I don't like harnesses being used on Corgis for several reasons: unless it fits perfectly, it can rub armpits where there is less hair; some harnesses look so cumbersome and can restrict a dog's movement, or the dog will walk differently putting strain on joints.

"Some are too loose, so the dog could suddenly get out of it. They also allow the dog to lean into its chest and pull. Finally, a harness is great for a sled dog which has long legs and needs to pull a sled!"

Here are some other comments: Piotr and Johnathan: "Harnesses are a strict no from us. While they are popular with trainers, it is a lazy way to train your dog and encourages pulling and not to walk to heel.

"In addition, some harnesses - if not all - can cause growth development issues. Being a dwarf breed and wide in the chest, a harness can cause restriction - and therefore development issues for bone and muscles - in a Corgi. We can often tell a pet Corgi that has been harness-raised, they are much narrower in the chest and they don't have the strong front that you'd expect to see.

"So, our advice is: Don't be lazy! Put the work in to collar and lead train your pup and you will have a much happier well-behaved Corgi - and one that doesn't look wrong!"

Photo: Thompsons Bengie, aged six months, who is quite happy with his collar and leash, courtesy of Lisa Thompson.

Linda: "I prefer a soft round leather slip collar and lead because I see lots of dogs going crackers on harnesses with zero control at the head. There seems to be lots of upward-pulling going on which must put pressure on the spine. I also don't like the appearance of harnesses on Corgis. They remind me of trussed up turkeys!"

Margaret E. Leighton: "I use a slip leash on all my Corgis; I do not use flexi leashes or halters. My dogs are often off leash because they come when called (mostly!) and we walk on country lanes and public footpaths where it is safe for them to be off leash. I don't really care for harnesses. I use the slip leash once they have been through training to walk nicely at heel."

Vicky Methuen: "I never use them. I think the Corgi is just the wrong shape; a harness is too restrictive for those short legs."

Jo Evans: "I have used collars, harnesses, haltis etc. – my dogs only pull when they meet someone! There are a lot of different views on harnesses, some like them and some don't. A halti headcollar (which goes over the dog's nose) can work well for a pulling dog, but I only use it for training, not all the time."

Sue Hardy does use a harness, but only when her Corgi Mambo takes part in canine activities: ""Harnesses. Yes. The best fit I've found is Perfect Fit. Mambo only uses it for Hide and Seek and Mantrailing. In normal circumstances, I don't think that you have a great deal of control with them if the dog is a strong puller."

A Perfect Fit harness is a series of straps that can be bought separately to ensure the best fit for your dog.

10. Specialist Training

The first part of this chapter tells the story of Maria Carter, Corgi trainer to the stars, and her film and TV work. Along the way, Maria gives an insight into the Corgi mind and shares some training tips.

Corgis are biddable dogs. But they are also clever, and some can be strong-willed. As one breeder said: "If you don't train your Corgi, they will train you!" So the second part of the chapter helps you to recognise when your Corgi is trying to get the upper hand and outlines techniques for dealing with unwanted behaviour.

Twice Bitten

Maria moved to England from her native Italy aged 18 and took a job as an au pair with a family who owned a Corgi. Maria loved Socks and Socks loved Maria, and when boyfriend Brian came to visit, Socks bit him!

"I liked that!" Maria said: "I liked the dog's spirit and the fact that he followed me everywhere, he even slept under my bed." Maria had also been bitten - by *'the Corgi bug!'* - and before long she had Pembrokes of her own. Brian was undeterred by the bite from Socks and the couple went on to marry.

She joined the local Cheltenham Dog Training Club, where she trained her Corgi, Flash, with other breeds. Despite having no previous experience, Maria and Flash were soon entering club Obedience competitions – and doing very well:

"We won most of them," Maria says matter-of-factly. "I found I had a natural ability for training. I think it's because we had horses in Italy and a German Shepherd called Tarzan; I loved that dog.

"I love animals, I feel a connection and training is all about building an understanding.

"Flash adored me, we built a very good understanding and she took to competition very well. Only thing was she didn't like other dogs - she was fine with other Corgis, I think they recognise their own - but not other breeds. "I wanted to get better at Obedience, so I used to take a stool to top competitions and watch others for hours on end."

Maria's determination paid off, her reputation as an animal handler and trainer spread and she and her dogs were in demand for film, advertisement and TV appearances. Her dogs' first major on-screen appearance was in a 1991 TV version of the Alan Bennett play *A Question of Attribution*, starring Prunella Scales as the Queen and James Fox as a spy.

They had numerous other engagements and in 2000, a video of four of them barking on cue to the tune of Happy Birthday was shown on TV to celebrate the Queen Mother's 100th birthday.

Photo above: Screen stars Ella, Carina and Laila.

Lights, Camera, Action!

In 2009, Maria found herself driving to London at the crack of dawn with her three Corgis, Ella, Carina and Laila, en route to filming *The King's Speech* with heartthrob Colin Firth!

Colin was playing future King George VI (Queen Elizabeth II's father) who learns to overcome his stammer before taking the British throne, after his elder brother Edward VIII unexpectedly abdicated with American divorcee Wallis Simpson.

In 1933, three years before his coronation, 'Bertie,' as the King was affectionately known, introduced the first Corgi, Dookie, to the Royal Family. Dookie was shortly followed by Jane and thereafter Corgis became an integral part of the Royal Family.

Maria recalls that first day of filming: "We have to wait a long time until we are called for filming and I'm anxious about the dogs. We walk around the hard London roads, but they won't even pee, so I get bossy and insist that someone shows me at least a small piece of grass!

"After a few phone calls, I am allowed to move my car close to the filming location in the park near Kensington Palace. I am surrounded by policemen who escort me through one gate and then another, and finally I can let the Corgis out after their long wait in the car and they duly perform.

"At last we are called on to the set. Nobody shows me what to do, it is all done by autocues, so it's just as well I have done it before and know my job. I simply put my Corgis in different places in the room, trying to cover the whole set; I could do with more dogs, but the cameraman will sort that out.

"The star and director are pleased with the Corgis; Colin Firth comes and speaks to me in excellent Italian - I think he's practising! I also meet Geoffrey Rush, Helena Bonham-Carter, who is playing the Queen Mother, and Timothy Spall, who plays Winston Churchill."

Maria, Laila, Ella and Carina went on to make the famous 2011 Freeview Corgi advertisement, timed to coincide with the marriage of Prince William and Kate Middleton. If you haven't seen it, it's a hilarious 60-second watch: www.youtube.com/watch?v=KInvdKF5-0Y

Maria's training came to the fore when her Corgis had to pose next to a 'wedding cake' made from liver and sausages during filming. "I don't know how, but somehow they managed to hold back for long enough!" she said.

In 2016, Maria and her Corgis landed the job of a lifetime as owner and trainer of the Corgis in the Netflix drama *The Crown*.

The series became a massive hit, watched in 73 million households, and was instrumental in raising the profile of the Pembroke from an endangered breed to almost top 10 in the USA, with registrations going up 25% in a year in the UK.

"It appears The Crown is making Corgis trendy again," said Kennel Club spokesman David Robson. Maria is proud to have played her part in that.

Photo: Maria's Corgis on the set of The Crown with members of the cast.

The Corgis worked their usual charm on the cast and Claire Foy, who played the Queen in the first two series, described the Corgis as "the real stars of the show."

She added: "'They love cheese. If you want a Corgi to come near you - top tip - just have a bit of cheeky Cheddar in your hand and they think you're amazing. That's the only convincing way I play the Queen, because I can say: 'Have the cheese, have the cheese,' and they come towards me!"

Maria has a thing or two to say about that: "Corgis only have to look at food to put on weight!" She adds that if you do give cheese as a treat, use Edam, not Cheddar as it's less fattening. Maria's Corgis are fed on a diet of raw chicken mince mixed with vegetables, and treats are tiny pieces of cooked liver.

At home in Gloucestershire, Maria takes on just three or four dogs at a time to train individually, a full-day session once a month for three months. She mostly trains for Obedience competitions, but has also developed a reputation for scent and behaviour training.

Over the years she has won prizes the length and breadth of the country and her indoor training centre is wallpapered in rosettes.

....

Maria's Tips for Training a Corgi

Maria says: "Some trainers don't understand that it's not just about the food or treats; the understanding between the dog and trainer or owner is most important.

"Corgis are a little-big dog. They are little in size, but have big personalities. Start training right away, as soon as you bring the puppy home; eight or nine weeks.

"They think they are playing, but you are training them. Do a little bit every day.

"They are very intelligent and by the time they get to about three years old, they know how to do things before you even ask them! By three they have their character.

Photo: Maria training Iucci, aged 18 months, on the weave poles.

"When you are training, talk to your dog the whole time. Tell them what you are doing, Corgis are very intelligent and they remember.

"Tone of voice is very important, it must be sing-song, upbeat. Tell your dog everything you are doing because Corgis remember.

"Use the same commands and say the dog's name a lot - all the time in the sing-song voice. They love their name because they connect it with something positive.

"Sometimes I say 'fish and chips and mashed potato' just to keep the dog listening!

"Corgis want to keep their minds occupied; I love that about them. When I am training one of mine, the other one moans because she isn't doing anything.

"If you had an old ball in one hand and a piece of steak in the other, Iucci would go for the old ball. Mine absolutely love training - they don't know it's training, they think they are playing games. Keep it short and fun. Sometimes I might do something silly just to break it up.

"A lot of Corgis don't like the Sit position. If you are teaching the Sit, caress their back and put gentle pressure on their back end, not the middle of the back.

"Don't reward every time with a treat, or they will come to expect it. We use a ball as well as a treat. Again, they think they are playing.

"Don't tell them off if they don't do something right. Say 'Do it again' in the same nice tone of voice. You'll learn from your dog. If it still doesn't work, repeat once then try something else - the dog is telling you it's not working.

"And if you see that your dog is tired or uninterested, cut the training session short."

Maria is currently training six Corgis on a weekly basis for obedience and showing. She takes tip-top care of her own beloved Pembrokes Ella and Iucci; she grooms them, cleans their teeth and checks their ears daily.

She's also got them used from puppyhood to their nails being regularly trimmed - and even trained them to walk up a plank on to the grooming table!

Photos: Maria says that building an understanding with your dog and talking to them throughout, so they listen to you, are key points when training a Corgi. Top: Maria and Ella during scent training in the indoor training centre. Below: Iucci walking to heel.

Dealing With Unwanted Behaviour

When treated well, socialised and trained, Corgis make wonderful canine companions. Once you've had one, no other dog seems quite the same. But sometimes they can be too smart for their own good, and a bored Corgi is a mischievous Corgi. Poor behaviour may show itself in different ways:

- ❧ Excessive barking
- ❧ Becoming overly protective of a person, toys or food
- ❧ Nipping – too much herding of people or animals!

- ❧ Aggression
- ❧ Snarling or lunging on the leash
- ❧ Chewing or other destructive behaviour
- ❧ Excessive digging
- ❧ Jumping up
- ❧ Soiling or urinating inside the house
- ❧ Constantly demanding your attention

These are the most common reasons for unwanted behaviour:

- ❧ Lack of socialisation
- ❧ Lack of training
- ❧ Poor breeding
- ❧ Boredom, due to lack of exercise or mental challenges
- ❧ Being left alone too long
- ❧ A change in living conditions
- ❧ Anxiety, insecurity or fear
- ❧ Being spoiled
- ❧ Being badly treated

If you are rehoming a Corgi, you'll need extra time and patience to help your new arrival unlearn some bad habits.

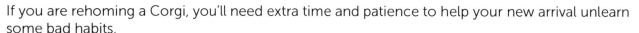

10 Ways to Avoid Bad Behaviour

Here are some tips to help you start out on the right foot:

1. **Buy from a good breeder**. They use their expertise to match suitable breeding pairs, taking into account factors such as good temperament, health and being *"fit for function."*

2. **Start socialisation right away**. Socialisation is EXTREMELY important for Pembrokes and Cardigans. Give a new puppy a couple of days to get used to his new surroundings and then start socialising him – even if this means carrying him places until the vaccination schedule is complete.

   Socialisation does not end at puppyhood. Dogs are social creatures that thrive on sniffing, hearing, seeing, and even licking. While the foundation for good behaviour is laid down during the first few months, good owners reinforce social skills and training throughout a dog's life.

   Corgis love to be at the centre of the action and it is important that they learn when young that they are not also the centre of the universe. Socialisation helps them to learn their place in that universe and to become comfortable with it.

3. **Start training early** - you can't start too soon. Start teaching your puppy to learn his own name as well as some simple commands a day or two after you bring him home.

4. **Basic training should cover several areas:** housetraining, chew prevention, puppy biting, simple commands like SIT, COME, STAY and familiarising him with collar and leash or puppy harness. Adopt a gentle approach and keep training sessions short. Start with five minutes a day and build up.

   Puppy classes or adult dog obedience classes are a great way to start; be sure to do your homework together afterwards. Spend a few minutes each day reinforcing what you have both learned in class - owners need training as well as dogs!

5. **Reward your dog for good behaviour.** All behaviour training should be based on positive reinforcement. Corgis love praise and rewards, and this trait speeds up the training process. The main aim of training is to build a good understanding between you and your dog.

6. **Ignore bad behaviour**, no matter how hard this may be. If, for example, your dog is chewing his way through your kitchen, shoes, or couch, jumping up or rounding up the kids, remove him from the situation and then ignore him. For most dogs even negative attention is some attention.

   Or if he is constantly demanding your attention, ignore him. Remove him or yourself from the room so he learns that you give attention when you want to give it, **not** when he demands it. If your pup is a chewer - and most are - make sure he has plenty of durable toys to keep him occupied.

7. **Take the time to learn what sort of temperament your dog has.** Is he by nature confident or reserved? What was he like as a tiny puppy, did he rush forward or hang back? Does he fight to get upright when on his back or is he happy to lie there? Is he laid-back or a ball of energy?

   Your puppy's temperament will affect his behaviour and how he reacts to the world. A nervous Corgi will certainly not respond well to a loud approach on your part, and an energetic, strong-willed one will require more exercise, games, patience and determination on your part.

8. **Exercise and stimulation.** A lack of either is another reason for dogs behaving badly. Regular daily exercise, games, toys and organised activities are all ways of stopping your Corgi from becoming bored or frustrated.

9. **Learn to leave your dog.** Just as leaving your dog alone for too long can lead to problems, so can being with him 100% of the time. The dog becomes over-reliant on you and then gets stressed when you leave; this is called *Separation Anxiety*.

   When your dog first arrives at your house, start by leaving him for a few minutes every day and gradually build it up so that after a while you can leave him for up to four hours.

10. **Love your Corgi – but don't spoil him,** however difficult that might be. You don't do your dog any favours by giving too many treats, constantly responding to his demands for attention, allowing him to boss other dogs or letting him behave exactly as he wants inside the house.

The Hierarchy of Treats

Treats are different things to different dogs. A treat is something the dog likes, so it could be food, a toy or praise. Most Corgis are highly motivated by food treats. Different treats have different values and using them at the right time will help you to get the best out of your dog:

4. **High Value Food** is human food - usually animal-based - such as sausage, ham, chicken, liver and cheese. All should be cooked if raw and cut into pea-sized treats – you're looking to reward your dog, not feed him. Place the tiny treats in a freezer bag in the freezer, which keeps them fresh, then you can grab a handful when you go out training. There's not much water content and they quickly thaw.

   When training, we want our dog to want more High Value Food. He smells and tastes it on his tongue but it is gone in a flash, leaving him wanting more. *So, all treats should be only as large as a pea - even if you're training a Great Dane!*

5. **Medium Value Food** such as moist pet shop treats or a healthy alternative like sliced apple or carrot.

6. **Low Value Food** such as kibble. Use your dog's own food if you feed dry, or buy a small bag if not.

IMPORTANT: Whenever you are asking your dog **to do something new,** make it worth his while. Offer a High Value treat like a tiny piece of liver. Once your dog understands what you are asking, you can move down to Medium Value treat.

When he does it every time use Low Value... reducing the frequency after a while and then only give it every other time... then only occasionally until you have slowly stopped giving any treat when asking for that task.

Excessive Barking

If your puppy is too fond of the sound of his own voice, it should be nipped in the bud as soon as possible as it's far harder to stop an adult Corgi barking. There are three main reasons why a dog is nuisance barking. He is:

❖ Over-excited

❖ Frightened

❖ Demanding something

Corgi puppies may bark or whine to demand something, usually your attention, such as when you put them in their crate or leave a room, or when they want something. We feel we have to do something, like we would with a crying baby or child.

STOP! Corgi puppies are smart. They will go through a repertoire of different behaviours to get you to do what THEY want you to do. If you give in, they store that information away and do it again. After several repetitions of this behaviour, it becomes a habit.

The best thing you can do for your puppy is to remove them or you from the situation and **ignore them.** Don't try and control them or give repetitive commands when they are not listening, simply remove your attention and leave them on their own.

Don't reward your puppy by talking to him or touching him. Intelligent dogs like the Corgi soon realise that their indiscriminate barking gets the opposite effect to what they want. And only ever give a treat when your dog is quiet.

If, for example, your puppy barks with excitement when you get out his collar and leash for a walk, stop your preparations. Give the Sit command and only reward him when he is sitting quietly and not barking. Don't make too much of a fuss when he stops, avoid eye contact and carry on calmy.

If he barks as he goes out into the garden to perform his business, put him on a loose lead and stand still until he stops barking.

Corgis make excellent watchdogs and you may actively want to encourage your puppy to bark when someone comes to the house. Be warned: you could soon end up with a dog that barks at everything. Our advice is: **Never encourage a Corgi puppy to bark!**

As pups mature, their guarding instinct kicks in at around six or seven months old, and a well-socialised Corgi is likely to bark without being taught.

As a breed with a working heritage, many Corgis have natural protective tendencies towards their home, fellow animals and humans. This is fine, in its place - you just have to ensure it doesn't get out of hand.

 The key is to socialise your young Corgi - expose him to new people, places, noises and animals in a positive manner while he is young. A well-socialised Corgi is relaxed in his surroundings and not barking through fear or excitement every time he encounters something new or different.

Some Corgis are reactive on the leash when they see other dogs. Although this may be excitement with a puppy, it is often grounded in fear.

FACT Just as we have different tones of voice, dogs have different barks, from a single bark to rapid, continuous barking, with the pitch ranging from deep to high-pitched, depending on the situation.

Your dog is talking to you! Learn to listen to what he is saying. Type *'AKC the meaning of your dog's barks'* into an online search engine for a better understanding of the noises your dog makes.

One very important thing to remember if your dog is aggressive, timid or reactive on the leash is that they will pick up on your fear. If you see another dog approaching, do NOT appear nervous by tightening the leash, picking your Corgi up or staring at the other dog.

Have a treat handy and **stay calm!** Before the other dog reaches you, get your dog's attention by showing him you have a treat and talking in a calm manner, using his name. Get him to sit, turned slightly away from the other dog and focusing on you as you feed him tiny treats until the other dog has passed. If you have to, start with High Value treats.

It may take lots of repetition if the habit is ingrained or your dog is very fearful, but this is a very effective technique - and don't forget to continue socialising him.

Speak and Shush!

The Speak and Shush technique teaches your dog or puppy to bark and be quiet on command. When your dog barks at an arrival at your house, gently praise him after the first few barks. If he persists, tell him **"Quiet."**

Get a friend to stand outside your front door and say **"Speak"** or **"Alert."** This is the cue for your accomplice to knock on the door or ring the bell - don't worry if you both feel like idiots, it will be worth the embarrassment!

When your dog barks, say **"Speak"** and praise him profusely. After a few good barks, say **"Shush"** or **"Quiet"** and then dangle a tasty treat in front of his nose.

If he is food-motivated, he will stop barking as soon as he sniffs the treat, because it is **physically impossible for a dog to sniff and woof at the same time.**

Praise your dog again as he sniffs quietly and give him the treat. Repeat this routine a few times a day and your Corgi will quickly learn to bark whenever the doorbell rings and you ask him to **"Speak."**

Eventually your dog will bark AFTER your request but BEFORE the doorbell rings, meaning he has learned to bark on command. Even better, he will learn to anticipate the likelihood of getting a treat following your **"Shush"** request and will also be quiet on command.

With Speak and Shush training, progressively increase the length of required shush time before offering a treat - at first just a couple of seconds, then three, five, 10, 20, and so on.

By alternating instructions to speak and shush, the dog is praised and rewarded for barking on request and also for stopping barking on request.

If you have a Corgi who is silent when somebody approaches the house, you can use the following method to get him to bark on the command of **"Speak."** This is also a useful command if you walk your dog alone, especially at night; your corgi's big bark will help to keep you safe:

1. Have some treats at the ready, waiting for that rare bark.

2. Wait until he barks - for whatever reason - then say **"Speak"** or whatever word you use.

3. Praise him and give a treat. At this stage he won't know why he is receiving the treat.

4. Keep praising him every time he barks and give a treat.

5. After you've done this for several days, hold a treat in your hand in front of his face and say **"Speak."**

6. Your dog will probably still not know what to do, but will eventually get so frustrated at not getting the treat that he will bark.

7. At which point, praise him and give the treat.

We trained a quiet dog to do this in a week and then, like clockwork, he barked enthusiastically every time anybody came to the door or whenever we gave him the "Speak" command, knowing he would get a treat for stopping.

Jumping Up

This common behaviour problem is something your dog has learned during puppyhood. When you - or your visitors - walk through the door, your Corgi jumps all over everybody. Some people love that about their Corgis, others not so much, especially if you have children or an elderly relative, when a Corgi can bowl them over.

Typically, you push the dog off, saying 'Down' or 'Off.' You are gently scolding him, but the truth is that your negative attention is better than no attention, so you are rewarding your dog for his behaviour every time.

ATTENTION = REWARD, so the trick here is to give a bigger, better reward for keeping all four paws on the ground.

For this exercise you need patience and persistence. If you are not prepared to put the effort in, then stay with a Corgi who jumps up and leave it at that!

Part 1 - Stop giving attention - positive and negative. As soon as your dog jumps up, turn your back. Cross your arms and do not speak or look at him. If he runs around trying to get your attention and keeps jumping up, keep turning away from him, but do not say anything or look at him. Or briefly leave the room, wait a moment then step back inside and repeat until the dog is calm enough to stop jumping up.

Part 2 - Reward good behaviour. Make sure you always have High Value treats to hand. As soon as your dog is in front of you with all four paws on the ground, throw him a treat. You can praise him, but keep all speech and praise low key; we don't want to excite him.

Then, practise, practise. Set up situations to practise with your dog. If the jumping happens when you come home, spend a little time coming and going from the house. Do not make a big fuss and step outside if he jumps up. **Only reward when all four paws are on the floor.**

Part 3 - Add the Sit. Once your dog is keeping his paws on the floor for a few seconds or more, ask for a Sit. Walk into the room through the front door and say "SIT." As soon as the dog sits, give a High Value treat

Part 4 - Practise with other people so, when anyone enters the room, he knows to sit.

 We have replaced the Jump with the Sit. Your dog still knows how to jump up; we cannot delete this from his brain, but we can make him feel that doing something else is much better.

Clicker Training

The first step towards being in control of a dog is by training him to listen to us.

The Clicker can be a good tool that bridges the language barrier between humans and their dogs. It can work very well with Corgis as they are quick learners - and they get a treat every time!

Corgis are also remarkable in that, unlike many other breeds, they respond to training regardless of the training method. A Clicker can be a simple and highly effective way of letting your Corgi understand that what he has just done is **EXACTLY** the thing you are asking for. Dogs love to please using a clicker, and it enforces the fact that he is doing it right. It is important that the click happens at the right moment as it means: 'Well done!'

One example is teaching the Sit. With the Clicker in your hand and treats in your pocket or in a bowl out of reach, ask your dog for a Sit. The moment his bottom touches the floor, **CLICK.** Think of it like pressing the shutter of a camera to take a picture of the behaviour.

After the click has happened, take out a treat and give your dog his prize. The Clicker is like the winning buzzer on a game show that tells a contestant he's just won the money! Through the Clicker, the trainer communicates precisely with the dog, and that speeds up training.

 You have to click the second your dog does as you ask. If you are too slow, he will think you are praising him for getting up out of a Sit - or if it is too soon, you will be praising him for looking at you.

NOTE: If the Clicker goes off randomly it can confuse your dog and the training will not be as effective. You can practise clicking (out of your dog's hearing) by bouncing a ball and clicking every time it hits the floor.

Separation Anxiety

It's not just dogs that experience Separation Anxiety - people do too. About 7% of adults and 4% of children suffer from this disorder. Typical symptoms for humans are:

- ❧ Distress at being separated from a loved one
- ❧ Fear of being left alone

Our canine companions aren't much different. When a puppy leaves the litter, his owner becomes his new pack.

It's estimated that as many as 10% to 15% of dogs suffer from Separation Anxiety, which is an exaggerated fear response caused by being apart from their owner.

Separation Anxiety affects millions of dogs and is on the increase. According to behaviourists, it is the most common form of stress for dogs – and it's stressful for the owner too.

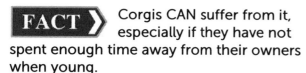 **Corgis CAN suffer from it, especially if they have not spent enough time away from their owners when young.**

Even if yours does not have Separation Anxiety, being over-reliant on you can lead to other insecurity issues, such as becoming:

Anxious, over-protective, territorial, too suspicious or aggressive with other people or dogs.

Separation Anxiety can be equally distressing for the owner - I know because one of our dogs suffered from it. He howled whenever we left home without him. He'd also bark if one of us got out of the car - even if other people were still inside.

Tell-Tale Signs

Does your Corgi do any of the following?

* ❈ Follow you from room to room - even the bathroom - whenever you're at home?

* ❈ Get anxious or stressed when you're getting ready to leave the house?

* ❈ Howl, whine or bark when you leave?

* ❈ Tear up paper or chew things he's not supposed to?

* ❈ Dig or scratch at the carpet, doors or windows trying to join you?

* ❈ Soil or urinate inside the house, even though he is housetrained? (This **only** occurs when left alone)

* ❈ Exhibit restlessness - such as licking his coat excessively, pacing or circling?

* ❈ Greet you ecstatically every time you come home – even if you've only been out to empty the bins?

* ❈ Wait by the window or door until you return?

* ❈ Dislike spending time alone in the garden or yard?

* ❈ Refuse to eat or drink if you leave him?

* ❈ Howl or whine when one family member leaves - even when others are still in the room?

If so, he may suffer from Separation Anxiety. Fortunately, in many cases this can be cured.

Causes

Dogs are pack animals and being alone is not a natural state for them - especially social breeds like the Corgi who thrive on the companionship of their 'family' - be it humans, other animals or both.

Puppies have to be taught to get used to periods of isolation slowly and in a structured way before they can become comfortable with being alone.

A puppy emotionally latches on to his new owner, who has taken the place of his mother and siblings. He will want to follow you everywhere initially and, although you want to shower him with love and attention, it's best to start leaving him, starting with a minute or two, right from the beginning.

 Even if you are at home all day, make an effort to leave the puppy on his own for short periods every day, starting with a few minutes and building up.

Adopted dogs may be particularly susceptible to Separation Anxiety. They may have been abandoned once already and fear it happening again.

One or more of these causes can trigger Separation Anxiety:

* ❈ Not being left alone for short periods when young

* ❈ Being left for too long by owners who are out of the house for most of the day

* ❈ Anxiety or lack of confidence due to insufficient socialisation, training or both

* ❈ Boredom

* ❈ Being given TOO MUCH attention

- All of the dog's attention being focussed on one person – usually because that person spends time with him, plays, feeds, trains and exercises him

- Making too much of a fuss when you leave and return to the house

- Mistreatment in the past, a rescue dog may well feel anxious when left alone

FACT ❯ It may be very flattering that your Corgi wants to be with you all the time, but Separation Anxiety is a form of panic that is distressing for your dog. Socialisation helps a dog to become more confident and self-reliant.

A different scenario is Separation Anxiety in elderly dogs. Pets age and their senses, such as scent, hearing and sight, diminish. They often become "clingier" and more anxious when they are separated from their owners - or even out of view.

You may even find that your elderly Corgi reverts to puppyhood and starts to follow you around the house again. In these cases, it is fine to spend more time with your old friend and gently help him through his final years.

So, what can you do if your dog is showing signs of canine Separation Anxiety? Every dog is different, but here are tried and tested techniques that have worked for some dogs.

Tips to Combat Separation Anxiety

1. After the first couple of days at home, leave your new puppy or adult dog for short periods, starting with a minute, then two, then gradually increasing the minutes you are out of sight.

2. Use a crate. Crate training helps a dog to become self-reliant.

3. Introduce your dog to other people, places and animals while young.

4. Get other members of your family to feed, walk and train him, so he doesn't become fixated on just one person.

5. Don't allow your Corgi to sleep in your bedroom, so he gets used to being away from you for eight hours a day.

6. Tire your Corgi out before you leave him alone. Take him for a walk, do an activity or play a game before leaving and, if you can, leave him with a view of the outside world, e.g. in a room with a patio door or low window.

7. Keep arrivals and departures low key and don't make a big fuss.

8. Leave him a *"security blanket,"* such as an old piece of clothing that still has your scent on it, a favourite toy, or leave a radio on softly in the room with the dog. Avoid a heavy rock station! If it will be dark when you return, leave a lamp on a timer.

9. Associate your departure with something good. Give him a rubber toy, like a Kong, filled with a tasty or frozen treat. This may take his mind off your departure. (Some dogs may refuse to touch the treat until you return home).

10. Structure and routine can help to reduce anxiety. Carry out regular activities, such as feeding and exercising, at the same time every day.

11. Corgis read body language very well; they may start to fret when they think you are going to leave them. One technique is to mimic your departure routine when you have no intention of leaving. Put your coat on, grab your car keys, go out of the door and return a few seconds later. Do this randomly and regularly and it may help to reduce your dog's stress levels when you do it for real.

12. However lovable your Corgi is, if he is showing early signs of anxiety when separating from you, do not shower him with attention all the time when you are there. He will become too reliant on you.

13. If you have to regularly leave the house for a few hours at a time, try to make an arrangement so the dog is not on his own all day every day during the week. Consider dropping him off with a neighbour, or doggie day care if you can afford it.

14. Getting another dog to keep the first one company can help greatly and Corgis usually get on well with other dogs in the household, but first ask yourself if you can afford double the food and veterinary bills.

15. There are many natural calming remedies available for dogs in spray, tablet or liquid form, such as CBD oils and chews, melatonin and pheromones.

Sit-Stay-Down

Another technique for helping to reduce Separation Anxiety is the *"sit-stay"* or *"down-stay"* exercises using positive reinforcement. The goal is to be able to move briefly out of your dog's sight while he is in the *"stay"* position. Through this, he learns that he can remain calmly and happily in one place while you go about your normal daily life.

You have to progress slowly. Get your dog to sit and stay and then walk away from him for five seconds, then 10, 20, a minute and so on. Reward your dog every time he stays calm. Then move out of sight or out of the room for a few seconds, return and give him a treat if he is calm, gradually lengthen the time you are out of sight.

If you're watching TV snuggled up with your dog and you get up for a snack, say *"Stay"* and leave the room. When you return, praise him quietly. It is a good idea to practise these techniques after exercise or when your dog is a little sleepy (but not exhausted), as he is likely to be more relaxed.

FACT ❯ Canine Separation Anxiety is not the result of disobedience or lack of training. It's a psychological condition; your dog feels anxious and insecure.

NEVER punish your dog for showing signs of Separation Anxiety – even if he has chewed your best shoes or dug a hole in your expensive rug. This will only make him more anxious.

NEVER leave your dog unattended in a crate for long periods or if he is frantic to get out, as it can cause physical or mental trauma. If you're thinking of leaving an animal in a crate all day while you are out of the house, get a rabbit or a hamster – definitely not a Corgi!

11. Exercise and Socialising

One thing all dogs have in common - including every Corgi ever born - is that they need daily exercise. Even if you have a large garden or back yard where your dog can run free, there are still lots of benefits to getting out and about.

Corgis love going for walks, but are happy to lounge around at home as well. Don't think that because they are happy to snuggle up on the sofa, they don't need regular exercise – THEY DO. Corgis were bred to herd and, like all breeds created to do a specific job, they require physical and mental challenges to be truly happy.

 Games, hide and seek, playing with other dogs, scenting, and activities that work your Corgi's mind can be just as tiring as going for a walk and all count as "daily exercise."

Daily exercise helps to keep your Corgi happy and healthy. It:

* Strengthens respiratory and circulatory systems
* Helps get oxygen to tissue cells
* Helps keep a healthy heart
* Wards off obesity
* Keeps muscles toned and joints flexible
* Aids digestion
* Releases endorphins that trigger positive feelings
* Helps to keep dogs mentally stimulated and socialised

FACT 〉 **One thing that surprises many new owners is the Corgi's active mind, which requires engagement (and training!) to stop them getting the upper hand.**

If you have the time and interest, an excellent way of keeping your Corgi's mind and body exercised is to take part in a canine activity or competition, such as Obedience or Agility. See **Chapter 12. The Active Corgi** for more information.

How Much Exercise?

The amount of exercise each adult Corgi needs varies from one dog to the next and depends on various factors, including:

* Temperament
* Natural energy levels
* Bloodline
* Your living conditions
* Whether your dog is kept with other dogs
* What they get used to

Some of your dog's natural temperament and energy levels will depend on the bloodline - ask the breeder how much exercise he or she recommends. Most Corgis enjoy toys and games and love a job to do - left to their own devices, most will herd anything in sight; the cat, birds, the kids, your visitors...

The UK Kennel Club says up to an hour of exercise a day. However, many experts involved in this book give their Corgis more. These hardy little dogs will take a lot more exercise, even all-day hikes, once they have built up to it.

 Much depends on your daily routine and what your dog gets used to. If your Corgi is used to lots of exercise, she won't be happy if it suddenly reduces or stops. Similarly, one used to little exercise will have to build up to extended or vigorous activities.

Owning more than one dog - or having friends with dogs - is a great way for your dog to get more exercise. A couple of dogs running around together get far more exercise than one on her own. Corgis are also very social dogs, and well-socialised Pems and Cardis enjoy being with other dogs - especially other Corgis.

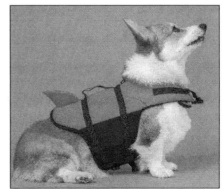

A garden or yard with a secure fence is great, but it should not be seen as a replacement for daily exercise away from the home, where your dog can experience new places, scents, people and dogs.

If you live in an apartment, you may have no outside space, so it is especially important to commit to and make time for daily walks.

Your Corgi will enjoy going for walks on the lead (leash), but will enjoy life much more when she is allowed to run free, following a scent or chasing. If your dog is happy just to amble along beside you, think about playing some games to raise her heartbeat, build muscle and get her fit.

Most Corgis have no road sense! Make sure it's safe, away from traffic and other hazards, before letting her off the lead - and only after she has learned the Recall.

Never underestimate a Corgi's natural instinct and keep them on a lead near livestock and wild animals if you are hiking in the countryside - unless you know they can be trusted not to herd or chase.

If you want to hike or take part in canine competitions with your dog, build up time and distance gradually. Always exercise within your dog's limits - on both land and water.

Corgis and Water

Whether your Corgi enjoys swimming very much varies from one individual to the next. If your dog is to be around water regularly, introduce them to the water in a positive manner; NEVER throw them in or entice them out of their depth.

Although most Corgis who want to swim can swim (despite their short legs and heavy bodies), a doggie life vest, **pictured,** is an option that gives you peace of mind if your dog spends a lot of time on boats or around deep water - and in an emergency you can grab the handle on top to pull her out. Remember that swimming is a very strenuous activity for any dog, so keep any swim sessions SHORT. Don't repeatedly throw a ball, stick or toy into water; your Corgi will not know when to stop and may get into difficulties.

If your dog does enjoy swimming, it is an excellent way to exercise; many veterinary clinics now use water tanks not only for remedial and IVDD therapy, but also for canine recreation.

Here's what some of our experts said, starting with Marian Your: "Tommy, our agility star, had one dock diving lesson. He was able to swim but was appalled at not having solid ground underfoot, so we decided not to pursue that.

"We don't have a boat and don't normally do water sports ourselves, so he hasn't had an opportunity to swim. I know people who use a life vest for their dogs when kayaking and I think that's an excellent idea."

Eileen Eby: "I had one Cardi who would use his paddling pool all year round - even if it meant breaking the ice so he could sit in it!

"He loved to swim whenever he had the opportunity (without a life vest) and always loved ditches, puddles, etc. Every day when we came home from our walks, he would jump into his paddling pool. I don't live near open water now, but one of my girls also likes to cool off in her paddling pool, though only in warm weather."

Sue Hardy: "We live withing walking distance of a canal. On a walk I crossed a lock bridge, leaving BenDog on the towpath the other side. He decided to jump in, doggy paddling across, gradually sinking. He had to be grabbed by the scruff of the neck and hoicked out! When another of my Corgis managed to fall off the back of a boat on the Norfolk Broads, we came to the conclusion that our Corgis were not swimmers!"

Margaret E. Leighton: "Owain is definitely a wader. However, if the weather is really hot, he'll swim. Corgis can be good swimmers if they like water. Bubbles does not like ponds, lakes or canals. She accidentally fell into our local canal and I think that is the reason she doesn't like water."

Jo Evans: "My youngest Corgi, Lucy, will go in the sea, but she doesn't go out of her depth if she can help it. Cara is not so keen.

"We live by the sea now and usually when I take a dip, I leave the dogs behind. But on one occasion my husband came too, just to stay on dry land and look after the dogs. However, the dogs were worried about me and swam right out to me at sea. I had to go ashore as their little legs were getting tired... Since that day they have watched from the beach!"

Lucy Badham-Thornhill: "Mine are not enthusiastic swimmers because we do not have local water, so a swim is rare. They can swim well and surprisingly strongly. I have a friend who lives by the sea and his Corgi swims daily and loves it."

Carole Turner: "Mine do go in water, they paddle and swim - no life vest. They are happy to be out of their depth and have no problems swimming. I wish they had more of a sense of danger!"

Linda Roberts: "Mine swim and paddle in our river and enjoy it. They're pretty strong - even when there's a current, but I don't swim them in the sea."

Vicky Methuen: "We live near the coast and it was not too long before our puppy Brona discovered what sea was for. She is a real water baby - anything from a puddle to the Celtic Sea!

"Her first real outing was when she was three months and we went to a nearby beach; the beaches here in West Wales tend to be long crescents of gently sloping sand. It was in the summer and she stuck initially to the tide line, but I went further into the water she followed, a little tremulously at first.

"The next few times we went anywhere near water she went in, but she's never out of her depth unless she is in a rockpool. We have one particular beach, Freshwater West, which is huge and there are a lot of deep rockpools. She knows we are there even when I'm parking the car - but all my Corgis have had this trait. Ball games often follow a swim so she dries off!"

Fran Fricker: "Mine do not mind water at all, they will walk through it rather than go round. They love being bathed and will join in the fun in a paddling pool or on the beach. They are very strong and have great power, even though they have short legs, but I have never taken them out of their depth. If I was to take them on a boat, I'd make sure they have a suitable flotation aid or lifejacket."

Mental Stimulation

Without mental challenges, dogs can become bored, destructive, attention-seeking and/or depressed. Corgis like to be involved and love a challenge. If this "drive" is not channelled in a positive manner, it can turn to naughtiness.

If you return home to find your favourite cushions shredded or the contents of the kitchen bin strewn around the floor, ask yourself: *"Is she getting enough exercise/mental stimulation?"* and *"Am I leaving her alone for too long?"* Have toys and chews available, and factor in regular play time with your Corgi - even gentle play time for old dogs.

Photo: Iucci (18 months) learns Scentwork, trained by owner and professional dog trainer Maria Carter, of Cheltenham, England. Many Corgis excel at Scentwork - and they love it!

Most Corgis are herders and many are chasers; they love running after birds, other dogs, small animals, etc.

In terms of retrieving balls and other objects, they will if they feel like it - so you might find that you are the one doing most of the retrieving! You can make *Fetch* more challenging by hiding the ball or toy and training your dog to find it.

 Sticks can splinter in a dog's mouth or stomach, and jumping up for a Frisbee can cause back damage. Balls should be big enough not to choke your dog.

A Corgi at the heart of the family getting regular exercise and mental challenges is a happy dog and an affectionate snuggle bug second to none!

NOTE: Both dognapping and dog attacks are on the increase - even in dog parks and public parks. Keep a close eye on your dog and, if you are at all worried, avoid popular dog walking areas and find other places where your dog can exercise safely. The UK police are advising owners not to walk their dogs at the same time and places each day, but to vary your routine.

Routine

Establish an exercise regime early in your dog's life. If possible, get your dog used to a walk or walks at similar times every day and gradually build that up as the puppy reaches adulthood. Start out with a regime you know you can stick to, as your dog will come to expect it and will not be happy if the walks suddenly stop.

 If you haven't enough time to give your Corgi the exercise she needs, consider employing a daily dog walker, if you can afford it, or take her to doggie day care once or twice a week. As well as the exercise, she will love the interaction with other dogs.

Corgis are curious and love investigating new scents and places, which is why you need to plug every little gap in your fence – they will be off given half a chance - and Corgi puppies can escape through the tiniest of gaps.

Older dogs still need exercise to keep their body, joints and systems functioning properly. They need a less strenuous regime – they are usually happier with shorter walks, but still enough to keep them physically and mentally active. Again, every dog is different; some are willing and able to keep on running to the end of their lives, others noticeably slow down.

If your old or sick dog is struggling, she will show you she's not up to it by stopping and looking at you or sitting/lying down and refusing to move. If she's healthy and does this, she is just being lazy!

Regular exercise can add months or even years to a dog's life.

Most Corgis love snow; they are hardy and have a thick double coat to protect them from the cold.

Salt or de-icing products on roads and pathways contain chemicals that can be poisonous to dogs and cause irritation – particularly if they try to lick it off. If your dog gets iced up, bathe paws and other affected areas in lukewarm - NOT HOT - water.

Exercising Puppies

There are strict guidelines for puppies. It's important not to over-exercise young pups as, until a puppy's growth plates close, they're soft and vulnerable to injury.

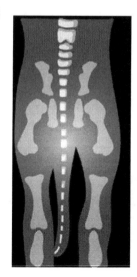

FACT Pembrokes and Cardigans are dwarf breeds and extra care has to be taken to ensure that their skeletons develop properly, without injury to their joints or back. Too much early impact can cause permanent damage.

This diagram shows the skeleton of a two-week-old puppy. The growth plates (tissue near the ends of long bones) have a long way to go before they close. Before that, over-exercise or impact can cause permanent damage.

So, playing Fetch for hours on end with your young Corgi is definitely a no-no, so is Frisbee or allowing a pup to freely run up and down stairs in your home.

You'll end up with an injured dog and a pile of vet's bills. Just like babies, puppies have different temperaments and energy levels; some need more exercise than others. Start slowly and build it up. The worst combination is over-exercise and overweight.

Don't take your pup out of the yard or garden until the all-clear after vaccinations - you can carry her around to start the socialisation process. Begin with daily short walks (literally just a few minutes) on the lead. Get yours used to being outside the home environment and experiencing new situations as soon as possible. The general guideline for exercise is:

Five minutes of on-lead exercise every day per month of age

So, a total of 15 minutes per day when three months (13 weeks) old

30 minutes per day when six months (26 weeks) old, etc.

This applies until around one year to 18 months old, when most of their growing has finished. Slowly increase the time as she gets used to being exercised and this will gradually build up muscles and stamina.

 It is OK for your young pup to have free run of your garden or yard, provided it has a soft surface such as grass. This does not count in the five minutes per month rule.

If the yard is stone or concrete, limit the time your dog runs around on it, as a hard surface impacts joints. It is fine for your pup to run freely around the house to burn off energy - although not up and down stairs or on and off furniture.

A pup will take things at her own pace and stop to sniff or rest. If you have other dogs, restrict the time pup is allowed to play with them, as she won't know when she's had enough. When older, your dog can go out for much longer walks.

One breeder added: "For the first 18 months whilst the puppy's bones are soft and developing, it's best not to over-exert and put strain on the joints. Daily gentle walking is great, just not constant fast and hard running/chasing in the puppy stage, as too much is a big strain."

And when your little pup has grown into a beautiful adult Corgi with a skeleton capable of carrying her through a long and healthy life, all your care and caution will have been rewarded:

A long, healthy life is best started slowly.

Corgi Exercise Tips

- ❖ Don't over-exercise puppies
- ❖ Don't allow them to run up and down stairs or jump on and off furniture
- ❖ Aim for one or two walks away from the house every day
- ❖ Vary your exercise route – it will be more interesting for both of you
- ❖ Triple check the fencing around your garden or yard

- Do not throw a ball or toy repeatedly if your dog shows signs of over-exertion. Corgis have no sense of their own limitations. Stop the activity after a while - no matter how much she begs you to keep playing

- The same goes for swimming; ensure any exercise is within your dog's capabilities - look out for heavy panting

- Don't strenuously exercise your dog straight after or within an hour of a meal as this can cause Bloat, which mainly affects deep-chested dogs.

- Corgis enjoy play time as well as walk time to keep their creative minds engaged - and they love interaction with their owners

- Corgis have thick coats, so exercise your dog early morning or in the evening in hot weather

- Exercise old dogs more gently - especially in cold weather when it is harder to get their bodies moving - and make sure they have a soft and warm place to rest afterwards

- Make sure your dog has constant access to fresh water. Dogs can only sweat a tiny amount through the pads of their paws; they need to drink water to cool down

Photo: An active Cardigan Corgi.

Admittedly, when it is raining or freezing cold, the last thing you may want to do is to venture outdoors with your dog.

But Corgis were bred for wet and windy conditions in Wales, so it's likely that the cold and rain will not deter them!

Make the effort; the lows are more than compensated for by the highs. And if your dog doesn't want to go out, don't let her dictate; it will only make her lazier, fatter and less sociable.

Walking the dog helps you bond with her, keep fit, see different places and meet new companions - both canine and human. In short, it enhances both your lives.

Socialisation

Your adult dog's character will depend largely on two things: inherited temperament and environment, or **NATURE AND NURTURE**. And one absolutely essential aspect of nurture for all dogs is socialisation.

FACT ⟩ Scientists now realise the importance that socialisation plays in a dog's life. There is a fairly small window regarded as the optimum time for socialisation - and this is up to the age of four to five months.

Socialisation means *"learning to be part of society,"* or *"integration."* This means helping dogs become comfortable within a human society by getting them used to different people, environments, traffic, sights, noises, smells, animals, other dogs, etc.

It actually begins from the moment the puppy is born, and the importance of picking a good breeder cannot be over-emphasised.

Not only will he or she breed for good temperament and health, but the dam (puppy's mother) will be well-balanced, friendly and unstressed, and the pup will learn a lot in this positive environment.

Learning When Young Is Easiest

Most young animals, including dogs, are naturally able to get used to their everyday environment until they reach a certain age. When they reach this age, they become much more suspicious of things they haven't yet experienced. This is why it often takes longer to train an older dog.

When you think about it, humans are not so different. Babies and children have a tremendous capacity to learn, we call this early period our *"formative years."*

As we age, we can still learn, but not at the speed we absorbed things when very young. Also, as we get older, we are often less receptive to new ideas or new ways of doing things.

This age-specific natural development allows a puppy to get comfortable with the normal sights, sounds, people and animals that will be a part of her life. It ensures that she doesn't spend her life jumping in fright, barking or growling at every blowing leaf.

The suspicion that dogs develop later also ensures that they react with a healthy dose of caution to new things that could really be dangerous - Mother Nature is clever!

It is essential that your dog's introductions to new things are all **positive**. Negative experiences lead to a dog becoming fearful and untrusting.

Your dog may already have a wonderful temperament, but she still needs socialising to avoid her thinking that the world is tiny and it revolves around her - don't let yours become an attention-seeker.

FACT Good socialisation gives confidence and helps puppies – whether bold or timid – to learn their place in society. The ultimate goal is to have a happy, well-adjusted Corgi you can take anywhere - and one that doesn't spend her entire life barking at, or suspicious/afraid of, at anything and everything.

Ever seen a therapy dog in action and noticed how incredibly well-adjusted to life they are? This is no coincidence. These dogs have been extensively socialised and are ready and able to deal in a calm manner with whatever situation they encounter. They are relaxed and comfortable in their own skin - just like you want your dog to be.

 Spend as much time as you can socialising your dog when young. It's just as important as training. Start as soon as you bring your puppy home. Regular socialisation should continue until your dog is around 18 months of age.

After that, don't just forget about it; socialisation isn't only for puppies, it should continue less intensively throughout life. As with any skill, if it is not practised, your dog will become less proficient at interacting with other people, animals, noises and new situations.

Developing the Well-Rounded Adult

Dogs that have not been properly integrated are more likely to react with fear or aggression to unfamiliar people, animals and experiences. Corgis who are relaxed around strangers, dogs, cats and other animals, honking horns, cyclists, joggers, veterinary examinations, traffic, crowds and noise are easier to live with than dogs who find these situations challenging or frightening.

And if you are planning on taking part in canine competitions, get yours socialised and used to the buzz of these events early on.

 **Well-socialised dogs live more relaxed, peaceful and happy lives than dogs that are constantly stressed by their environment.**

Socialisation isn't an *"all or nothing"* project. You can socialise a puppy a bit, a lot, or a whole lot. The wider the range of positive experiences you expose her to (positively) when young, the better.

Socialisation should never be forced, but approached systematically and in a manner that builds confidence and curious interaction.

If your pup finds a new experience frightening, take a step back, introduce her to the scary situation much more gradually, and make a big effort to do something she loves during the situation or right afterwards. For example, if your puppy seems to be frightened by noise and vehicles at a busy road, a good method would be to go to a quiet road, sit with the dog away from - but within sight of - the traffic. Every time she looks towards the traffic say *"YES!"* and reward her with a treat.

If she is still stressed, you need to move further away. When your dog takes the food in a calm manner, she is becoming more relaxed and getting used to traffic sounds, so you can edge a bit nearer - but still just for short periods until she becomes totally relaxed. Keep each session short and **POSITIVE**.

Meeting Other Dogs

When your gorgeous and vulnerable little pup meets other dogs for the first few times, you may be a bit apprehensive. Try and stay calm, Corgis are hardy little dogs who usually get on well with other dogs.

However, the initial introductions are all-important and should always be positive.

To begin with, introduce your puppy to just one other dog - one that you know to be friendly, rather than taking her straight to the park where there are lots of dogs of all sizes racing around, which might frighten the life out of your timid little darling.

On the other hand, your pup might be full of confidence right from the off, but you still need to approach things slowly.

If your puppy is too cocksure, she may get a warning bite from an older dog, which could make her more anxious when approaching new dogs in the future.

Always make initial introductions on neutral ground, so as not to trigger territorial behaviour. You want your Corgi to approach other dogs with friendliness, not fear.

From the first meeting, help both dogs experience good things when they're in each other's presence. Let them sniff each other briefly, which is normal canine greeting behaviour. As they do, talk to them in a happy, friendly tone of voice; never use a threatening or hysterical tone.

Don't allow them to sniff each other for too long as this may escalate to an aggressive response. After a short time, get the attention of both dogs and give each a treat in return for obeying a simple command, e.g. *"Sit"* or *"Stay."* Continue with the *"happy talk,"* and rewards.

Learn to spot the difference between normal rough and tumble play and interaction that may develop into fear or aggression. Here are some signs of fear to look out for when your dog interacts with other canines:

* Running away or freezing on the spot
* Trembling or panting, which can be a sign of stress or pain
* Frantic/nervous behaviour, e.g. excessive sniffing, drinking or playing frenetically with a toy
* A lowered body stance or crouching
* Lying on her back with paws in the air – this is submissive, as is submissive urination
* Lowering of the head or turning the head away, when you may see the whites of the eyes as the dog tries to keep eyes on the perceived threat
* Growling and/or hair raised on her back (raised hackles)
* Licking the lips or lips pulled back
* Tail lifted in the air - or ears high on the head, *as in this photo. This Pembroke may be nervous as the other dog is much larger and on a lead (leash), which can make some dogs more reactive when their 'fight or flight' instinct kicks in.*

Some of these responses are normal. A pup may well crouch on the ground or roll on to her back to show other dogs she's not a threat. If the situation looks like escalating, calmly distract the dogs or remove your puppy – don't shout or shriek. The dogs will pick up on your fear.

Another sign to look out for is **eyeballing.** In the canine world, staring a dog in the eyes is a challenge and may cause an aggressive response.

NOTE: Whereas we might look someone in the eye when we are first introduced, it is normal for dogs to sniff the scent glands in another dog's bottom!

 Your puppy has to learn to interact with other dogs. Don't be too quick to pick her up; she will sense your anxiety, lose confidence and become less independent. The same is true when walking on a lead – don't be nervous every time you seen another dog – your Corgi will pick up on it and may react by barking, lunging or snapping.

Always follow up a socialisation experience with praise, petting, a fun game or a special treat.

One positive sign from a dog is the *"play bow" pictured on the next page,* when she goes down on her front elbows but keeps her rear end up in the air. This is a sign that she's feeling friendly towards the other dog and wants to play. Relaxed ear and body position and wagging tail are other positive signs.

Although Corgis are not normally aggressive towards other dogs, aggression is often grounded in fear, and a dog that mixes easily is less likely to be combative. Similarly, without frequent and new experiences, some dogs can become timid or anxious.

Take your new dog everywhere you can. You want her to feel relaxed and calm in any situation, even noisy and crowded ones. Take treats with you and praise her when she reacts calmly to new situations.

An excellent way of getting your new puppy to meet other dogs in a safe environment is at a puppy class. We highly recommend this for all puppies. Ask around locally if any classes are being run.

Local vets and dog trainers often run classes for very junior pups who have had all their vaccinations. These help pups get used to other dogs of a similar age.

What the Experts Say

We'll start with some comments from experienced Pembroke owners. Sue Hardy: "They will take as much or as little as you like. Brainwork tires them out as much as, if not more than, exercise, and Scentwork is good for that."

Kevin Egan: "We do a first walk of 30 minutes duration at 7.30am each day. Second walk for an hour late morning, and third and final walk of 30 minutes at 3pm, which, is more field and game play engaged, and not necessarily about distance travelled."

Margaret E. Leighton: "I find mine do not need much exercise, but we go up to three miles on a nice day. I've cut that down in the winter as my older dog can only manage about two miles now. On other days I take them for a short walk three times a day because I do not have a garden."

Vicky Methuen: "My Corgis follow the routine of the house. I take them out after breakfast, and I'll find them behind me directing me to the hall where the leads are kept, and then to the internal door into the garage which leads to outside! When I get her lead out, Brona puts her head down as I put her collar on."

Lucy Badham-Thornhill: "Mine get a minimum of 2 hours per day."

Corgis are social dogs. Lucy's photo of her and Carole Turner's Pembrokes.

Now some comments from Pembroke breeders, starting with Wisconsin-based Lisa Thompson: "We live on a farm, they exercise all the time. They can handle a lot of exercise and love to be outside.

"They also need to be socialized from the beginning, and training is **sooooo** important, starting at birth."

Hungarian breeder Alexandra Trefán-Török: "Mine get one to two hours three or four times a day, weather dependent."

Linda Roberts: "My adults receive two good walks every day of around 45 minutes each. One will be primarily roadwork and one will be primarily loose exercise in safe enclosed fields. On top of this they have lots of free time to chase each other around the garden and lots of loose time together in the house.

"It is important that exercise is age-appropriate. Please never over-tire a growing puppy. It is hard to overstate how important adequate rest is to youngsters.

"Puppy socialisation is extremely important. I would encourage all puppy buyers to enrol at a suitable local puppy class (often run by vet practices) as soon as their vaccinations are complete. Socialisation can begin before the vaccinations are complete by carrying the puppy through busy environments so it can experience traffic, lots of other people, strange noises and sights etc.

"Please be extremely careful when introducing puppies to strange dogs; happy experiences are excellent, but anything untoward will remain with the dog for life. Following on, it is a good idea to continue basic obedience training and the Kennel Club Good Citizen Dog Training Scheme (AKC Canine Good Citizen in the US) runs excellent courses throughout the country - highly recommended!"

Kevin Dover: "Corgis respond to a schedule, they like to get up and go out at a set time, be fed at the same time and be exercised at the same time. Just because it's raining is no reason for them not be exercised, which should all be taken into consideration before buying any animal."

Photo: Kevin grooming Polly (Pemslife Another Brick on the Wall for Pemcader) at Crufts Dog Show.

"Living deep in the countryside my dogs have the freedom to run free in the adjacent forest. I ensure they go out for at least two and sometimes three walks a day. They are usually out for half an hour to an hour at a time and, as several go together, they chase each other around, building up muscle tone.

"Whilst many new owners are surprised at the amount of exercise a Corgi can take, you have to remember that these are still working dogs regardless and as such should be able to handle this type of exercise easily - they are not couch potato dogs!

"It's very important to have a well-socialised puppy. Most towns will hold puppy parties and some vets have them to help with being examined, which is a must - especially the mouth. Obviously from a showing perspective, having a dog's mouth examined is a priority, so all our dogs have their mouths examined regularly as well as feet, should nails require attention.

"In respect to mixing with other dogs, I've never encountered any issues as they do get very close to many breeds at the shows and just ignore them, but again this is down to having a close relationship with your dog and setting what is allowed and what isn't.

"I have a rescue cat and all of our Corgis like to run up to her, but then just ignore her - in fact she likes to come out for a walk with the dogs!"

Piotr and Johnathan Mazur-Jones: "Adult Pems can walk as little as 15 mins and as long as 10 miles. It is important that you let puppies develop; they are a dwarf breed and so their structure is different. We see many who get on long walks too soon; we advise our owners to take at least 18 months to slowly build up the amount of exercise - as if you were training for a marathon.

"Socialisation is as important as feeding and toileting. Although we do a lot of this in the first 10 weeks of a puppy's life, it is important that a new family then retraces foundations already laid and introduces them to new smells, sounds, places, people, routine etc. We always advise even when taking an adult dog to new places to allow the dog time to adjust.

"From our experience, socialisation plays a huge part in the acceptance of new animals Pems get on well with all breeds of dogs and cats, but introduction is not a five-minute wonder, it should be taken slowly and in gradual steps. If done correctly, harmony will prevail."

Photo: Plenty of training and socialisation ahead! Ruby (Creslow River Sheppey) bred by Piotr and Johnathan, takes a breather.

Now comments from some Cardigan breeders. Fran Fricker: "My dogs free run for around half an hour in the paddock, then they have a concrete run (great for keeping the nails in trim) where they will exercise themselves running back and forth and also jumping up and down on their legs - not onto items such as sofas or climbing stairs; this is not good for them.

"But they are great for long walks once they are over 18 months. And for the exercise enthusiasts - once the growing stages are over with structured exercise to allow for growth and development - they are keen walkers and will go for miles.

"Socialisation and training are two very important issues. It all starts at a very young age when mum keeps them in check whilst nursing. As they progress, they become used to household noises, voices, darkness and light.

"A responsible breeder will introduce them all gradually so they can become familiar with them as part of growing up. Being handled correctly to avoid accidents and injury to the young puppy. As they grow, they are introduced to new experiences on walks and on car journeys. Even grooming plays a big part being used to stand on a table to be groomed and have nail trims from an early age prepares them well for the future."

Karen Hewitt: "One of the things I love about Cardigans is that they can manage really long walks (when adult) but don't feel the need to tear up your home if you can't take them too far for whatever reason.

"Mine get a short morning walk if I'm working and a longer walk in the evening.

"Socialising and training are both incredibly important, Cardis are clever little souls but they do need direction and exposure to as many experiences as possible. They do need to know that their owner is in charge and that they must learn to follow the rules of the house and family.

"They need to see and hear as many different animals and people as possible during their early formative years so that they accept other animals and individuals without nervousness or aggression."

Photo of the attractive Sally (Cardhew La Salle), aged 18 months, bred by Karen.

12. Corgi Activities

In this chapter some leading lights in the Corgi world share their passion for the breed - and show you just what these dogs are capable of!

Pembrokes in Agility

By Marian Your

Marian, who lives in Texas, has bred Tri-umph Corgis since 1984. She has won numerous accolades in the world of conformation (showing) and is an AKC judge for Pembrokes, Cardigans, Australian Shepherds and German Shepherd Dogs.

Her Pembroke Tommy has achieved his MACH2 (the second Masters Agility Championship) and qualified for the AKC National Agility Championships for the last three years. This is her story.

I've had Pembrokes since 1979. I only had to have my first, Aimee Lee, for a short time before I realized that she had more energy and mischievousness than I had anticipated!

I enrolled her in obedience class, with the primary objective being to keep her from slipping out the door every time it opened. Being a typical Corgi, she only needed a job to do to channel her energies - and she flourished in her class!

I was soon encouraged to show her in Obedience Trials. If life was a movie, dramatic music would have played when this suggestion was made, as it transformed not only her life, but mine over the next 22 years.

Aimee excelled at Obedience and soon earned her Companion Dog, Companion Dog Excellent, and Utility Dog Obedience titles with Dog World Awards for high scores, and then at age 10 earned her Tracking Dog title. Meanwhile, I had acquired Rocky and Sukey for conformation showing, and they also earned their Utility and Tracking titles. As Agility became popular, many dogs I'd bred did well in it, and eventually I decided to give it a try.

Lure Coursing

Interestingly enough, my adventure didn't start at an Agility Trial at all! It began at a Coursing Aptitude Test (CAT), which is great fun for dogs with chase instinct.

Coursing is open to all breeds and involves dogs running individually and chasing an artificial lure over a 300 or 600-yard course. The lure is attached to a pulley in a configuration in a wide-open field. The length of course depends on the height of the dog; Pembrokes and other under-12" dogs run the 300-yard course.

Born to Run! Tommy showing his natural ability at a Fast CAT trial. Photo by Allison Schmidt.

Dogs must finish the course in less than one-and-a-half minutes, which is not difficult, and either pass or fail. Dogs must be 12 months old, and can be neutered or unneutered.

Bitches in season may not compete, which is where this story begins. I'd driven an hour to a lure coursing trial with my girl, Larch, and when we checked in, I was informed she was in season... She wasn't when we left home! I had prepaid five runs for that weekend, so this wasn't anything I wanted to hear. The event chair told me under the circumstances they would allow me to substitute another dog, so I drove home, thinking all the way about which dog would run instead.

Tommy (Tri-umph Tommy Wonder) was my two-year-old conformation Grand Champion with a lot of attitude and time on his hands. I thought he would probably run... and run he did!

We really had fun that day, and he earned his CA (Coursing Ability) title. It was so much fun, I urged a friend to go with me the following two days. Her Pembroke bitch also earned her CA. Tommy and I enjoyed it so much that I started thinking of other things we could do, and I came up with Fast CAT and Agility.

Like CAT, Fast CAT takes no training or preparation, although it helps to have a dog with prey drive. As a friend of mine said: "There are dogs that want to chase and those that are completely confused by the situation. No in-between." I think that's pretty accurate.

Because it took no training, I started with a Fast CAT trial nearby. In Fast CAT, the dogs run in a straight line for 100 yards in a fenced enclosure. A lure is attached to a straight-line pulley. It's very exciting to watch your dog race down the course, and your qualifying ribbon has your dog's speed in miles per hour.

Believe it or not, Corgis can run about 18 mph, with some getting up to 22 or 23 mph! Pembrokes aren't quite as fast as Usain Bolt (who reached a top speed of 27mph), but some breeds are even faster - 35-45 mph! There is a formula for calculating points based on speed, and dogs earn a BCAT for 150 points, a DCAT for 500 points and an FCAT for 1,000 points.

The best thing about Fast CAT is that you and your dog have fun in the fresh air, and there is absolutely no stress since your dog is only competing against his previous speed and your personal goals.

Tommy Finds His Niche

At the same time, January 2019, Tommy was enrolled in Beginner Agility. After our first class, I knew we had found our niche.

The most important benefit to any dog sport is that it enriches your relationship with your dog while letting your dog do something he or she really enjoys. Tommy enjoyed showing in conformation well enough and had a lot of fun chasing the lure, but Agility classes had him going out of his mind with joy!

Balancing on the teeter (see-saw), running through tunnels, scrambling over the A-Frame, with food rewards for everything he did... what was not to like?

Photo: Tommy in full flight by Phyllis Ensley Photography.

In his Beginner Class, Tommy learned the basics of performing every obstacle. Some, like the jumps, were introduced in the first lesson and then incorporated in every lesson afterwards. Obstacles that were more difficult to master were introduced in stages. Weave poles and the see-saw are more difficult and were introduced gradually.

The two objectives in the Beginner Class, as in Agility at all levels, are to build enthusiasm and drive while keeping the dogs safe. There are no negative corrections. It's all positive!

If you decide to try an Agility class, don't be surprised if you see a side of your Corgi you have never seen before, as he gains confidence and drive. I've found it useful to have my dog able to "Sit," "Stay," and "Come" before starting class.

The Sit, Stay and Come are training management tools used in all training classes. They make the dog easier to manage while teaching obstacles. Some instructors require an obedience class before they will accept a dog for training. Others merely suggest that these skills would be useful.

Once being introduced to all the equipment and assessed for their ability to perform in Agility, dogs move on to Intermediate Classes. In these classes, they progress to sequencing skills and to perfecting their performance on all the equipment. They learn how to negotiate a course and learn what the handler's position, movement, and verbal cues mean.

They are also introduced to various distractions they might encounter at a show. Handlers are also encouraged to have their dogs get used to being in a crate, being around other dogs, and hearing all the sounds of an Agility Trial.

Overall, Tommy trained in Beginner and Intermediate for nine months before he was able to start competing at trials. Even then, he was still uncertain in the weave poles, so we restricted ourselves to a "game" class, called FAST, in which the handler chooses which obstacles to take on.

Photo: Tommy masters the weave poles by Phyllis Ensley Photography.

Anyone attempting agility should get a minimum of a set of weave poles and a few jumps as soon as possible because daily practice really does help. Often, more experienced exhibitors are replacing their equipment and will sell used obstacles for a fraction of their original cost. Tommy continues to attend classes twice a week and we train regularly at home.

There are three types of Agility courses: Standard, Jumpers with Weaves, and FAST; more details can be found on the AKC website.

There are also three levels: Novice, Open, and Excellent/Masters. Novice Classes are for the dog just starting out, and have fewer obstacles, 14-16. The focus of the course is to perform the obstacles with minimum handling technique. When a dog has successfully completed three Novice courses and earned its Novice titles of NA, NAJ, and NF, it can compete in Open.

Open Classes have 16-18 obstacles and require more handling skill. After successfully completing each Open course three times and earning the titles OA, OAJ, and OF, the dog can then compete at Excellent/Masters level.

This level has 18-20 obstacles, and requires close communication between dog and handler. It is more challenging and, at the Masters level, requires a perfect score of 100 for a qualifying score. Time faults are allowed at the Excellent level. A dog can then progress, via a 'double Q,' - getting perfect scores in both Jumpers and Standard on the same day - all the way to a MACH, a Masters Agility Championship.

Premier Agility is an optional titling class designed to challenge dogs and handler teams at an increased speed and skill level above those set for Masters classes. There are varied approach angles, spacing, and obstacle discriminations.

As AKC states in their Agility Brochure, "Once the judge has set up the course and determined the sequence of obstacles, handlers are allowed a 'walk through,' which is done as a group without the dogs. Handlers follow the numbers set at each obstacle to become familiar with the course. Most handlers walk the course as many times as they can in the time allotted, to plan their handling strategy.

"Exhibitors may even gather in small groups to discuss potential challenges on the course and how best to handle them. The handler and dog team runs the course individually, off-leash. The "timer" tells the handler when he or she may begin, starting a stopwatch as soon as any part of the dog crosses the start line and stops the clock when any part of the dog crosses the finish line.

"As each dog runs, the judge indicates the faults, if any, that the dog commits. These faults are recorded by a scribe on a score sheet for that individual dog. The dog's time is also placed on the scribe sheet. This information is then given to a scorekeeper, who calculates the qualifying performances and top placements of each team."

Does all of this sound like something you would like to do with your dog? I will warn you that it is somewhat addictive!

The adrenaline rush of a good run is second to none, and every run deepens the bond you have with your dog. You literally become a team as you develop communication with body language, verbal and nonverbal commands, eye contact, and more.

If you're considering getting a Corgi with an eye to Agility at some point, buying from a breeder who can spot the potential star at a young age is a good start. Drive and biddability are important.

Temperament Testing, done at seven weeks, is a useful tool, but so is daily observation for 10 weeks by someone who knows what they are looking for. If your breeder doesn't do Agility, try borrowing someone who does for an evaluation of a puppy or adult any time after seven weeks.

Tommy and I are fortunate to have local trials almost every weekend, and most of them are three-day trials. Since Tommy is the first agility dog I have taken past the Open level, we have learned together about handling techniques and communication. We started Novice in June of 2020 and by August of that year he had completed all the levels and earned his first Double Q!

Our bond continues to deepen as we've earned MACH titles and have begun competing in Premier. Tommy, now known as GCH CH MACH2 Tri-umph Tommy Wonder MXS MJG MFS TQX T2B2 CA FCAT TKN, and I continue to hone our skills, with our ultimate goal being an Agility Grand Championship.

To get started on your own journey with your best friend, look for classes near you with instructors who successfully compete in agility at the higher levels. And have fun!

Coursing: https://www.akc.org/sports/coursing/coursing-ability-test/

Fast CAT: https://www.akc.org/sports/coursing/fast-cat

Agility: https://www.akc.org/sports/agility/

Herd Mentality

By Mary Ann Wehmueller

Mary Ann Wehmueller, of Fairyfyre Pembroke Welsh Corgis, lives in Indiana and describes herself as "a herding addict." She trains and handles all her own dogs, and over the years they have earned numerous herding High and Reserve High in Trial awards.

Mary Ann is extremely proud of the accomplishments of her first "serious" herding dog, Wilson (GCh DC Sua Mah Beach Boy HXAcds, HXBd, HIAs, HSAcd, PT, HT). He is not only a Grand Champion show dog, but completed his AKC Herding Champion to become only the seventh Pembroke to achieve AKC Dual Champion (DC).

In the days of old, the Pembroke and Cardigan Welsh Corgi acted as the Welsh farmer's all-around farm dog and work partner. They served as guardian of the farmstead, protecting home and farmyard from intruders of the two-and four-legged varieties.

Their herding skills were highly valued, aiding the farmer in managing and moving cattle, sheep and other livestock to and from market and from pasture to pasture. Today, Welsh Corgis continue to work livestock on farms worldwide.

Off the farm, they successfully compete against other breeds at herding competitions, called *'herding trials,'* around the world. As stewards of the breed, we should take great pride in preserving the work ethic so valued by the Welsh farmers of old.

Starting Out

In 2004, I acquired my first Pembroke Welsh Corgi (PWC). My children were at an age to bear some responsibility for a family pet and I thought a Corgi would help fill the void of the inevitable empty nest that would occur in the coming years.

Festus (Little Red Festus), a darling red and white puppy, entered our lives and immediately captured our hearts with his bold, inquisitive and biddable character. A few months later, my husband stumbled upon a nearby herding trainer's website that offered *'herding instinct tests.'*

Mary Ann and Wilson having a quiet discussion before the run. Wilson always checked in at the beginning of a run - then off they'd go! Photo by Linda Dossett Photography.

The following Sunday, we loaded up our little red dog and headed to the country for what we believed would be a nice, one-time outing and introduction to sheep.

Six-month-old Festus was delighted to meet the sheep and exhibited natural instinct for a pup so young. By the end of our Sunday outing, I had caught *'the herding bug'* and the rest, as they say, is history!

While I'd caught the bug, I quickly found out I had a lot to learn - and I do mean a LOT! I was fortunate enough to find nearby herding instructors who graciously shared their years of knowledge and experience with me.

Equipped with some rudimentary knowledge of the sport and by no means an expert, I volunteered at various herding trials, watched, listened and learned from judges and handlers.

Watching handlers *'run'* or compete with their dogs, I observed what I thought were good runs and those that were less than stellar. I then approached the handlers to pepper them with questions about how they trained, who they trained with, and for tips or guidance on training.

I also researched various herding clubs and events in my area, and soon started attending herding clinics, sometimes with a dog and others as an auditor to watch and learn from others who were working their dogs. Throughout this period, I continued to take herding lessons with my PWC.

Eventually, I summoned the courage to enter Festus in a herding test at a local trial. Neither of us having ever competed, I was a nervous wreck. But Festus took the exercise in his stride and earned his first American Kennel Cub (AKC) herding title, known as Herding Tested, or HT.

Festus later went on to earn his AKC herding Pre-Trial (PT) title. He retired from herding after earning his test titles and I went looking for my next herding partner.

The Next Steps

My next PWC, Ella (Fairyfyre Ellatude), was a dynamo from the start. A fierce little, black-headed tri bitch with two speeds: fast and faster! She was willing to share her loud opinion with anyone or anything within earshot.

Vastly different in working style from my sweet, biddable Festus, Ella was by far a harder dog to train. She was more talented, but constantly fought and challenged me as a trainer. In retrospect, she made me a better trainer and handler because I was forced to learn how to train and handle a difficult dog.

Ella totally focused on herding. Photo by Moonshots Photography, LLC.

She earned her AKC PT title quickly, but I ran her in 10 PT tests until I felt she and I were both ready to enter trial competition at the starter level.

In the AKC herding program, a dog must gain three qualifying trial scores in order to earn a title. There are three levels of AKC trials: Started, Intermediate and Advanced. Generally, the Started classes allow the handler to move around the course to help the dog, and so is viewed as an easier course because the handler has the freedom to move and help the dog.

Unfortunately, Ella's trial career was short-lived. At the age of five she began exhibiting periodic lameness due to a bad hip, so I made the decision to retire her to avoid permanent and irreparable injury. Prior to retirement, she earned her AKC started sheep title.

She is now nearly 17, still suffers from occasional lameness and is as opinionated as ever!

As one door closes, another opens. As it became clear that Ella's herding career would end prematurely, I started the search for my next herding partner. I was determined to find a reputable breeder who was dedicated to breeding for proper structure, temperament and work ethic. My search for the total package took over four years, but was more than worth the wait.

Judy Hart, of Sua Mah Pembroke Welsh Corgis, was the answer. Having owned a herding and dual champion herself, she knew exactly what I wanted in my next dog. I travelled to Judy's and came home with Wilson (GCh DC Sua Mah Beach Boy HXAcds HXBd). I promised Judy that I would finish - or at least attempt to finish - Wilson's conformation championship and shared with her my desire to focus on his herding career.

Photo: Wilson herding ducks, by Linda Dossett Photography.

Different types of stock require different training techniques. The foundation skills are the same; however, because of differences in the size, speed and behavior of various livestock, application of these skills needs to be adjusted in order to be successful in competition and in managing livestock on the farm.

Wilson is responsible for many of my firsts: he is my first conformation dog, and as such, my first conformation Champion and Grand Champion. He is the first herding dog I trained to Advanced Levels and is my first herding champion with championship points on cattle, ducks and sheep.

Completion of his herding championship also resulted in him being my first Dual Champion (showing and herding). What a journey with such a solid and sensible working partner! Wilson has taught me so much about herding, training and handling.

He is now 13 and has retired to a life of leisure, but occasionally has time to herd ducks when he has nothing better to do. I am thrilled that he has passed on his good looks, structure and herding acumen to his progeny. I am currently training a son and granddaughter of Wilson and have high hopes that they can follow in his paw prints.

Training Tips

Finding a trainer who has experience with Pembrokes or other 'loose-eyed' breeds is extremely helpful, although there are many things one can learn from Border Collie trainers who are willing to work with other breeds. (A loose-eyed herding breed is one that does not herd with the intense eye and concentration of a Border Collie or Kelpie).

Early and consistent exposure to livestock is important. Some pups *'turn on'* to livestock immediately, while others may take several lessons before their instinct to herd kicks in. Don't be discouraged if your young pup doesn't immediately take to stock.

When a pup or young dog stays focused on the livestock for 10 to 15 minutes, it is time to start lessons. The foundation skills necessary for a good herding dog are rather simple in theory, but are skills that must be continually practiced and reinforced throughout the dog's herding career. There are five basic commands your dog must learn:

1. **A reliable stop**.

2. **How to 'walk-up'** or walk straight at/into the stock.

3. **Flanks** (directions): a clockwise flank, meaning the dog must travel around the stock in a clockwise direction, referred to as a 'come-by' flank; and moving around the stock in a counter-clockwise direction; referred to as an 'away' or 'away-to-me' flank.

4. **An out**, meaning the dog must turn in the opposite direction from and move away from the stock, thus releasing pressure on the livestock.

5. **A call off**, often referred to as "That'll Do," to indicate to the dog that the exercise or chore is done and to stop working.

Once you've mastered these, you then work on fetching livestock, where the dog moves out and around the livestock and brings them to you (the handler) with the dog holding the back side of the livestock as the handler and stock move from point A to point B.

As skills progress, you will work on your dog's driving skills - meaning the dog controls the livestock and moves the stock away from the handler. Pembrokes are a droving breed, so for most, driving may come more naturally than fetching. Both are important for farm work and competition, so it is critical to work on both skills.

Wilson learning to drive sheep. Photo by John Saracen.

Training and competing in herding trials can be physically and mentally exhausting for your dog. Ensuring your PWC stays trim and in good working condition to handle the demands of training and competing is something that should not be overlooked or underrated.

I have been fortunate to successfully compete in herding trials around the United States, mostly at all breed trials, with my PWCs. I assure you Pembrokes can hold their own in competitions against Border Collies and other breeds.

Competition aside, my Pembrokes still work on a farm and help manage and care for sheep. There is nothing more enjoyable to me than working as a herding partner with my dogs in the barnyard or on the trial field. I take great satisfaction in knowing that the work ethic so valued by the Welsh farmers of old lives on and strong in our beloved, versatile breed.

For more information about herding venues, please visit:

American Kennel Club: https://www.akc.org/sports/herding/

American Herding Breed Association (AHBA): http://www.ahba-herding.org/

Australian Shepherd Club of America: https://asca.org/stockdog/

In the UK, herding trials are currently only for Border Collies. However, there are many other activities you can take part in with your Corgi, including Obedience, Scentwork, Rally and Agility. Type *'Kennel Club events and activities'* into a search engine for more information.

The World's Your Oyster!

By Sue Hardy

Sue Hardy from Wiltshire, England, has owned Pembrokes for over 30 years. A lover of outdoor sports, it was at an airfield in the Brecon Beacons, Wales, in the 1980s that she came across a Corgi called Sammy. She says: "I fell for him hook line and sinker - and never looked back!"

Over the years her Corgis have loved being involved in her and her husband's active lifestyle: caravanning, boating, gliding and radio-controlled model aircraft flying. But when Sue started to slow down, her seven-month-old Pembroke Mambo was raring to go!

She looked around for something to challenge him and here she shares her experience on activities Mambo has taken part in; all of which stimulate the Corgi mind and body and deepen the bond between dog and owner.

Mambo is a very intelligent boy and can be quite demanding if his brain is not kept occupied. Many years ago, I remember being told that Corgis have the attention span of a six-year-old child.

Mambo was seven months old when he came to us in 2019. It was a long time since I'd had such a young dog, so I decided to enlist some help and looked around for a training school. Because he wasn't a young puppy, it took us a while, but when we found Frome K9 Dog Training (www.fromek9.co.uk), it was fantastic.

I tried a few things that we could do together. The training school has a lot to choose from: Agility, Canicross (canine cross country), Bikejor (the dog pulls you on a bike - more suitable for big, strong adult dogs), 26-mile walks around Salisbury Plain, hikes up Snowden, Water Rescue, Hide and Seek, Obedience, Scentwork.

Hide and Seek

The first thing we tried together was Hide and Seek. This takes place in an enclosed area with natural and man-made *'hides.'* The owner walks away from the dog with the dog watching and enters one of the hides.

The dog is held by the instructor and when the owner is out of sight, given the *'Find'* command and released. They are never allowed to fail, being guided by the instructor, if necessary, until the dog understands what he is being asked to do.

This progresses to *'blind searches',* where the dog does not know where the owner has gone. More experienced dogs can be given someone else's scent and then tasked to find them. Nowadays, I usually manage to *'persuade'* someone else to hide! It is all done off-lead and the dogs love it.

Mantrailing

Mantrailing is where the dog follows a scent to find someone. It is utilised by search and rescue teams to find missing people, but is also a popular sport in several countries and is establishing itself as an exciting new canine sport in the UK.

Mantrailing can be done anywhere outdoors and the dog wears a harness with a 10m line attached to their owner or handler. The Misper (missing person) goes and hides somewhere out of view and the dog has to find them. When they find the Misper they are rewarded by a high-value treat which the Misper was given prior to the search. The dog usually does not know the Misper.

As well as providing physical exercise, Mantrailing engages the olfactory (smell) sense, which gives the dogs an intense mental and stimulating session along the way - and it's fantastic to watch the dog's confidence grow as he gets used to following the scent.

To start Mantrailing you need to enrol in a beginner's introductory session and then you can do as many sessions as you like. We have had sessions in country parks, school grounds, polo club fields and local industrial estates, to name but a few.

There are many instructors springing up around the country, take a look at www.mantrailinguk.com or www.mantraillingscentdogs.co.uk and other websites for instructors in your area.

In the US, visit www.akc.org/expert-advice/sports/mantrailing-for-the-scent-driven-dog for more information.

Scentwork

Corgis are not a breed that people naturally associate with Scentwork, but Mambo, **pictured,** loves it. In fact, the training school recently said he is one of the best scent dogs they have ever trained! To quote my instructor: "He is one hell of a dog."

In Scentwork, a dog uses his incredible sense of smell to identify and locate a specific scent. They start with simple scents and move on to more difficult ones, or ones harder to locate. The training is initially held in group classes. The dog starts with finding food - which is easy for a Corgi!

They then progress to finding a scent next to food, and the next step is for the dog to find the scent without the food as a distraction. Our school uses boxes with a scent article inside to encourage the dog's indication. The dog puts his nose in the box when he finds the scent.

Initially, the lid of the box is removed and a reward is dropped in. Then the reward is placed alongside the box, and finally the handler has the reward and gives it the dog after releasing him from the task. Obviously, this takes place over a number of sessions – but there is always a big party with lots of high-value treats.

Scentwork really engages a dog's brain and it's very tiring for them; it wears Mambo out. He also gets very thirsty and I need to keep him well-hydrated. We practise Scentwork most days to keep his nose and brain active.

We have a dedicated Scentwork collar and lead. As soon as it comes out, on comes his smile and his tail (flag) starts to wag. He definitely knows what this particular combination means - and whoever said dogs don't smile has not met Corgis!

We have been taught to what is called *'operational standard.'* This is where the dogs learn to find a scented article in hedgerows, open fields, in the barn, holes in the ground etc. Mambo can also find a mobile phone, coins and keys in the field and the barn - both mine and other people's.

Some of the areas in which the scented article is placed are difficult for him to reach. The taller dogs only have to stretch their necks, while Mambo has to stand on his back legs and point at where the scent is.

He does not like what we call *'bondhu bashing'* (a military term for hacking your way through the bush or scrub). He especially dislikes the nettles, which is no doubt due to his short legs! This apart, Scentwork really suits his independent temperament.

All dogs are individuals. While Mambo needs a challenge and excels at Scentwork, he is slightly wary of strangers. My 12-month-old Samba is totally different; he is a snuggle bunny and loves everyone. He is very biddable (less independent-minded than Mambo) and has already shown the aptitude to make a good Rally Obedience dog.

When training, both dogs are motivated by food, praise, consistency and repetition. Neither of them likes a grumpy owner or handler!

This picture shows the scent article I use the most (on the left). As you can see it is the same size as an English 5p piece (or American nickel). It includes the head of one cotton bud that has been dipped in clove oil.

There is also a small magnet inside which means that it can be hidden on a car, manhole cover, door hinges/handles or any metal object. www.scentdog.co.uk is where I get my scent articles from.

During Lockdown we built a *'scent wall,'* which is a cheap wallpaper paste table that we drilled holes in and placed 'cups' in the hole. A piece of metal was glued to the back of each cup. Then my magnetic scent article was placed out of sight attached to the metal.

The idea was for Mambo to find the scent article, place his *'shonk'* (nose) in the correct hole and keep it there until given the release command. In his case an over-the-top **"YEE HAW!"**

Mambo has an unusual 'positive indication' when he finds the scent. The flag always stops wagging and either stays upright or goes down, as in this picture. This invariably makes other members of any training class chuckle.

Scentwork and Hide and Seek turned out be Mambos 'favourtest' things.

As Mambo became more experienced and confident, we looked to expand his Scentwork skills. SCUK (Scentwork UK www.scentworkuk.com) is the main group in UK and their website is well worth a look. They take Scentwork in a different direction, in that dogs go to different locations and search for the scents in many and varied situations, inside and outdoors; on tables/chairs, boxes/luggage, cars, hidden in walls etc.

 So far, we have tested Mambo's nose in railway stations, village halls, aviation museums, riding stables, factory buildings - it is definitely not boring! There are a number of instructors who teach to SCUK standard.

Initially the dogs learn with clove oil and then build up to gun oil and truffle oil. They can take part in trials starting at Level 1 right through to Level 8. So far, we have completed Levels 1 and 2. Each trial tests a different aspect of the dog's training. The main thing is the partnership between the dog and handler; no negative handling is allowed.

Generally, the trials we attended last around four hours, depending on how many dogs are taking part. Each dog only works for about 10 minutes at a time and then rests while another dog works.

Both my boys have Kennel Club Good Citizen qualifications. Mambo achieved his Bronze and is waiting for the opportunity to take his Silver. Samba completed his puppy course in the minimum required time and is now waiting to take his Bronze.

Our main aim is just to continue enjoying what we are doing.

UK: www.scentworkuk.com

USA: https://www.akc.org/sports/akc-scent-work/getting-started There is also K9 Nose Work at www.k9nosework.com

Find a training group that suits you and your dog, we travel 30 minutes for ours. Train regularly with like-minded people, enjoy your dogs and have fun.

Pembroke Corgis are intelligent, enthusiastic, loving, happy, willing, they love life and their owners. They make you laugh and brighten up your day.

Find out what you and they love and the world's your oyster!

----

13. Corgi Health

Both Pembrokes and Cardigans are regarded as relatively robust, healthy breeds with a typical lifespan of 12 to 15 years - even longer if you're lucky.

Health should always be a major consideration when choosing and raising a dog. Firstly, select a puppy from a breeder who produces Welsh Corgis sound in both body AND temperament. Secondly, play your role in helping to keep your dog healthy throughout his or her life.

NOTE: This chapter is intended to be used as an encyclopaedia to help you to identify potential health issues and act promptly in the best interests of your dog. Please don't read it thinking your Corgi will get lots of these ailments – he or she WON'T!

First, let's put things in perspective: the UK Kennel Club has a **Breed Watch Fit For Purpose** campaign that identifies potential faults that could lead to health issues. There are three categories:

1 Breeds with no current points of concern reported

2 Breeds with Breed Watch points of concern

3 Breeds where some dogs have visible conditions or exaggerations that can cause pain or discomfort.

The good news is that both the Pembroke and the Cardigan are classed in Category 1.

Health Testing

It is becoming increasingly evident that genetics can have a huge influence on a person's health and even life expectancy, with lots of time and money currently being devoted to genetic research.

A human is more likely to suffer from a hereditary illness if the gene or genes for that disorder is passed on from parents or grandparents. That person is said to have a *"predisposition"* to the ailment if the gene is in the family's bloodline. Well, the same is true of dogs.

There is not a single breed without the potential for some genetic weakness. For example, many Cavalier King Charles Spaniels have heart problems and 25% of all West Highland White Terriers have a hereditary itchy skin disease.

Anyone thinking of getting a Pembroke or Cardigan puppy today can reduce the chance of their dog having a genetic disease by choosing a puppy from healthy bloodlines.

If you're actively searching for a puppy, you might be considering a breeder based on the look or colour of her dogs or their success in the show ring, but consider the health of the puppy's parents and ancestors as well.

Could they have passed on unhealthy genes along with the good genes for all those features you are attracted to?

The way to reduce those hereditary diseases that can be screened for is for breeders to carry out DNA testing and NOT to mate an *Affected* dog with another *Affected* dog or *Carrier.*

Many inherited diseases are *"Autosomal Recessive,"* below are all possible outcomes – these are average results over thousands of litters. They are the same averages for all autosomal recessive genetic diseases.

PARENT CLEAR + PARENT CLEAR = pups clear

PARENT CLEAR + PARENT CARRIER = 50% will be carriers, 50% will be clear

PARENT CLEAR + PARENT AFFECTED = 100% will be carriers

PARENT CARRIER + PARENT CLEAR = 50% will be carriers, 50% will be clear

PARENT CARRIER + PARENT CARRIER = 25% clear, 25% affected and 50% carriers

PARENT CARRIER + PARENT AFFECTED = 50% affected and 50% carriers

PARENT AFFECTED + PARENT CLEAR = 100% will be carriers

PARENT AFFECTED + PARENT CARRIER = 50% affected and 50% carriers

PARENT AFFECTED + PARENT AFFECTED = 100% affected

COI (Coefficient of Inbreeding)

Carriers carry the faulty gene(s) but do not show signs of the disease. The reason Corgi breeders don't remove all *Carriers* from their breeding stock is that the gene pool would become too small (resulting in a high *COI,* see below), which can cause inbred health issues.

As long as a *Carrier* is bred to a dog with a *Clear* result, no puppies will be affected by the disease.

Breeding two closely-related dogs can increase the risk of health issues. In the UK you can check the COI on the Kennel Club website by typing the registered name of your puppy into their COI calculator: www.thekennelclub.org.uk/search/inbreeding-co-efficient

The breed average for Pembrokes is 8.9% and for Cardigans 10% This or **lower** is acceptable. For

example, if you breed the dam or sire (mother or father) to one of their offspring, the COI is 25%, and breeding first cousins results in a COI of 6.25%.

So you can see that the gene pool is not huge for either type of Welsh Corgi - and a factor to consider when choosing a puppy. Good breeders of Welsh Corgis take COI into consideration when choosing a mate for their dog.

There's an excellent guide to COI at: www.dogbreedhealth.com/a-beginners-guide-to-coi

The good news is that once you have got your puppy there is plenty you can do to help your Pembroke or Cardigan live a long and healthy life.

Health Certificates for Puppy Buyers

Pembrokes

The Genetics Committee of the Pembroke Welsh Corgi Club of America has this advice for anyone buying a Pembroke puppy in the USA: "When evaluating a breeder and considering the purchase of a puppy, do not hesitate to ask questions such as:

* Are the sire and dam screened clear of **hip dysplasia** via an OFA (Orthopedic Foundation for Animals) or PennHIP evaluation?

* Are the **eyes** certified clear of inherited conditions by a certified veterinary ophthalmologist?

* Describe the **temperament** of both the sire and dam. Any noise sensitivity or other observed fears? How do they react to new situations?

* What **other inherited conditions** are found in Pembrokes? (Hint: if the answer is "none," that's not the right answer!). Does the breeder openly talk about reproductive issues, cancer, cardiac issues, neurologic disorders, autoimmune diseases, hips and eyes?"

UK Pembrokes tend to have fewer hereditary issues than their American counterparts. There are no compulsory DNA tests that Kennel Club Assured Breeders have to carry out on their breeding stock.

The UK Kennel Club does, however, recommend that all breeders check the COI of the two mates.

Two other diseases that can affect older Pembrokes and Cardigans are DM (Degenerative Myelopathy) and IVDD (Intervertebral Disc Disease) - more on these later.

Cardigans

The Cardigan Welsh Corgi Club of America says: "While the Cardigan Welsh Corgi is in general a very healthy breed, there a several diseases that can be of concern, and all of which, in fact, can affect many other purebred and crossbred dogs."

These include:

* **Hip Dysplasia**, a malformation of the hip joints that causes arthritis and pain

* **Progressive Retinal Atrophy (PRA),** a disease that causes blindness and for which there is a genetic test, and

* **Degenerative Myelopathy (DM),** a disease that causes progressive paralysis and seems to only affect very old Cardigans. Its cause appears to be multigenetic and the currently available genetic test identifies dogs that may be at risk of developing the disease

In the UK, the Kennel Club's Assured Breeders **must** use the following schemes, all other breeders are strongly advised to also use these:

* DNA test for PRA(rcd3), a hereditary eye disease that can lead to blindness

* Eye screening scheme (BVA/KC/ISDS)

* It is strongly recommended that ALL breeders check the COI of the two mates

Karen Hewitt, Chairperson of the Cardigan Welsh Corgi Association, outlined extra measures taken in the UK: "The marker for PRA was identified in the 1990s, and at the Cardigan Welsh Corgi Association AGM in 2002, members passed a motion that only genetically Clear Cardigans would be used in breeding programs.

"In 2015 the Kennel Club put into place a control order, meaning that only litters from Clear parents could be registered. In addition, any Cardis imported into the UK must be tested clear of PRA before they are accepted for registration."

 If you are buying a puppy, check what DNA tests the parents have had and ask to see original certificates where relevant - a good breeder will be happy to provide them.

As well as asking to see health certificates, prospective buyers should always find out exactly what contract the breeder is offering with the puppy. Good breeders offer a Puppy Contract.

FACT › **If a puppy is sold as "Vet Checked," it does not mean that the parents have been health screened. It means that a veterinarian has given the puppy a brief physical and visual examination, worming and vaccinations are up to date, and the pup appears to be in good health on the day of the examination.**

If you have already got your dog, don't worry! There is plenty of advice in this book on how to take best care of your Corgi. Being careful with your puppy's exercise, feeding a quality food, monitoring your Corgi's weight, regular grooming and check-overs, plenty of socialisation - and exercise for adult dogs - all help to keep your Corgi in tiptop condition.

Good owners can certainly help to extend the life of their dog.

 NOTE: A pedigree certificate from the Kennel Club or AKC does NOT mean that that puppy or its parents have been health screened. A pedigree certificate simply guarantees that the puppy's parents can be traced back several generations and that the ancestors were registered purebred Pembrokes or Cardigans.

Corgi Insurance

Insurance is another point to consider for a new puppy or adult dog. Puppies from many reputable breeders in the UK come with four weeks' or 30 days' insurance that can be extended before it expires.

USA breeders may or may not provide insurance, if not, ask if they can recommend a plan. If you are getting an older Welsh Corgi, get insurance BEFORE any health issues develop, or you may find any pre-existing conditions are excluded.

If you can afford it, take out life cover. This may be more expensive, but will cover your dog throughout his or her lifetime - including for chronic (recurring and/or long term) ailments, such as joint, heart or eye problems, epilepsy and cancer.

Insuring a healthy puppy or adult dog is the only sure-fire way to ensure vets' bills are covered before anything unforeseen happens - and you'd be a rare owner if you didn't use your policy at least once during your dog's lifetime.

Costs in the UK range from around £15 a month for Accident Only to around £30-£50 per month for Lifetime Cover, depending on where you live, how much excess you are willing to pay and the total in pounds covered per year.

The average cost of dog insurance in the US is around $50 per month. This varies a lot, depending on location, the excess, and total coverage per year in dollars. With advances in veterinary science, there is so much more vets can do to help an ailing dog - but at a price.

Surgical procedures can rack up bills of thousands of pounds or dollars. Below are Trupanion real examples of insurance claims:

> Hip Dysplasia $7,815, Diabetes $10,496, Ingestion of foreign body $2,964, Parvo gastroenteritis $5,084, Cruciate ligament tear $5,439, Cancer $5,351
> ($1.35 = approx. £1 at the time of writing)

Of course, if you make a claim your monthly premium will increase. But if you have a decent insurance policy BEFORE a recurring health problem starts, your dog should be covered if the ailment returns. You have to decide whether insurance is worth the money. On the plus side:

1. Peace of mind financially if your beloved Corgi falls ill, and

2. You know exactly how much hard cash to part with each month, so no nasty surprises.

Three Health Tips

1. **Buy a well-bred puppy** - Good Corgi breeders select their stock based on:

   * General health and genetic health of the parents

   * Conformation (physical structure)

   * Temperament

   * COI

   Believe it or not, committed breeders are not in it for the money, often incurring high bills for stud fees, health screening, veterinary costs, specialised food, etc. Their main concern is to produce healthy, handsome puppies with good temperaments that are *"fit for function."*

2. **Get pet insurance as soon as you get your dog** - Don't wait until he has a health issue and needs to see a vet as most insurers exclude all pre-existing conditions on their policies. Check the small print to make sure all conditions are covered and that if the issue recurs, it will continue to be covered year after year. When working out costs of a dog, factor in annual or monthly pet insurance fees and trips to a vet for check-ups, vaccinations, etc.

3. **Find a good vet** - Ask around, rather than just going to the first one you find. A vet that knows your dog from his or her puppy vaccinations and then right through their life is more likely to understand your dog and diagnose quickly and correctly when something is wrong. If you visit a big veterinary practice, ask for the vet by name when you make an appointment.

We all want our dogs to be healthy - so how can you tell if yours is? Well, here are some positive things to look for in a healthy Corgi:

Health Indicators

1. **Eyes** - Corgis have black or dark eye rims. Paleness around the eyeball (conjunctiva) could also be a sign of something amiss. A cloudy eye could be a sign of cataracts. Sometimes the dog's third eyelid (nictating membrane) is visible at the inside corner - this is normal. But there should be no thick, green or yellow discharge from the eyes.

2. **Movement** - Healthy dogs move at all speeds freely and without pain. Look out for warning signs of stiffness when getting up from lying, limping, a reluctance to move, get in the car or go up steps.

3. **Nose** - A dog's nose is an indicator of health. Corgi noses are black, except some blue merle Cardigans who have a **butterfly nose** (with patches of pink). They should be free from clear, watery secretions. Any yellow, green or foul-smelling discharge is not normal - in younger dogs this can be a sign of canine distemper. Corgi pups often have a pink or butterfly nose that usually darkens in a few weeks or months.

4. **Ears** - If you are choosing a puppy, gently clap your hands behind the pup - not so loud as to frighten him - to see if he reacts. If not, this may be a sign of deafness. The Corgi's pricked-up ears make him less prone to ear infections than floppy-eared breeds, but ears should still be checked when grooming to make sure they are clean and not smelly, which is a sign of yeast infection.

5. **Mouth** - Corgi gums are usually pink or pink and black. Paleness or whiteness can be a sign of anaemia, Bloat or lack of oxygen due to heart or breathing problems. Blue gums or tongue are a sign that your dog is not breathing properly. Red, inflamed gums can be a sign of gingivitis or other dental disease. Young dogs have sparkling white teeth, whereas older dogs have darker teeth, but they should not have any hard white, yellow, green or brown bits. Your dog's breath should not smell unpleasant.

6. **Energy** - Corgis are alert dogs. Yours should have good amounts of energy with fluid movements. Lack of energy or lethargy could be a sign of an underlying problem.

7. **Coat and Skin** - These are easy-to-monitor indicators of a healthy dog. A healthy Corgi has a clean, double coat with a soft, dense undercoat and harsher topcoat. Their short legs mean that they pick up a lot of dirt and mud, so a rinse or towel dry after a wet walk will help to keep the coat and skin healthy.

Any dandruff, bald spots, a dull, lifeless, discoloured or oily coat, or one that loses excessive hair, can all be signs that something is amiss. Skin should be smooth without redness or rashes. If a dog is scratching, licking or biting a lot, he may have a condition that needs addressing.

Open sores, scales, scabs, red patches or growths can be a sign of a skin issue or allergy. Signs of fleas, ticks and other external parasites should be treated immediately; check for small black or dark red specks, which may be fleas or flea poop, on the coat or bedding.

8. **Weight** - Obesity can be an issue within the breed – and it's not the dog's fault! Corgis were bred as working dogs and are also notoriously greedy, so it's up to you to monitor calories and make sure yours is getting plenty of exercise.

Your Corgi's stomach should be **above** the bottom of his rib cage when standing, **pictured,** and you should be able see a visible waistline and feel the ribs beneath his coat without too much effort. If the stomach is level or hangs below, your Corgi is overweight - or may have a pot belly, which can also be a symptom of other conditions.

9. **Temperature** - The normal temperature of a dog is 101°F to 102.5°F. (A human's is 98.6°F). Excited or exercising dogs may run a slightly higher temperature. Anything above 103°F or below 100°F should be checked out. The exceptions are female dogs about to give birth that will often have a temperature of 99°F. If you take your dog's temperature, make sure he is relaxed and *always* use a purpose-made canine thermometer.

10. **Stools** - Poo, poop, business, faeces - call it what you will - it's the stuff that comes out of the less appealing end of your dog on a daily basis! It should be mostly firm and brown, not runny, with no signs of blood or worms. Watery stools or a dog not eliminating regularly are both signs of an upset stomach or other ailments. If it continues for a couple of days, consult your vet.

    If puppies have diarrhoea, they need checking out much sooner as they can quickly dehydrate.

11. **Smell** - Corgis who regularly run free in the countryside can sometimes have a doggie smell, particularly in wet weather. But if yours has a musty, 'off' or generally unpleasant smell, it could be a sign of a yeast infection. There can be a number of causes; it could be a food allergy or anal sac issue, which may be accompanied by *'scooting'* (dragging the rear end across the floor). Whatever the cause, you need to get to the root of the problem quickly before it develops into something more serious.

12. **Attitude** - A generally positive attitude is a sign of good health. Welsh Corgis are alert – *like this Cardigan pictured* - engaged and involved. Symptoms of illness may include one or all of the following: a general lack of interest in his surroundings, tail not wagging (if yours has one!), lethargy, not eating food and sleeping a lot more than normal.

The important thing is to look out for any behaviour that is out of the ordinary for YOUR Corgi.

There are many different signs that may indicate your canine companion isn't feeling great. If you don't yet know your dog, his habits, temperament and behaviour patterns, then spend some time getting acquainted with them.

What are his normal character and temperament? Lively or calm, playful or serious, a joker or an introvert, bold or nervous, happy to be left alone or loves to be with people?

How often does he empty his bowels, does he ever vomit? (Dogs will often eat grass to make themselves sick, this is perfectly normal and a natural way of cleansing the digestive system).

Tip **You may not think your Corgi can talk, but he most certainly can!**

If you really know your dog, his character and habits, then he CAN tell you when he's not well. He does this by changing his patterns. Some symptoms are physical, some emotional and others are behavioural. It's important to be able to recognise these changes, as early treatment can be the key to keeping a simple problem from snowballing into something more serious.

If you think your dog is unwell, it is useful to keep an accurate and detailed account of his symptoms to give to the vet, perhaps even take a video of him on your mobile phone. This will help the vet to correctly diagnose and effectively treat your dog.

Three Vital Signs of Illness

1. **Temperature** - A new-born puppy has a temperature of 94-97°F (34.4-36.1°C). This reaches the normal adult body temperature of around 101°F (38.3°C) at four weeks old. A vet takes a dog's temperature reading via the rectum. If you do this, only do it with a special rectal thermometer, like this electronic one **pictured**, which can also be used in the mouth. Infrared forehead thermometers are also widely available.

   NOTE: Exercise or excitement can cause temperature to rise by 2°F to 3°F (1-1.5°C) when your dog is actually in good health, so wait until he is relaxed before taking his temperature. If it is above or below the norms and the dog seems under par, give your vet a call.

2. **Respiratory Rate** - Another symptom of illness is a change in breathing patterns. This varies a lot depending on the size and weight of the dog. An adult dog will have a respiratory rate of anything from 10 to 30 breaths per minute when resting and up to 200 when panting. You can easily check this by counting your dog's breaths for a minute with a stopwatch handy. Don't do this when he is panting.

3. **Behaviour Changes** - Classic symptoms of illness are any inexplicable behaviour changes. If there has NOT been a change in the household atmosphere, such as another new pet, a new baby, moving home, the absence of a family member or the loss of another dog, then the following symptoms may well be a sign that all is not well:

* Depression or lethargy

* Tiredness - sleeping more than normal or not wanting to exercise

* Lack of interest in his surroundings

* Loss of appetite

* Being more vocal - grunting, whining or whimpering

* Abnormal posture

* Restlessness, not settling, walking in circles, etc.

* Aggression

* Anxiety and/or shivering, which can be a sign of pain

* Falling or stumbling

If any of them appear for the first time or worse than usual, you need to keep him under close watch for a few hours or even days. Quite often he will return to normal of his own accord. Like humans, dogs have off-days too.

If he is showing any of the above symptoms, then don't over-exercise him, and avoid stressful situations and hot or cold places. Make sure he has access to clean water. Keep a record and it may be useful to take a fresh stool sample to your vet. If your dog does need professional medical attention, most vets will want to know:

WHEN the symptoms first appeared in your dog

WHETHER they are getting better or worse, and

HOW FREQUENT the symptoms are - intermittent, continuous or increasing?

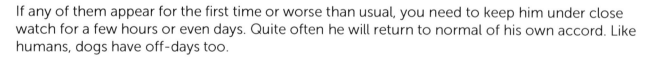

DM (Degenerative Myelopathy)

DM is a degenerative fatal neurological disease, similar to ALS (Amyotrophic Lateral Sclerosis or Lou Gehrig's disease) in humans. It can affect many breeds in later life, including Pembrokes and Cardigans, particularly in the US.

DM is not painful; it causes a loss of movement and sensation rather than pain. As yet there is no cure - although physiotherapy can help some dogs stay mobile for longer. Owners often decide to put the dog to sleep before the disease progresses to its final stages.

According to Dr Jerold S. Bell, DVM, Chairman of the Hereditary Disease Committee, World Small Animal Veterinary Association, and Director of CHIC: "Affected dogs begin to show signs of the disorder usually between eight and 14 years of age. The average age of onset in Pembroke Welsh Corgis is 11 years of age."

The full article can be read here: https://pembrokecorgi.org/about-pembrokes/canine-degenerative-myelopathy-and-genetic-testing-in-pwcs

Typical signs are:

* Weakness of the hind legs
* Hindlimb ataxia (swaying when moving)
* Scuffing of the hind toes
* Crossing of the hind legs
* Progressing to dragging of the hind legs

Dr Bell says: "The progression is slow, occurring over six months to two years. With excellent nursing care (and a canine wheelchair, *pictured*, affected dogs can progress to advanced disease."

Advanced symptoms are:

* Losing urine and bowel control
* Weakness or paralysis of the forelimbs
* Eventually, loss of control of breathing

Dr Bell: "All affected dogs are eventually euthanized - most prior to these later stages. DM is not a painful disease, but one of loss of motor (muscular) and sensory (feeling) function.

"There is no treatment that alters the clinical progression of DM. As several different disorders can mimic the clinical signs of DM, a confirmed diagnosis can only be made through a pathological examination of the spinal cord" (a microscopic exam of spinal tissue post mortem).

FACT ❯ Since 2008, there has been a DNA test for DM. While the test is very accurate at determining whether a Corgi is carrying the gene for DM, it is NOT a good indicator of whether that dog will go on to develop the disease.

However, DM should not be ignored as it does affect Corgis. A number of breeders already test for it. Ultimately, the way to reduce DM in the Corgi population is:

A. For a more reliable DNA test to be developed to determine which At Risk dogs will go on to actually develop the disease, and

B. For breeders to have their breeding dogs screened and NOT to breed an At Risk dog with another At Risk or Carrier.

According to the latest statistics from the USA's OFA (Orthopedic Foundation for Animals), of 4,699 tested Pembrokes, 53.4% were Abnormal (i.e. At Risk of developing DM), 33.3% were Carriers and 13.3% were Normal (equivalent to Clear in the UK). DM is more commonly diagnosed in the US than Europe. The figures for the 817 US tested Cardigans were: 17% Abnormal, 33.3% Carrier, 49.7% Normal.

NOTE: The vast majority of Abnormal/At Risk dogs <u>DO NOT</u> go on to develop DM. In 2021 Dr Bell added: "Clinical degenerative myelopathy needs to be put back in the RARE and INFREQUENTLY DIAGNOSED category where it belongs."

The Cardigan Welsh Corgi Club of America (CWCCA) says: "So far it appears that the incidence of this gene is relatively low in Cardigans. Not every dog that is "at risk" develops clinical DM and there are other neurological diseases like intervertebral disk disease (IVDD) that can be mistaken for it."

Linda Roberts, Breed Health Co-ordinator for The Welsh Corgi League (Pembroke Corgi), added: "The incidence of DM may be higher in certain bloodlines and the race is on (in the USA primarily) to identify modifying SOD genes which affect whether a genetically At Risk dog will go down in later life.

"Some people wonder why we just don't breed Clear to Clear, or Clear to Carrier, but many breeders feel that making decisions based on a weak test is not the way forward. We have lots of other considerations to contend with of course – overall health, breed-type, structure, soundness, temperament etc. The reality is that most affected dogs will succumb to other diseases or conditions before showing symptoms.

"We are in discussions with the Kennel Club about the way forward and we hope for a refined, more accurate test soon."

....

IVDD (Intervertebral Disc Disease)

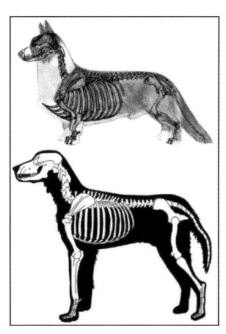

IVDD is the specific name given to a variety of back problems, such as "slipped," ruptured, herniated or bulging disk(s), and it's the most common spinal disease in dogs.

Both types of Corgi are dwarf breeds, having been bred down from larger dogs. They are also *"chondrodystrophic,"* meaning they have short, curved limbs and relatively long bodies, making them prone to back problems, *see diagram.*

To reduce the chances of IVDD developing, it is especially important that Corgi puppies avoid high impact activities and that they are not over-exercised.

Cartilage is a connective tissue, softer and more elastic than bone, found all over the body, particularly in joints. Intervertebral disks are fibrous cartilage cushions between the vertebrae (series of small bones that form the backbone).

The disks allow movement, provide supportive and act as shock absorbers.

There are two main types of IVDD: Type 1 and Type 2. Type 2, often called a **bulging disk,** happens gradually and more commonly affects older large breed dogs.

Corgis typically suffer from Type 1, also known as a **ruptured disk.** It occurs when the gel-like inner layer of the disk suddenly breaks through the top of the outer layer, causing sudden pressure on the spinal cord. It's sometimes called IVDE (Disk Extrusion) and symptoms are noticeable within one to five days.

IVDD can affect Corgis of all ages and the onset might be quite sudden. Symptoms vary according to severity and include:

- Stiffness of the neck, limbs or back
- Reluctance to go up or down a step
- Hanging head when standing
- Reluctance to lift or lower the head
- Arched back
- Knuckling (paws upside down)
- Swollen or hard abdomen
- Wobbliness, stumbling, unusual gait – often mainly affecting the hind legs
- Yelping, either unprovoked or when touched - a sign of pain
- Trembling, panting or licking the lips
- Dragging the rear leg(s)

In very extreme cases: paralysis, loss of bladder control and inability to feel pain

 Choosing a puppy from bloodlines with no history of back problems is a good place to start. But if you've already got yours, there's still lots you can do to help keep your Corgi free from back pain.

1. VERY IMPORTANT: Don't let your Corgi get overweight - it puts strain on the spine.

2. Don't let your dog run up and down stairs or jump on and off furniture.

3. Don't over-exercise puppies.

4. Learn how to handle a Corgi puppy properly - and teach the kids how to do it.

5. Don't play vigorous games with a Corgi - avoid Tug-o-War, Frisbee, etc.

6. Avoid any activity where your dog's spine may twist, **pictured.**

7. Mixing with other dogs is fine, but avoid roughhousing with bigger or boisterous dogs.

8. Hiking and long walks (for healthy <u>adult</u> Corgis) help to strengthen muscles around the spine.

Follow this advice and the likelihood is that your Corgi will remain untroubled by IVDD.

Diagnosis and Treatment

If your dog is showing any symptoms of IVDD get him to the vet. It's important to get the right diagnosis straight away as a delay may cause a more serious rupturing of the disk(s). Ask if your vet has experience of canine spinal issues; IVDD is sometimes misdiagnosed as arthritis, muscle pain or a gastro problem.

IVDD cannot be diagnosed with normal X-rays or a blood test. A special type of X-ray called a *myelogram* can detect spinal cord problems, but an MRI or CT scan is better. Extensive diagnostic tests and treatment are expensive - another reason to have good pet insurance in place.

If IVDD is confirmed, the vet will give a grading. Grade 1 is the least serious, when a dog is walking normally, but feels some pain. Grade 5 is 'very serious,' with paralysis, incontinence and complete loss of deep sensation in affected limbs. Even then, there is a 50%-60% chance that the dog will walk again after surgery, although many have an odd gait. With Grades 1 and 2, recovery can be as high as 95%.

For all but the most severe cases, there are *"conservative (non-surgical) treatments."* Painkillers and anti-inflammatories (NSAIDS), crate rest, rehabilitation exercises, massage, acupuncture, hydrotherapy and physiotherapy can all help to reduce the severity of the symptoms.

In more serious cases mobility devices may help the dog, and in extreme cases surgery may be recommended. The procedure is often carried out by a veterinary neurologist, rather than a general veterinary surgeon.

Recovery varies according to severity; the dog can start walking again within anything from one to 12 weeks, although full recovery may take the best part of a year in severe cases.

Dr Marianne Dorn, The Rehab Vet, says: "There is no single "magic cure" for IVDD. Depending on how severely they are affected, your dog will need a combination of medicine (including painkillers), nursing care, and home care, with or without an operation as well.

"If a surgical operation is required, then your dog will still need special home care afterwards: Put down plenty of mats to provide a safe grippy surface if your floors are slick.

"Confine your dog so they cannot use stairs, jump on furniture, rush through the home or access slick flooring.

"An XXL or giant crate may be needed for the first few weeks, or use a pen if your dog will not try to jump out. You must keep your dog slow on lead and harness whenever outside their pen or crate and, if they cannot walk, you will also have to support them with a sling.

"Many dogs come home from the operation unable to walk, but then go on to make a good recovery with the help of dedicated home care.

"Each recovering dog has different home care needs, so follow your vet's advice specific to your own dog. If your dog has recently been diagnosed with IVDD, or if you are struggling to care for a long-term sufferer, then do not despair.

"With care and attention to detail, many dogs with IVDD eventually return to a happy lifestyle."

There is much more advice on IVDD and how to look after an affected dog on Marianne's website at https://therehabvet.com/ivdd

 The owner plays a large part in the dog's return to normal or near-normal, as prolonged periods of crate rest, carefully-monitored exercise, a healthy diet and bucketloads of patience are all essential.

IVDD is a painful and debilitating condition. If surgery is unsuccessful or the damage is too far gone, it may be time to consider putting the dog to sleep. No matter how hard it is to make that decision, it may be the kindest option.

Tips for Crate Rest

This can be a challenging time for the owner as well as the dog. Here are a few tips if your dog does need crate rest:

* Crate-train your puppy, so if a problem arises later in life, he will be used to a crate
* Place the crate near the family, don't leave him isolated
* A recovering dog needs a calm environment
* Use a Vetbed or folded blanket for him to lie on
* When you open the crate door, get down to your dog's level and be ready to put on a lead – don't let him dash out
* Take your dog outside to eliminate on a lead, don't allow him to freely wander
* If your dog is likely to be mainly in two places, consider getting a second crate
* DAP (Dog Appeasing Pheromone) diffusers, melatonin, hemp oil and other natural products help some dogs to stay calm and relaxed
* Some dogs do well with part of their crate covered with a sheet (leave a gap at the bottom for air flow)

* A Kong or puzzle toy may help to stave off boredom, or a drive in the car
* **Finally - DON'T stop the crate rest too early** - it's a mistake many owners make when they see their dog improving. Stick to what the vet says

Use a pen if there's no danger of your Corgi jumping out, his body will not be so restricted and you can access him easier. Dr Dorn adds that these are her recommended good welfare pen and crate sizes for Corgis during IVDD recovery:

For approximately the first three weeks following injury or surgery, or as advised by your vet:

* PEN: 80x80cm (31.5"x31.5") square or up to an 80x160cm (31.5"x63") rectangular
* CRATE (for likely escapees): XXL crate - 122x74cm (48"x29") floor area or, for larger individuals, a Giant crate 137x94cm (54"x37") floor area

After the first three weeks. Again, take advice from your vet regarding timings:

❖ PEN: 120x120cm (47"x47") square pen. For a large dog, 160x160cm (63"x63") square pen. Avoid crates if possible.

Most of the research into IVDD has been done with Dachshunds. To read more information and personal experiences from owners of Daxies with IVDD, visit https://www.dachshund-ivdd.uk/ and https://dodgerslist.com

....

Hip Dysplasia

Hip Dysplasia, or *Canine Hip Dysplasia (CHD),* is the most common inherited orthopaedic problem in dogs of all breeds. While Hip Dysplasia is not a major issue with UK Corgis, the breed clubs for Pembrokes and Cardigans in the US recommend that hip screening is carried out on all breeding dogs.

Of the 15,046 Pembrokes tested by OFA in the USA, one in five had abnormal hips. The figure was nearly one in four for the 3,261 Cardigans tested.

Comparable figures for the UK are not available as it is not regarded as an inheritable problem and almost no Corgis are tested.

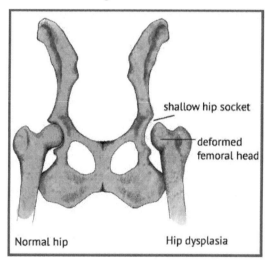

shallow hip socket

deformed femoral head

Normal hip   Hip dysplasia

The hips are the uppermost joints on the rear legs of a dog, either side of the tail, and *"Dysplasia"* means *"abnormal development."* Dogs with this condition develop painful degenerative arthritis of the hip joints. The hip is a ball and socket joint.

Hip dysplasia is caused when the head of the femur, or thigh bone, fits loosely into a shallow and poorly developed socket in the pelvis. The joint carrying the weight of the dog becomes loose and unstable, muscle growth slows and degenerative joint disease often follows.

Symptoms often start to show at five to 18 months of age. Occasionally, an affected dog will have no symptoms at all, while others may experience anything from mild discomfort to extreme pain.

Diagnosis is made by X-ray, and an early diagnosis gives a vet the best chance to tackle HD, minimising the chance of arthritis.

While there is a genetic disposition, there are also other risk factors, including:

Symptoms are:

❖ Hind leg lameness, particularly after exercise

❖ Difficulty or stiffness when getting up, climbing stairs or walking uphill

❖ A reluctance to jump, exercise or climb stairs

❖ A "bunny hop" gait or waddling gait

❖ A painful reaction to stretching the hind legs, resulting in a short stride

❖ Side-to-side swaying of the croup (area above the tail)

❖ Wastage of the thigh muscles

 **FACT** While a predisposition to hip dysplasia is often inherited, other factors can trigger or worsen it, including:

❖ Obesity

❖ Frequent use of stairs, especially while still growing

❖ Slippery floors

Prevention and Treatment

There is a system called *hip scoring,* run by PennHIP or OFA in the USA and the BVA and Kennel Club in the UK. UK dogs' hips are X-rayed at a minimum age of 12 months; in the US, dogs must be 24 months old before they can receive their final hip certification.

In the UK, the X-rays are submitted to a specialist panel at the BVA who assess nine features of each hip, giving each feature a score. **The lower the score, the better the hips,** so the range can be from **0** NO DYSPLASIA to **106** BADLY DYSPLASTIC (53 in each hip). A hip certificate shows the individual score for each hip.

It is far better if the dog has evenly matched hips, rather than a low score for one and a high score for the other. Listed here are the American ratings, with the UK ratings in brackets:

❖ **Excellent** (0-4, with neither hip higher than 3)

❖ **Good** (5-10, with neither hip higher than 6)

❖ **Fair** (11-18)

❖ **Borderline** (19-25)

❖ **Mild** (26-35)

❖ **Moderate** (36-50)

❖ **Severe** (51-106)

Section C – TO BE COMPLETED BY SCRUTINEERS			
CERTIFICATE OF SCORING			
HIP JOINT	Score Range	Right	Left
Norberg angle	0-6	O	I
Subluxation	0-6	2	3
Cranial acetabular edge	0-6	2	2
Dorsal acetabular edge	0-6	—	—
Cranial effective acetabular rim	0-6	—	—
Acetabular fossa	0-6	—	—
Caudal acetabular edge	0-5	—	—
Femoral head/neck exostosis	0-6	—	—
Femoral head recontouring	0-6	—	—
TOTALS	(max possible 53 per column)	4	6	10

This section of a UK BVA certificate, pictured, shows a hip score of 10, which is good.

There is no 100% guarantee that a puppy from low scoring parents will not develop hip dysplasia, as the condition is caused by a combination of genes, rather than just one. However, the chances are significantly reduced with good hip scores.

Treatment is geared towards preventing the hip joint getting worse. If the dysplasia is not severe it is often dealt with by restricting exercise, **keeping body weight down** and managing pain with analgesics and anti-inflammatory drugs.

Glucosamine, chondroitin and/or a daily supplement such as Yumove, which contains glucosamine, vitamins C and E, hyaluronic acid and green-lipped mussels, are also often recommended by vets. Good quality hydrotherapy has been shown to help.

Very severe cases may require surgery to replace part or all of the damaged hip. If you are buying a Corgi puppy in the US, ask to see the hip scores of the parents.

Elbow Dysplasia

The elbow is at the top of a dog's front leg, near the body, and bends backwards. Like Hip Dysplasia, Elbow Dysplasia is a painful inherited disease that occurs when cells, tissue or bone don't develop correctly. This causes the elbow to form abnormally then to degenerate (arthritis).

Although not a major problem, recent OFA studies in America involving over 2,500 Welsh Corgis found that 4% had elbow abnormalities.

A test called **elbow scoring** is available in the USA, and there is the BVA (British Veterinary Association)/KC Elbow Dysplasia Scheme in the UK. Results are graded 0-3, with 0 being the best score.

Symptoms begin during puppyhood, typically at four to 10 months of age, although not all young dogs show signs. Look out for:

- ❧ Stiffness followed by temporary or permanent lameness aggravated by exercise
- ❧ Pain when extending or flexing the elbow
- ❧ Holding the affected leg away from the body
- ❧ Groaning when getting up
- ❧ Swelling around the joint
- ❧ In advanced cases: grating of bone and joint when moving

Diagnosis is made by a veterinary examination and X-rays, requiring the dog to be anaesthetised. Treatment depends on age and severity, and may involve Non-steroidal Anti-inflammatory Drugs (NSAIDs) or injections.

Thanks to advances in veterinary medicine, surgery is now an option for many dogs who are severely affected. According to Embrace Pet Insurance, it costs $1,500-$4,000, (£1,100-£3,000) and results in partial or full improvement in the vast majority of cases.

Treatment is similar to that for Hip Dysplasia. Keeping your dog's weight in check and feeding the right diet are important; supplements mentioned earlier can also help to relieve pain and stiffness.

NOTE: Screening for Hip Dysplasia is compulsory for breeders of Pembrokes and Cardigans to qualify for Canine Health Information Center (CHIC) certification in the US.

---

von Willebrand's Disease

Von Willebrand's Disease is the most common inherited bleeding disorder in dogs and humans; it's similar to haemophilia in humans. In Von Willebrand's Disease (vWD), the dog lacks a substance which helps to form blood clots. This substance (**von Willebrand's factor**) normally forms clots and stabilises something called Factor VIII in the normal clotting process.

Dogs that show symptoms of von Willebrand's Disease bleed excessively as their blood does not clot properly. However, many dogs diagnosed with vWD show no symptoms, or none until later life.

The disease is caused by an inherited gene mutation and certain breeds have a higher incidence of vWD than average - including Pembrokes - who can be affected by the least severe form of the disease: vWD1 (Type 1 von Willebrand's).

It is named after Erik Adolf von Willebrand **(pictured),** a Finnish doctor who documented and studied a rare bleeding disorder in an isolated group of people in 1924. He showed that the disease was inherited, rather than caught by infection.

vWD1 can be diagnosed with a special blood test or a DNA test. At one time it was thought that the faulty gene(s) was recessive, meaning BOTH parents had to have it for the puppy to be affected. Latest research shows that it may be a dominant gene, so it's possible that one affected parent can pass the disease on to a puppy.

The DNA test for vWD is not compulsory for Kennel Club breeders of Pembrokes, but some do test for it. Affected dogs should not be used for breeding.

Symptoms

The main symptom is excessive bleeding:

- ❧ Nosebleeds
- ❧ Blood in the faeces (black or bright red blood)
- ❧ Bloody urine
- ❧ Bleeding from the gums
- ❧ Females bleeding excessively from the vagina
- ❧ Bruising of skin
- ❧ Prolonged bleeding after surgery or trauma
- ❧ Blood loss anaemia if there is prolonged bleeding

If bleeding occurs in the stomach or intestine, you may notice something unusual in your dog's faeces; his stools may have blood in them or be black and tarry or bright red. Some dogs will have blood in their urine, while others may have bleeding in their joints. In this last case, the symptoms are similar to those of arthritis.

There is no cure for vWD. Treatment usually involves transfusions of blood or plasma and/or administration of a synthetic hormone.

Some dogs with von Willebrand's Disease are also **hypothyroid**, meaning they have lower than normal levels of thyroid hormone. These dogs benefit from thyroid hormone replacement therapy.

A synthetic hormone called desmopressin acetate (DDVAPP) may also be given in mild cases to help the dog increase its level of von Willebrand factor, although results are variable.

The Eyes

There are a number of eye issues that can affect dogs of all breeds and we have included the most common ones here. All US Pembroke and Cardigan breeding stock must have an eye examination by a veterinary ophthalmologist to qualify for a CHIC certificate (the gold standard of health testing in America).

Cardigans: A DNA test for PRA3 is compulsory for CHIC certification in the US as well as UK Kennel Club Assured Breeders.

Progressive Retinal Atrophy (PRA-rcd3)

PRA is the name for several progressive diseases causing degeneration of the retina that lead to blindness. First recognised at the beginning of the 20th century in Gordon Setters, this inherited condition has been documented in over 100 breeds, including Cardigan Welsh Corgis.

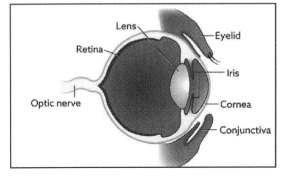

The type of PRA that can affect Cardigans is called **PRA-rcd3, or PRA3**.

The retina is the light-sensitive layer at the back of the eye with cells called photoreceptors. When light enters the eye, the lens focusses it on to the retina. This is converted into electrical signals that are sent to the brain, which processes the signals and interprets them as images.

The two main photoreceptor cells of the retina are the **rod cells** and the **cone cells**. Dogs' eyes contain many more rods than cones.

Rod cells are responsible for vision in low light and for detecting and following movement. Cone cells are responsible for detecting colour. (Cone cells do not work very well in low light).

In PRA-rcd3 in Cardigans, the rod cells begin to die, often before the age of one year old, and the dog quickly becomes night-blind. At two to three years old, the dog's cone cells also degenerate and die, leading to a loss of colour vision and complete blindness. Unfortunately, there is no cure for PRA.

Symptoms

If your dog has PRA, you may first notice that he lacks confidence in low light; is perhaps reluctant to go down stairs or along a dark hallway.

If you look closely into his eyes, you may see the pupils dilating (becoming bigger) and/or the reflection of greenish light from the back of his eyes.

In some dogs the lenses may become opaque or cloudy. As the condition worsens, they might then start bumping into things, first at night and then in the daytime too. PRA is not painful and many dogs' eyes appear normal - without redness, tearing or squinting.

PRA-rcd3 is a genetic disorder associated with a **recessive** gene mutation. This means that the faulty gene must be inherited **from both parents** for a puppy to be affected.

 It is worth bearing in mind that while sight is important for dogs, it is not as important as it is for humans. Dogs have incredibly well-developed senses of smell and hearing, and many dogs who become blind manage perfectly well - with help and patience from their owners - and go on to live happy, otherwise healthy lives.

....

Glaucoma

Glaucoma is a painful condition that puts pressure on the eye, and if it worsens or continues without treatment, it will eventually cause permanent damage to the optic nerve, resulting in blindness.

Both Pembrokes and Cardigans have a slightly higher than average risk of Glaucoma and there are two types:

- ❧ **Primary Glaucoma,** which is inherited, and
- ❧ **Secondary Glaucoma,** which is caused by another problem such as a wound to the eye, cataracts or cancer – this is believed to be twice as common as Primary Glaucoma

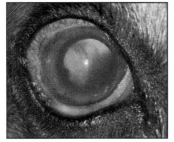 A normal eye contains a fluid called aqueous humour to maintain its shape, and the body is constantly adding and removing fluid from inside of the eye to maintain the pressure inside the eye at the correct level. *Our photo shows an eye with acute Glaucoma.*

Glaucoma occurs when the pressure inside the eyeball becomes higher than normal. Just as high blood pressure can damage the heart, excessive pressure inside the eye can damage the eye's internal structures. The increased pressure is most frequently caused by this fluid not being able to properly drain away from the eye.

When the pressure starts to rise, similar to a water balloon, the balloon stretches more and more. A balloon will eventually burst, but the eye is stronger so this does not happen. Instead the eye's internal structures are damaged irreparably.

Symptoms

The age of onset varies a lot from one Corgi to the next, but Glaucoma is a serious disease and it's important for an owner to be able to immediately recognise initial symptoms. If treatment is not started within a few days - or even hours in some cases - of the pressure increasing, the dog may well lose sight in that eye. Here are the early signs:

* Pain

* A dilated pupil or one pupil looks bigger than the other

* Rapid blinking

* Red eyeballs

* Cloudiness in the cornea at the front of the eye

* The whites of an eye look bloodshot

* One eye looks larger or sticks out further than the other one

* Loss of appetite, which may be due to headaches

* Change in attitude, less willing to play, etc.

 Most dogs will not display all of these signs at first, perhaps just one or two. A dog rubbing his eye with his paw, against the furniture or carpet or your leg is a common - and often unnoticed - early sign. Some dogs will also seem to flutter the eyelids or squint with one eye.

The pupil of the affected eye will usually dilate in the early stages of Glaucoma. It may still react to all bright light, but it will do so very slowly. If the pupil in one eye is larger than in the other, something is definitely wrong.

If you suspect your dog has Glaucoma, get him to the vet as soon as possible, i.e. immediately, not the day after; this is a medical emergency. The vet will carry out a manual examination and test your dog's eye pressure using a tonometer on the surface of the eye. The dog may lose sight in this eye, but the vet will have a much better chance of saving the second eye.

Treatment revolves around reducing pressure within the affected eye, draining the aqueous humour and providing pain relief. There are also surgical options for the long-term control of Glaucoma. As yet it cannot be cured.

A predisposition to Primary Glaucoma can be detected by a test called a *gonioscopy*, which looks for an abnormality in the eye and is part of eye testing schemes.

Cataracts

The lens is transparent and its function is to focus rays of light to form an image on the retina. A cataract occurs when the lens becomes cloudy. Less light enters the eye, images become blurry and the dog's sight diminishes as the cataract becomes larger.

Age-related or *late onset cataracts* can develop in any breed any time after the age of eight years and usually have less impact on a dog's vision that those seen in younger dogs. This is the type that may affect some older Corgis.

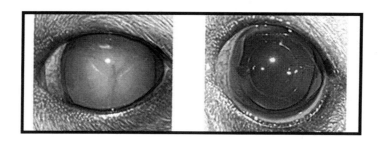

Left: eye with cataracts. Right: same eye with artificial lens

If the cataract is small, it won't disturb the dog's vision too much, but owners must monitor cataracts because the thicker and denser they become, the more likely they will lead to blindness or glaucoma.

 Diabetes is a known trigger for cataracts, and overweight dogs are more susceptible to diabetes than dogs of a healthy weight.

Depending on the cause, severity and type of cataract, surgery is an option for some dogs; the lens is removed and replaced with a plastic substitute. It costs around $3,000-$4,000 per eye in the US and £2,500-£3,500 in the UK, but if the dog is a suitable candidate, it is successful in 90% of cases. In less severe cases, dogs can live a perfectly normal life with daily eye drops and vigilance on the part of the owner.

 Beware of miracle cures! If you do try drops, look for some containing the effective ingredient N-Acetyl Carnosine, or NAC.

As well as a cloudy eye, other signs are the dog bumping into things, especially in dimly-lit situations, squinting or pawing at the eye, eye redness, an inflamed eye socket, or a bulging eye. If you suspect your Corgi has cataracts, get him to the vet for an examination as soon as possible. Early intervention can prevent complications developing.

Distichiasis

This occurs when eyelashes grow from an abnormal spot on the eyelid. (*Trichiasis* is ingrowing eyelashes and *Ectopic Cilia* are single or multiple hairs that grow through the inside of the eyelid - *cilia* are eyelashes). *Our photo shows a healthy eye.*

With Distichiasis, an eyelash or eyelashes abnormally grow on the inner surface or the very edge of the eyelid, and both upper and lower eyelids can be affected. The affected eye becomes red, inflamed, and may have a discharge.

The dog typically squints or blinks a lot, just like a human with a hair or other foreign matter in the eye. The dog can make matters worse by rubbing the eye against furniture, other objects or the carpet. In severe cases, the cornea can become ulcerated and it looks blue.

Often, very mild cases require no action. Mild cases may require lubricating eye drops and in more severe cases, surgery may be the best option to remove the offending eyelashes and prevent them from regrowing. Left untreated, Distichiasis can cause corneal ulcers and infection which can ultimately lead to blindness or loss of the eye.

Exercise Induced Collapse (EIC)

This inherited disease is occasionally found in Pembroke Welsh Corgis. Severely affected dogs typically become weak in the hind legs and can collapse after five to 20 minutes of high intensity exercise, and in some cases simple fetch and retrieve. Other dogs only collapse sporadically and, as yet, scientists are not sure why this is the case.

ALWAYS stop the dog from exercising at the first signs of something amiss - which is usually wobbliness. The good news is that most dogs recover quickly and are usually back to normal within half an hour with no lasting weakness or stiffness.

The wobbliness is followed by the rear legs becoming weak and affected dogs may continue to run while dragging their back legs. In some dogs this progresses to front leg weakness and occasionally a total inability to move. Some dogs appear to be uncoordinated and have a loss of balance, particularly as they recover. It's common for the symptoms to worsen for three to five minutes, even after the dog has stopped exercising.

According to one study, dogs that experience EIC are most likely to have intense, excitable personalities, and it seems that their level of excitement plays a role in causing the collapse. It is thankfully rare in Pembrokes, as one experienced breeder who regularly exercises her Corgis said: "I'm more likely to collapse than my dogs!"

Epilepsy

Epilepsy means repeated seizures (also called fits or convulsions) due to abnormal electrical activity in the brain. Epilepsy affects around four or five dogs in every 100 across the dog population as whole.

Epilepsy can be classified as *structural,* when an underlying cause can be identified in the brain, or *idiopathic,* when the cause is unknown. The type of epilepsy affecting most dogs of all breeds is *idiopathic epilepsy.*

In some cases, the gap between seizures is relatively constant, in others it can be very irregular with several occurring over a short period of time, but with long intervals between *"clusters."* Affected dogs behave normally between seizures. If they occur because of a problem somewhere else in the body, such as heart disease (which stops oxygen reaching the brain), this is not epilepsy.

Seizures are not uncommon; however, many dogs only ever have one. If your dog has had more than one, it may be that he is epileptic. Anyone who has witnessed their dog having a seizure knows how frightening it can be. The good news is that, just as with people, there are medications to control epilepsy in dogs, allowing them to live happy lives with normal lifespans.

Symptoms

Some dogs seem to know when they are about to have a seizure and may behave in a certain way. You will come to recognise these signs as meaning that an episode is likely. Often dogs just seek out their owner's company and come to sit beside them. There are two main types of seizure:

❖ **Petit Mal**, also called a Focal or Partial Seizure, which is the lesser of the two as it only affects one half of the brain. This may involve facial twitching, staring into space with a fixed glaze and/or upward eye movement, walking as if drunk, snapping at imaginary flies, and/or running or hiding for no reason. Sometimes this is accompanied by urination. The dog is conscious throughout

❖ **Grand Mal,** or Generalised Seizure, affects both hemispheres of the brain and is more often what we think of when we talk about a seizure. Most dogs become stiff, fall onto their side and make running movements with their legs. Sometimes they will cry out and may lose control of their bowels, bladder or both

 With Grand Mal the dog is unconscious once the seizure starts – he cannot hear or respond to you. While it is distressing to watch, the dog is not in any pain - even if howling.

It's not uncommon for an episode to begin as Petit Mal, but progress into Grand Mal. Sometimes, the progression is pretty clear - there may be twitching or jerking of one body part that gradually increases in intensity and progresses to include the entire body – other times the progression happens very fast.

 Most seizures last between one and three minutes - it is worth making a note of the time the seizure starts and ends – or record it on your phone because it often seems to go on for a lot longer than it actually does.

If you are not sure whether or not your dog has had a seizure, look on YouTube, where there are many videos of dogs having epileptic seizures.

Dogs behave in different ways afterwards. Some just get up and carry on with what they were doing, while others appear dazed and confused for up to 24 hours afterwards. Most commonly, dogs will be disorientated for only 10 to 15 minutes before returning to their old self.

FACT Most seizures occur while the dog is relaxed and resting quietly, often in the evening or at night; it rarely happens during exercise. In a few dogs, seizures can be triggered by particular events or stress.

They often have a set pattern of behaviour that they follow - for example going for a drink of water or asking to go outside to the toilet. If your dog has had more than one seizure, you may well start to notice a pattern of behaviour that is typically repeated.

The most important thing is to **STAY CALM.** Remember that your dog is unconscious during the seizure and is not in pain or distressed. It is probably more distressing for you than for him. Make sure that he is not in a position to injure himself, for example by falling down the stairs, but otherwise do not try to interfere with him.

NEVER try to put your hand inside his mouth during a seizure or you are very likely to get bitten.

It is very rare for dogs to injure themselves during a seizure. Occasionally, they may bite their tongue and there may seem to be a lot of blood, but it's unlikely to be serious; your dog will not swallow his tongue.

If it goes on for a very long time (more than 10 minutes), his body temperature will rise, which can cause damage to the liver, kidneys or brain. In very extreme cases, some dogs may be left in a coma after severe seizures. Repeated seizures can cause cumulative brain damage, which can result in early senility (with loss of learned behaviour and housetraining, or behavioural changes).

When Should I Contact the Vet?

Generally, if your dog has a seizure lasting more than five minutes or is having them regularly, you should contact your vet. When your dog starts fitting, make a note of the time.

If he comes out of it within five minutes, allow him time to recover quietly before contacting your vet. It is far better for him to recover quietly at home rather than be bundled into the car right away.

If your dog does not come out of the seizure within five minutes, or has repeated seizures close together, contact your vet immediately, as he or she will want to see your dog as soon as possible. Call the vet before setting off to make sure there is someone who can help when you arrive.

The vet may need to run a range of tests to ensure that there is no other cause of the seizures. These may include blood tests, X-rays or an MRI scan of your dog's brain. If no other cause can be found, then a diagnosis of epilepsy may be made. If your Corgi already has epilepsy, remember these key points:

- Don't change or stop any medication without consulting your vet

- See your vet at least once a year for follow-up visits

- Be sceptical of *"magic cure"* treatments

Treatment

As yet, it is not possible to cure epilepsy, so medication is used to control seizures – in some cases even a well-controlled epileptic may have occasional fits. There are many drugs available; two of the most common are Phenobarbital and Potassium Bromide (some dogs can have negative results with Phenobarbital).

There are also a number of holistic remedies advertised, but we have no experience of them or any idea if any are effective.

FACT ❯ **Factors that have proved useful in some cases are: avoiding dog food containing preservatives, adding vitamins, minerals and/or enzymes to the diet and ensuring drinking water is free of fluoride.**

Each epileptic dog is an individual and a treatment plan will be designed specifically for yours, based on the severity and frequency of seizures and how he responds to different medications. Many epileptic dogs require a combination of one or more types of drug for best results.

Keep a record of events in your dog's life, note down dates and times of episodes and record when you have given medication. Each time you visit your vet, take this diary along with you so he or she can see how your dog has been since his last check-up. If seizures are becoming more frequent, it may be necessary to change the medication.

 Owners of epileptic dogs need patience and vigilance. Treatment success often depends on owners keeping a close eye on the dog and reporting any physical or behavioural changes to the vet.

It is also important that medication is given at the same time each day, as the dog becomes dependent on the levels of drug in his blood to control seizures. If a single dose of treatment is missed, blood levels can drop, which may be enough to trigger a seizure.

It is not common for epileptic dogs to stop having seizures altogether. However, provided your dog is checked regularly by your vet, *there is a good chance that he'll live a full and happy life; most epileptic dogs have far more good days than bad ones.*

LIVE *WITH* EPILEPSY NOT *FOR* EPILEPSY.

....

Endocrine and Hormones

The endocrine system comprises the glands and organs that make hormones and release them into the bloodstream so they can travel to tissues and organs all over the body.

Hormones are the body's chemicals and they control many of its processes, including metabolism, growth and development, emotions, energy levels - and even sleep and behaviour.

Sometimes the system goes a bit haywire and produces too much or too little of a certain hormone, resulting in a hormonal imbalance. Here we list a few of the main ones that affect the dog population in general.

Hypothyroidism (Low Thyroid)

Hypothyroidism is a fairly common hormonal disorder in dogs and is due to an under-active thyroid gland. The gland (located on either side of the windpipe in the dog's throat) does not produce enough of the hormone thyroid, which controls the speed of the metabolism. Dogs with very low thyroid levels have a slow metabolic rate.

It occurs mainly in dogs of either gender over the age of five. It is hard to diagnose as the symptoms are often non-specific and quite gradual in onset, and they may vary depending on breed and age. Most forms of hypothyroidism are diagnosed with a blood test and the OFA provides a registry for thyroid screening in the USA.

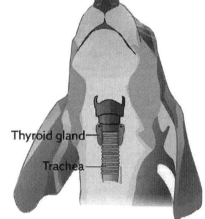

Common Symptoms

These have been listed in order, with the most common ones at the top:
- ❧ High blood cholesterol
- ❧ Lethargy
- ❧ Hair loss
- ❧ Weight gain or obesity
- ❧ Dry coat or excessive shedding
- ❧ Hyper pigmentation or darkening of the skin, seen in 25% of cases
- ❧ Intolerance to cold, seen in 15% of dogs with the condition

Treatment

Although hypothyroidism is a type of auto-immune disease that cannot be cured, symptoms are usually easily diagnosed with a blood test and treated.

The most commonly recommended treatment is a synthetic thyroid hormone replacement tablet of levothyroxine (Thyro-Tabs Canine, Synthroid). Blood samples are taken periodically to monitor him and adjust the dose accordingly. Once treatment has started, he will be on it for the rest of his life.

NOTE: **Hyper**thyroidism (as opposed to **hypo**thyroidism) is caused by the thyroid gland producing **too much** thyroid hormone. It is quite rare in dogs, more often seen in cats. A common symptom is the dog being ravenously hungry, but losing weight.

Cushing's Disease

This complex ailment, also known as *hyperadrenocorticism,* is caused when a dog produces too much Cortisol hormone. Often it is the gland that is over-producing the hormone, although Cushing's can also be caused by a tumour.

It develops over a period of time, which is why it is more often seen in middle-aged or senior dogs, usually over seven years of age in Corgis.

Cortisol is released by the adrenal gland near the kidneys. Normally it is produced during times of stress to prepare the body for strenuous activity. Think of an adrenaline rush. While this hormone is essential for the effective functioning of cells and organs, too much of it can be dangerous.

The disease can be difficult to diagnose, as the most common symptoms are similar to those for old age. A dog may display one or more:

* A ravenous appetite
* Drinking excessive amounts of water
* Urinating frequently or urinary incontinence
* Hair loss/thinning or recurring skin issues
* Lack of energy, general lethargy
* Pot belly
* Muscle wastage
* Insomnia
* Panting a lot

Cushing's Disease cannot be cured, but it can be successfully managed and controlled with medication, giving the dog a longer, happier life. Some dogs with mild symptoms do not require treatment, but should be closely monitored for signs of them worsening.

Lysodren (mitotane) or Vetoryl (trilostane) are usually prescribed by vets to treat the most common pituitary-dependent Cushing's disease. Both can have a number of side effects - so your dog needs monitoring - and the dog remains on the medication for life.

Addison's Disease

Addison's disease in dogs is also known as *hypoadrenocorticism* and is the opposite of the more common Cushing's disease. It occurs when the adrenal glands produce too **little** of the hormones cortisol and aldosterone, which helps regulate water and electrolytes in a dog's body.

Addison's more often affects young to middle-aged female dogs; however, a dog of any age and either sex can develop the disease. The causes are not yet known, although they are generally thought to be genetic, often related to autoimmune disorders.

The symptoms are similar to many other ailments, which makes diagnosis difficult and sometimes only arrived at by a process of elimination. This has earned Addison's the nicknames 'the Great Mimic' and 'the Great Imitator'. But once correctly diagnosed, it can be successfully treated and the dog can live a normal active life.

The symptoms can be vague and may initially simply appear as if the dog is off-colour. Here are some general signs to look out for: lethargy, lack of appetite, vomiting, diarrhoea, weight loss, tremors or shaking, muscle weakness or pain in the hindquarters

The most important thing to remember is that you know your dog better than anyone, so if something seems not right, get it checked out by a vet.

Diagnosis is confirmed by a blood test called the ACTH stimulation test. However, because the disease is not very common and has a wide variety of symptoms, the test is usually done after several other tests have been done to eliminate more common diseases.

Treatment

One effective option is the injection about every 25 days of Percorten-V (DOCP), which may be supplemented with an oral medication. DOCP is not for every dog, and some Addison's patients do best just on an oral medications such as Florinef.

In addition, the cortisol, or glucocorticoids, must also be replaced. This is typically done with a low dose of prednisone, *pictured,* or hydrocortisone given orally.

An affected dog will need medication and monitoring for the rest of his life, but the good news is that the vast majority have a good to excellent prognosis once it has been diagnosed and they are receiving the right medications.

The dog's diet and activity levels can often remain unchanged.

Diabetes

Diabetes can affect dogs of all breeds, sizes and both genders, and obese dogs are particularly prone to it. There are two types:

* *Diabetes insipidus* is caused by a lack of vasopressin, a hormone that controls the kidneys' absorption of water

* *Diabetes mellitus* occurs when the dog's body does not produce enough insulin and therefore cannot successfully process sugars

Dogs, like us, get their energy by converting the food they eat into sugars, mainly glucose. This travels in the bloodstream and then, using a protein called *insulin,* cells remove some of the glucose from the blood to use for energy.

Most diabetic dogs have Type 1 diabetes; their pancreas does not produce any insulin. Without it, the cells can't use the glucose that is in the bloodstream, so they *"starve"* while the glucose level in the blood rises.

Diabetes mellitus (sugar diabetes) is the most common form and affects mostly middle-aged and older dogs. Both males and females can develop it, although unspayed females have a slightly higher risk. Vets take blood and urine samples in order to diagnose diabetes. Early treatment helps to prevent further complications developing.

 The condition is treatable and need not shorten a dog's lifespan or interfere greatly with quality of life. Due to advances in veterinary science, diabetic dogs undergoing treatment now have the same life expectancy as non-diabetic dogs of the same age and gender.

Symptoms of Diabetes Mellitus:

- Extreme thirst
- Excessive urination
- Weight loss
- Increased appetite
- Coat in poor condition
- Lethargy
- Vision problems due to cataracts

If left untreated, diabetes can lead to cataracts or other ailments. Treatment and Exercise

It is EXTREMELY IMPORTANT that Corgis are not allowed to get overweight, as obesity is a major trigger for diabetes.

 Many cases of canine diabetes can be successfully treated with a combination of a diet low in sugar, fat and carbs (a raw diet is worth considering), alongside a moderate and consistent exercise routine and medication. More severe cases may require insulin injections.

In the newly-diagnosed dog, insulin therapy begins at home after a vet has explained how to prepare and inject insulin. Normally, after a week of treatment, you return to the vet for a series of blood sugar tests over a 12 to 14-hour period to see when the blood glucose peaks and troughs.

Adjustments are made to the dosage and timing of the injections. You may also be asked to collect urine samples using a test strip of paper that indicates the glucose levels.

 If your dog is already having insulin injections, beware of a "miracle cure" offered on the internet. It does not exist. There is no diet or vitamin supplement that can reduce a dog's dependence on insulin injections, because vitamins and minerals cannot do what insulin does in the dog's body.

If you think that your dog needs a supplement, discuss it with your vet first to make sure that it does not interfere with any other medication.

Exercise burns up blood glucose the same way that insulin does. If your dog is on insulin, any active exercise on top of the insulin might cause him to have a severe low blood glucose episode, called *"hypoglycaemia."*

Keep your dog on a reasonably consistent exercise routine. Your usual insulin dose will take that amount of exercise into account. If you plan to take your dog out for some demanding exercise, such as running around with other dogs, you may need to reduce his usual insulin dose.

Tips

- ❖ Specially-formulated diabetes dog food is available from most vets

- ❖ Feed the same type and amount of food at the same times every day

- ❖ Most vets recommend twice-a-day feeding for diabetic pets (it's OK if your dog prefers to eat more often)

- ❖ Help your dog to achieve the best possible blood glucose control by NOT feeding table scraps or treats between meals

- ❖ Watch for signs that your dog is starting to drink more water than usual. Call the vet if you see this happening, as it may mean that the insulin dose needs adjusting

Food raises blood glucose - Insulin and exercise lower blood glucose - Keep them in balance

For more information visit www.caninediabetes.org

....

The Heart

Just as with humans, heart issues are relatively common among the canine population in general.

The heart is a mechanical pump. It receives blood in one half and forces it through the lungs, then the other half pumps the blood through the entire body.

Heart failure, or *Congestive Heart Failure (CHF)*, occurs when the heart is not able to pump blood around the dog's body properly. One disorder that can affect Corgis is *Dilated Cardiomyopathy (DCM)*, also known as *enlarged heart, pictured.*

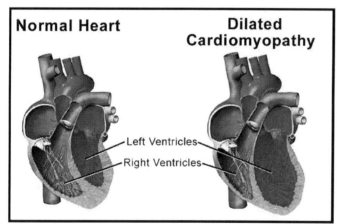

The ventricles, or heart chambers, become larger and the cardiac muscle surrounding them becomes thinner, causing the heart to change shape.

This then restricts muscle contractions and the effectiveness of the valves, which can lead to irregular heartbeats and the backflow or leakage of blood through the valves.

In people, heart disease usually involves the arteries that supply blood to the heart muscle becoming hardened over time, causing the heart muscles to receive less blood than they need. Starved of oxygen, the result is often a heart attack.

FACT ❯ In dogs, hardening of the arteries (arteriosclerosis) and heart attacks are very rare. However, heart disease is quite common, and in dogs it is often seen as heart failure, which means that the muscles "give out."

This is usually caused by one chamber or side of the heart being required to do more than it is physically able to do. It may be that excessive force is required to pump the blood through an area and over time the muscles fail.

Unlike a heart attack in humans, *heart failure in a dog is a slow process* that occurs over months or years. Once symptoms appear, they usually worsen over time until the dog requires treatment.

Symptoms and Treatment

- ❧ Tiredness

- ❧ Decreased activity levels

- ❧ Restlessness, pacing around instead of settling down to sleep

- ❧ Intermittent coughing - during exertion or excitement, at night or when he wakes up in the morning - in an attempt to clear the lungs

As the condition progresses, other symptoms may appear:

- ❧ Lack of appetite

- ❧ Rapid breathing

- ❧ Abdominal swelling (due to fluid)

- ❧ Noticeable loss of weight

- ❧ Fainting (syncope)

- ❧ Paleness

A vet will carry out tests that may include listening to the heart, chest X-rays, blood tests, electrocardiogram (a record of your dog's heartbeat) or an echocardiogram.

If the heart problem is due to an enlarged heart or valve disease, the condition cannot be reversed.

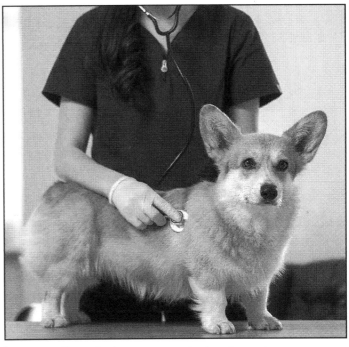

Treatment focuses on managing exercise and various medications, which may change over time as the condition progresses. The vet may also prescribe a special low salt diet, as sodium determines the amount of water in the blood.

There is some evidence that fatty acids and other supplements may be beneficial for a heart condition; discuss this with your vet.

The prognosis for dogs with congestive heart failure depends on the cause and severity, as well as their response to treatment.

A dog can't recover from congestive heart failure, but once diagnosed, he can live a longer, more comfortable life with the right medication and regular check-ups.

The prognosis for dogs with congestive heart failure depends on the cause and severity, as well as their response to treatment. A dog can't recover from congestive heart failure, but once diagnosed, he can live a longer, more comfortable life with the right medication and regular check-ups.

Tip **Pay attention to your Corgi's weight and oral health, as obesity and dental problems can increase the risk of heart disease.**

NOTE: There is a growing discussion as to whether diet can be a trigger for DCM. You can read more here: www.whole-dog-journal.com/food/diet-dogs-and-dcm

PDA (Patent Ductus Arteriosus)

This is one of the most common birth defects in dogs and Corgis are thought to be at a higher risk than some other breeds, but it's still fairly rare.

In the foetus (unborn puppy), the Ductus Arteriosis (DA) is a blood vessel which bypasses the lungs to circulate oxygen until birth. *Patent* in medical terms means *failing to close*.

At birth the lungs take over and the DA naturally closes within the first week of life. With PDA, the DA fails to close and blood continues to be diverted to the lungs rather than the body in the opposite direction to how blood flowed when in the womb.

This is often referred to as a *left-to-right shunt.* The heart then has to work much harder than normal to deliver oxygen-rich blood around the body.

Diagnosis and Treatment

A vet uses a stethoscope to carefully listen to heart and lung sounds. Normally, the heartbeat has two sounds – *lub dub.* A murmur is a swishing sound heard when there is turbulent blood flow across a heart valve or through an abnormal conduit like a PDA.

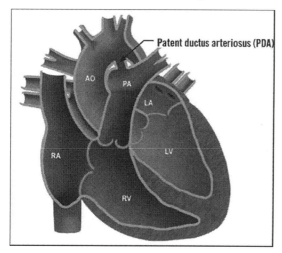

Dogs with PDAs have a characteristic murmur that sounds like a washing machine. It is often called a *continuous or machinery murmur.* X-rays, ECG and echocardiogram (ultrasound) will follow.

Some dogs develop breathing problems and start to fail because their hearts are working too hard, while others don't have any symptoms associated with PDA; they just have a heart murmur.

Surgery should be performed as soon as possible – without treatment two in three puppies die before one year age.

Early correction of a PDA (generally before five months of age) usually results in a normal life for the dog.

VCA Animal Hospitals says: "Provided that the condition is treated before heart failure develops, the success rate associated with surgical closure is very high and the prognosis for a normal life after surgery is excellent.

"If irreversible heart damage was already present before surgery, the dog may require heart medication in the future."

There are two possible procedures:

* Surgical Ligation, where the PDA is tied off – this involves major heart surgery
* Coil/Vascular Plug or Ductor Device – this is less invasive

Coil embolization is a specialist technique where a coil is inserted via a catheter (narrow tube) through an artery in the neck or hind leg and into the PDA. Small clots gradually form on the coil and block it. Vascular plugs or doctor devices perform a similar task.

Heart Murmurs

Heart murmurs are not uncommon in dogs and are one of the first signs that something may be amiss. One of our dogs was diagnosed with a Grade 2 murmur several years ago and, of course, your heart sinks when the vet gives you the terrible news.

But once the shock is over, it's important to realise that there are several different severities of the condition and, at its mildest, it is no great cause for concern. Our dog lived an active, healthy life and died at the age of 13.

Literally, a heart murmur is a specific sound heard through a stethoscope, which results from the blood flowing faster than normal within the heart itself or in one of the two major arteries. Instead of the normal **lub dub** noise, an additional sound can be heard that can vary from a mild *"pshhh"* to a loud **whoosh.** The different grades are:

- ❧ **Grade 1** - barely audible
- ❧ **Grade 2** - soft, but easily heard with a stethoscope
- ❧ **Grade 3** - intermediate loudness; most murmurs that are related to the mechanics of blood circulation are at least Grade 3
- ❧ **Grade 4** - loud murmur that radiates widely, often including opposite side of chest
- ❧ **Grade 5 and Grade 6** - very loud, audible with the stethoscope barely touching the chest; the vibration is strong enough to be felt through the dog's chest wall

Murmurs are caused by a number of factors; it may be a problem with the heart valves or could be due to some other condition, such as hyperthyroidism, anaemia or heartworm.

In puppies, there are two major types of heart murmurs, often detected by a vet at the first or second vaccination visit. The most common type is called an innocent *"flow murmur."*

This type of murmur is soft - typically Grade 2 or less - and is not caused by underlying heart disease. An innocent flow murmur typically disappears by four to five months of age. However, if a puppy has a loud murmur - Grade 3 or louder - or if it is still easily heard with a stethoscope after four or five months of age, it's more likely that the pup has an underlying heart problem.

The thought of a puppy having congenital heart disease is worrying, but it is important to remember that the disease will not affect all puppies' life expectancy or quality of life.

Canine Cancer

This is the biggest single killer and will claim the lives of one in four dogs, regardless of breed. It is the cause of nearly half the deaths of all dogs aged 10 years and older, according to the American Veterinary Medical Association.

As with all breeds, many different types of cancer that have been reported in Corgis. Some of the more common include: Hemangiosarcoma, Lymphoma, Mammary, Nose and Mouth Tumours.

Hemangiosarcoma is an aggressive cancer of the blood vessel walls, most commonly found in the spleen, heart or liver, and can affect dogs of any age. Symptoms include:

- ❧ Pale gums
- ❧ Disorientation, tiredness or collapse
- ❧ Lack of appetite
- ❧ Rapid breathing

❀ Extreme thirst

Unfortunately, Hemangiosarcoma has a high mortality rate. Affected dogs can die from internal bleeding or the cancer spreading to other parts of the body. However, in some cases if the cancer is in the spleen and discovered early, the spleen may be removed before the malignant cells spread to other organs.

Lymphoma is one of the more common canine cancers. It is a blanket term used to describe more than 30 types of canine cancer that stem from **lymphocytes,** a type of white blood cell that helps the immune system fight infection.

They are highly concentrated in organs that play a role in the immune system, like the lymph nodes, spleen and bone marrow. While lymphoma can affect any organ in the body, these organs tend to be where most lymphoma cancers are found.

Multicentric lymphoma is by far the most common of these types: 80-85% of all lymphomas. This type causes swelling of the lymph nodes, which are located under the chin, on either side of the neck, behind the knees on the back legs, armpits, chest and groin.

Other symptoms are lethargy, fever, anorexia, weakness and dehydration, and diagnosis is usually made by doing a biopsy (taking a tiny sample) of the affected organ.

Treatment normally involves chemotherapy and the prognosis (outlook) varies from one dog to another: which organs are affected, how far the disease has progressed are two factors. It is true to say that outcomes have improved dramatically with the advancement of veterinary science.

Other Cancers

Typical symptoms of other types of cancer include:

❀ Swellings anywhere on the body or around the anus

❀ Sores that don't heal

❀ Weight loss

❀ Lameness, which may be a sign of bone cancer, with or without a visible lump

❀ Laboured breathing

❀ Changes in exercise or stamina level

❀ Change in bowel or bladder habits

❀ Increased drinking or urination

❀ Bad breath, which can be a sign of oral cancer

❀ Poor appetite, difficulty swallowing or excessive drooling

❀ Vomiting

FACT ❯ There is evidence that the risk of mammary, testicular and uterine cancers decreases after neutering and spaying. However, recent studies also show that EARLY neutering may affect development in some breeds. See Chapter 16. The Facts of Life for more detailed information.

Treatment and Reducing the Risk

Just because your dog has a skin growth doesn't always mean that it's serious. Many older dogs develop fatty lumps *(lipomas)* which are often harmless, but it's still advisable to have the first one checked.

Your vet will make a diagnosis following an X-ray, scan, blood test, biopsy or a combination of these.

If your dog is diagnosed with cancer, there is hope. Advances in veterinary medicine and technology offer various treatment options, including chemotherapy, radiation and surgery. Unlike with humans, a dog's hair does not fall out with chemotherapy.

We had a happy ending. We had a four-year-old dog who develop a lump like a black grape on his anus. We took him down to the vet within a day or so of first noticing it and got the dreaded diagnosis of T-cell lymphoma, a particularly aggressive form of cancer.

The vet removed the lump a couple of days later and the dog went on to live into his teens.

 Every time you groom your dog, get into the habit of checking his body for lumps and bumps. Lift his top lip to check for signs of paleness or whiteness in the gums. As with any illness, early detection often leads to a better outcome.

We have all become aware of the risk factors for human cancer: stopping smoking, protecting ourselves from over-exposure to strong sunlight and eating a healthy, balanced diet all help to reduce cancer rates.

We know to keep a close eye on ourselves, go for regular health checks and report any lumps to our doctors as soon as they appear.

The same is true with your dog.

The outcome depends on the type of cancer, treatment used and, importantly, how early the tumour is found. The sooner treatment begins, the greater the chances of success.

While it is impossible to completely prevent cancer, the following points can help to reduce the risk:

❧ Feed a healthy diet with few or no preservatives

❧ Don't let your Corgi get overweight

❧ Consider dietary supplements, such as antioxidants, Vitamins, A, C, E, beta carotene, lycopene or selenium, or coconut oil – check compatibility with any other treatments

❧ Give pure, filtered or bottled water (fluoride-free) for drinking

❧ Give your dog regular daily exercise

❧ Keep your dog away from chemicals, pesticides, cleaning products, etc. around the garden and home

❧ Avoid passive smoking

❧ Consider natural flea remedies (check they are working) and avoid unnecessary vaccinations

- ❖ Check your dog regularly for lumps and any other physical or behavioural changes
- ❖ If you are buying a puppy, ask whether there is any history of cancer among the ancestors

Canine cancer research is currently being conducted all over the world, and medical advances are producing a steady flow of new tests and treatments to improve survival rates and cancer care.

....

With thanks to Linda Roberts and The Welsh Corgi League, Karen Hewitt and The Cardigan Welsh Corgi Association, Dr Marianne Dorn, the Rehab Vet, and Dr Jerold S. Bell for assistance with this chapter.

NOTE: Vaccinations, dental issues, parasites, allergies, skin problems, food sensitivities, spaying and neutering are covered in other chapters.

Disclaimer: The author is not a vet. This chapter is intended to give owners an outline of some of the main health issues and symptoms that may affect their Corgi(s). If you have any concerns regarding your dog's health, our advice is always the same: consult a veterinarian

14. Corgi Skin & Allergies

Visit any busy veterinary clinic these days – especially in spring and summer – and you'll see itchy dogs. Skin conditions, allergies and intolerances are on the increase in the canine world as well as the human one. While Corgis generally have few allergies, some individuals can have them and be susceptible to skin issues.

....

How many children did you hear of having asthma or a peanut allergy when you were at school? Not too many, I'll bet. Yet allergies and adverse reactions are now relatively common – and it's the same with dogs.

The reasons are not clear; it could be connected to genetics, diet, environment, over-vaccination – or a combination. As yet, there is no clear scientific evidence to back this up.

The skin is a complicated topic and a whole book could be written on this subject alone. While many dogs have no problems at all, some suffer from sensitive, itchy, dry or oily skin, hot spots, bald spots, yeast infections or other skin disorders, causing them to scratch, bite or lick themselves excessively. Symptoms vary from mild itchiness to a chronic reaction.

Canine Skin

The skin is the dog's largest organ. It acts as the protective barrier between your dog's internal organs and the outside world; it also regulates temperature and provides the sense of touch. Surprisingly, a dog's skin is actually thinner than ours, and it is made up of three layers:

1. **Epidermis** or outer layer, the one that bears the brunt of your dog's contact with the outside world.

2. **Dermis** is the extremely tough layer mostly made up of collagen, a strong and fibrous protein. This is where blood vessels deliver nutrients and oxygen to the skin, and it also acts as your dog's thermostat by allowing her body to release or retain heat, depending on the outside temperature and your dog's activity level.

3. **Hypodermis** is a dense layer of fatty tissue that allows your dog's skin to move independently from the muscle layers below it, as well as providing insulation and support for the skin.

 **FACT** ❯ Human allergies often trigger a reaction within the respiratory system, causing us to wheeze or sneeze, whereas allergies or hypersensitivities in a dog often cause a reaction in her SKIN.

❧ Skin can be affected from the **INSIDE** by things that your dog eats or drinks

❧ Skin can be affected from the **OUTSIDE** by fleas, parasites, or inhaled and contact allergies triggered by grass, pollen, man-made chemicals, dust, mould, etc.

None of the breeders involved in this book has had a problem with allergies, and most Corgis can run through fields, dig holes and roll around in the grass with no after-effects. This shouldn't be surprising; after all, they were originally bred as herders and were expected to run though the countryside for hours on end.

Their dense double coats are so effective at keeping out the cold and wet. However, they can also be very good at trapping allergens, causing an allergic reaction in a few Corgis. This may result in itching, hot spots, bald patches or recurring ear infections.

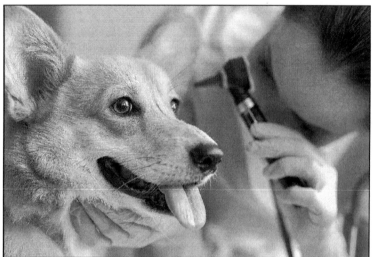

Similarly, most Corgis can eat pretty much anything and everything with no issues at all, while owners of others spend a lot of time trying to find the magic bullet – the ideal food for their Corgi's sensitive stomach.

It's by no means possible to cover all of the issues and causes in this chapter. The aim here is to give a broad outline of some of the more common ailments and how to deal with them.

We have also included remedies tried with some success by ourselves (we had a dog with skin issues) and other owners of affected dogs, as well as advice from a holistic specialist. This information is not intended to take the place of professional help; always contact your vet if your dog appears physically unwell or uncomfortable. This is particularly true with skin conditions:

 SEEK TREATMENT AS SOON AS POSSIBLE. If you can find the cause(s) early, you reduce the chances of it taking hold and causing secondary issues and infections.

Whatever the cause, before a vet can make a diagnosis, you'll have to give details of your dog's diet, exercise regime, habits, medical history and local environment. The vet will then carry out a physical examination, possibly followed by further tests, before a course of treatment can be prescribed.

One of the difficulties with skin ailments is that the exact cause is often difficult to diagnose, as the symptoms are similar to other issues.

If environmental allergies are involved, specific and expensive tests are available. You'll have to take your vet's advice on this, as the tests are not always conclusive. And if the answer is pollen, it can be difficult - if not downright impossible - to keep your dog away from the triggers. You can't keep a Corgi permanently indoors, so it's often a question of managing rather than curing the condition.

FACT ❯ There are many things you as an owner can do to reduce the allergen load – and many natural remedies and supplements that can help as well as veterinary medications.

Types of Allergies

"Canine dermatitis" means inflammation of a dog's skin and it can be triggered by numerous things, but the most common is allergies. Vets estimate that as many as one in four dogs they see has some kind of allergy. Symptoms are (your dog may have one or more of these):

* Chewing, most commonly the feet or belly
* Itchy ears, head shaking
* Rubbing her face on the floor
* Scratching
* Scratching or biting the anus
* Hair loss
* Flaky or greasy skin, perhaps with sore or discoloured patches or hot spots
* The skin can smell of corn chips

Corgis who are allergic to something show it through skin problems and itching; your vet may call this *"pruritus."* It may seem logical that if dogs are allergic to something inhaled, like certain pollen grains, their nose will run; if allergic to something eaten, they may vomit, or if allergic to an insect bite, they may develop a swelling. But in practice this is seldom the case.

Dogs with allergies often chew their feet until they are sore and red. You may see yours rubbing her face on the carpet or couch, or scratching her belly and flanks.

Because the ear glands produce too much wax in response to the allergy, ear infections can occur - with bacteria and yeast (which is a fungus) often thriving in the excessive wax and debris.

Digestive health can play an important role. Holistic vet Dr Jodie Gruenstern says: "It's estimated that up to 80% of the immune system resides within the gastrointestinal system; building a healthy gut supports a more appropriate immune response.

"The importance of choosing fresh proteins and healthy fats over processed, starchy diets (such as kibble) can't be overemphasized. Grains and other starches have a negative impact on gut health, creating insulin resistance and inflammation."

Allergic dogs may cause skin lesions or *hot spots* by constant chewing and scratching. Sometimes they will lose hair, which can be patchy, leaving a mottled appearance, or the coat may change colour. The skin itself may be dry and crusty, reddened, swollen or oily, depending on the dog. It is common to get secondary bacterial skin infections due to these self-inflicted wounds.

An allergic dog's body is reacting to certain molecules called *allergens.* These may come from:

* Tree, grass or plant pollens
* Flea bites
* Grain mites

- ❖ Specific food or food additives, such as cooked or raw meat or poultry, grains, colourings or preservatives
- ❖ Milk products
- ❖ Fabrics, such as wool or nylon
- ❖ Rubber and plastics
- ❖ House dust and dust mites
- ❖ Mould
- ❖ Chemical products used around the home or garden

FACT ❯ These allergens may be INHALED as the dog breathes, INGESTED as the dog eats, or caused by CONTACT with the dog's body when walking or rolling.

Regardless of how they arrive, they all cause the immune system to produce a protein called IgE, which releases irritating chemicals like histamine inside the skin, hence the scratching.

Managing allergies is all about **REDUCING THE ALLERGEN LOAD.**

Inhalant Allergies (Atopy)

Some of the most common allergies are inhalant and seasonal - at least at first; some allergies may develop and worsen. Look at the timing of the reaction. Does it happen all year round? If so, this may be mould, dust or some other permanent trigger. If the reaction is seasonal, then pollens may well be the culprit.

There is a serum test called **VARL Liquid Gold** widely used in the USA. A simple blood sample is taken and tested for reactions to different types of pollen in your area, other environmental triggers and food. VARL claims it's at least as effective as the more intrusive **intradermal skin testing** (around 75%), which involves sedating the dog, injecting a small amount of antigen into the skin and then inspecting it for an allergic reaction.

They say a further advantage is that it does not give false positives. Depending on the results, treatment may involve avoidance or an immunotherapy programme consisting of a series of injections or tablets. A similar serum test called **Avacta** is used by vets in the UK.

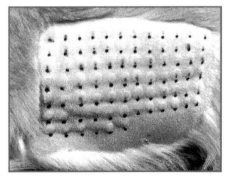
Our photo shows a Golden Retriever that has undergone intradermal skin testing. This dog was tested for over 70 allergens, which is a lot. The injections are in kits. If you consider this option, ask the vet or specialist how many allergens are in the kit.

Other blood tests work by checking for antibodies caused by antigens. The two standard tests are **RAST** and **ELISA**. Many vets feel that the ELISA test gives more accurate results, although both can give false positives.

Some owners of dogs with allergies consider changing to an unprocessed diet (raw or cooked) and natural alternatives to long-term use of steroids, which can cause other health issues.

Environmental or Contact Irritations

These are a direct reaction to something the dog physically comes into contact with, and the triggers are similar to inhalant allergies. If grass or pollen is the issue, the allergies are often seasonal. An affected dog may be given treatments such as tablets, shampoo or localised cortisone spray for spring and summer - with a steroid injection to control a flare-up - but be perfectly fine the rest of the year. This was the case with our dog with allergies.

It's a bit of a nightmare if your Corgi does develop environmental or contact allergies as you are not going to stop them going into the pollen-laden Great Outdoors. However, there's plenty you can do to reduce the symptoms.

 If you suspect your Corgi has outdoor contact allergies, rinse them down after walks. Washing their feet and belly will get rid of some of the pollen and other allergens, which in turn reduces scratching and biting. Try them on a natural, unprocessed diet and reduce chemicals around the house and garden.

The problem may be localised - such as the paws or belly. Symptoms are a general skin irritation or specific hotspots - itching (pruritus) and sometimes hair loss. Readers of our website sometimes report that their dog will incessantly lick or try to lick one part of the body, often the paws, anus, belly or back.

Flea Bite Allergy

This is a common allergy affecting lots of dogs. It's typically seasonal, worse during summer and autumn - peak time for fleas - and in warmer climates where fleas are prevalent. Unfortunately, some dogs with a flea allergy also have inhalant allergies.

This allergy is not to the flea itself, but to proteins in flea saliva left under the dog's skin when the insect feeds. Just one bite to an allergic dog will cause red, crusty bumps *(pictured)* and intense itching.

Affected dogs usually have a rash at the base of their tails and rear legs, and will bite and scratch the area. Much of the skin damage is done by the dog's scratching, rather than the flea bite, and can result in hair falling out or skin abrasions.

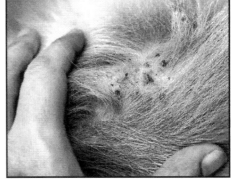

Some dogs also develop hot spots, often along the base of the tail and back.

A vet can make a diagnosis with a simple blood test. If fleas are the cause, you'll also have to make sure your dog's bedding and your home are flea-free zones.

Most flea bite allergies can be treated with medication, but they can only be totally prevented by keeping all fleas away from the dog. Various flea prevention treatments are available – see the section on **Parasites**.

Acute Moist Dermatitis (Hot Spots)

A hot spot can appear suddenly and is a raw, inflamed and often bleeding area of skin. The area becomes moist and painful and begins spreading due to continual licking and chewing. They can become large, red, irritated lesions in a short pace of time. The cause is often a local reaction to an insect bite.

 Some owners have had good results after dabbing hot spots, interdigital cysts and other skin irritations with an equal mixture of the amber-coloured Listerine Original *(pictured)*, baby oil and water. US owners have also reported success with Gold Bond Powder.

Once diagnosed and with the right treatment for the underlying cause, hot spots often disappear as soon as they appeared. Treatments may come in the form of injections, tablets or creams – or a combination of all three. The affected area is first clipped and cleaned by the vet.

Bacterial infection (Pyoderma)

Pyoderma literally means **pus in the skin** (yuk)! The offending bacteria is staphylococcus, and the condition may also be referred to as a **staph infection.** Early signs are itchy red spots filled with yellow pus, similar to pimples or spots in humans. They can sometimes develop into red, ulcerated

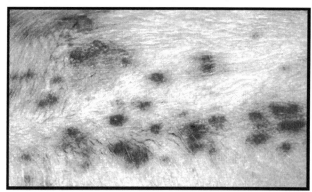

skin with dry and crusty patches. Fortunately, the condition is not contagious.

Pyoderma is caused by several things: a broken skin surface, a skin wound due to chronic exposure to moisture, altered skin bacteria, or poor blood flow to the skin.

Allergies to fleas, food, parasites, yeast or fungal skin infections, thyroid disease, hormonal imbalances, heredity and some medications can all increase the risk.

FACT One of the biggest causes of infection is a dog with a skin disorder excessively licking or biting an itchy patch.

Puppies can develop **puppy pyoderma** in thinly-haired areas, such as the groin and underarms. If you notice symptoms, get to the vet quickly before the condition develops from **superficial pyoderma** into **severe pyoderma**, which is very unpleasant and takes a lot longer to treat.

Superficial and puppy pyoderma are usually successfully treated with a two to six-week course of antibiotic tablets or ointment. Severe or recurring pyoderma looks awful, causes your dog some distress and can take months to completely cure.

Medicated shampoos and regular bathing, as instructed by your vet, are also part of the treatment. It's also important to ensure your dog has clean, dry, padded bedding. Bacterial infection, no matter how bad it may look, usually responds well to medical treatment.

Malassezia Dermatitis and Yeast Infections

Yeast infections affect many dogs, and Malassezia Dermatitis is a specific type. **Malassezia** is a yeast (fungus) that gets into the surface layers of the skin. These organisms cause no harm to the vast majority of animals, but cause inflammation in some dogs when numbers multiply.

Like all yeast infections, they like humid conditions - so climate can be a factor - and especially warm, damp areas on a dog's body like ear canals and skin folds. One trigger is saliva with repetitive licking – which explains why feet are often stained and itchy; saliva stains them and Malassezia grows. Corgis that already have poor skin condition, allergies or a hormonal disorder are more prone to Malassezia infection.

Symptoms are:

❖ Itchy, flaky skin at inflamed areas around the lips, ear canals, neck and armpits, between the toes and in skin folds on the face

❖ Greasy or flaky skin

- Unpleasant smell
- In long-term cases, the skin becomes thicker and darker
- Reddish-brown discolouration of the claws

The condition is easily diagnosed with a skin scraping and is often effectively treated with anti-fungal shampoos, wipes and creams, or tablets. If another skin disorder is causing the Malassezia to spread, this will have to be addressed to rid the dog of the problem.

Interdigital Cysts

If your Corgi gets a fleshy red lump between the toes that looks like an ulcerated sore or a hairless bump, then it's probably an interdigital cyst - or *interdigital furuncle*. These can be very difficult to cure as they are often not the main problem, but a symptom of some other ailment.

They are not cysts, but the result of *furunculosis*, a skin condition that clogs hair follicles and creates chronic infection. Causes include allergies, obesity, poor foot conformation, mites, yeast infections, ingrowing hairs or other foreign bodies.

 Bulldogs are the most susceptible breed, *see photo,* but any dog can get them - often the dog also has allergies.

These nasty-looking bumps are painful, will probably cause a limp and can be a nightmare to get rid of. Vets might recommend a whole range of treatments to get to the root cause, and it can be very expensive to have a barrage of tests or biopsies - even then you're not guaranteed to find the underlying cause.

Here are some remedies your vet may suggest:

- Antibiotics and/or steroids and/or mite killers
- Soaking the feet in Epsom salts
- Testing for allergies or thyroid problems
- Starting a food trial if food allergies are suspected
- Shampooing the feet
- Cleaning between the toes with medicated (benzoyl peroxide) wipes
- A referral to a veterinary dermatologist
- Surgery (this is a last-resort option)

If you suspect your Corgi has an interdigital cyst, visit the vet as soon as possible for a correct diagnosis and to discuss the various options. A course of antibiotics may be suggested initially, along with switching to a hypoallergenic diet if a food allergy is suspected.

If the condition persists, many owners get discouraged, especially when treatment continues for several weeks.

 Be wary of agreeing to a series of steroid injections or repeated courses of antibiotics, as this means that the underlying cause of the furuncle has not been diagnosed. In such cases, it is worth exploring natural diets and remedies – and trying to lower the overall allergen load on your dog.

Before you resort to any drastic action, first try soaking your Corgi's affected paw in Epsom salts for five or 10 minutes twice a day. After the soaking, clean the area with medicated wipes, which are antiseptic and control inflammation.

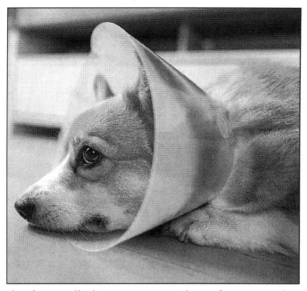

Surgery is a drastic option. Although it can be effective in solving the immediate issue it doesn't deal with the underlying problem. Interdigital cysts are not simple to deal with and it's important to **get the right diagnosis as soon as possible.**

If your dog has a skin issue - or surgical procedure - she may have to wear an E-collar, which is very stressful for everybody. No dog likes the cone, but it's especially difficult for an energetic dog like the Corgi.

Most Corgis hate the *"Cone of Shame"* - they may slump down like you've hung a 10-ton weight on their neck or sink into a depression. Even compliant dogs are miserable as they wander round banging into door frames and furniture. Fortunately, they don't usually have to wear them for more than a few days.

If your dog is resistant and the problem is with the paws, try putting socks on the affected area instead. This works well while they sleep, but you have to watch them like a hawk when they are awake to stop them biting.

An alternative to prevent dogs licking damaged skin on their bodies is an *inflatable comfy collar, pictured.*

 Anecdotally, some owners have reported that adding a spoonful of live yoghurt or a daily probiotic supplement to their dog's feed can improve the dog's gut health and help reduce allergic reactions and yeast infections.

Parasites

Demodectic Mange (Demodex)

Also known as red mange, follicular mange or puppy mange, this skin disease is caused by the tiny mite Demodex canis, *pictured.* The mites actually live inside the hair follicles on the bodies of virtually every adult dog and most humans without causing any harm or irritation.

In humans, the mites are found in the skin, eyelids and the creases of the nose...try not to think about that!

The mite spends its entire life on the host dog. Eggs hatch and mature from larvae to nymphs to adults in 20 to 35 days and the mites are transferred directly from the mother to the puppies within the first week of life by direct physical contact.

Demodectic mange is not a disease of poorly-kept or dirty dogs or kennels. It is generally a disease of young dogs with inadequate or poorly-developed immune systems - or older dogs suffering from a suppressed immune system.

Virtually every mother carries and transfers mites to her puppies, and most are immune to the mite's effects, but a few puppies are not and they develop full-blown mange. They may have a few (less than five) isolated lesions and this is known as *localised mange* – often around the head.

Puppy Mange is quite common, usually mild and often disappears on its own.

Generalised mange is more serious and covers the entire body or region of the body. Bald patches are usually the first sign, usually accompanied by crusty, red skin which sometimes appears greasy or wet. Usually hair loss begins around the muzzle, eyes and other areas on the head. The sores may or may not itch.

In localised mange a few circular crusty areas appear, most frequently on the head and front legs of three to six-month-old puppies. Most self-heal as the puppy becomes older and develops their own immunity, but a persistent problem should be treated.

Photo: A healthy Pembroke puppy with a good coat.

With generalised mange there are bald patches over the entire coat, including the head, neck, body, legs, and feet. The skin on the head, side and back is crusty, often inflamed and oozes a clear fluid.

The skin itself will often be oily to touch and there is usually a secondary bacterial infection. Some puppies can become quite ill and can develop a fever, lose their appetites and become lethargic.

If you suspect your puppy has generalised demodectic mange, get them to a vet straight away.

There is also a condition called *pododermatitis*, when the mange affects a puppy's paws. It can cause bacterial infections and be very uncomfortable, even painful. Symptoms include hair loss on the paws, swelling of the paws (especially around the nail beds) and red, hot or inflamed areas that are often infected. Treatment is always recommended and can take several rounds to clear it up.

Diagnosis and Treatment – The vet will make a diagnosis after he or she has taken a skin scraping or biopsy, in which case the mites can be seen with a microscope. As these mites are present on every dog, they do not mean that the dog necessarily has mange. Only when they are coupled with lesions will a diagnosis of mange be made. Treatment usually involves topical (on the skin) medication and sometimes tablets.

Traditional treatments for Demodex have included the FDA-approved heartworm drug Ivermectin, given at a higher dose as a tablet or liquid. For dogs that don't tolerate Ivermectin, including herding breeds, other treatments have included another heartworm medication, Milbemycin. Sometimes the anti-parasitic dip Mitaban has been dispensed as a last resort.

FACT ❯ All of these treatments can have side effects. Some dogs, especially Toy breeds, don't respond well to Mitaban as it can make them nauseous. Discuss treatment and other options fully with your vet.

The latest treatment to prove highly effective is *Bravecto,* given in chewable tablets. It not only gets rid of the mites, but also remains effective for 12 weeks following treatment. A bonus is that it is also effective against ticks and fleas during those 12 weeks.

One UK veterinarian added: "One very effective treatment for Demodex is Bravecto, recently licensed for this, and now the best one available."

Dogs with generalised mange may have underlying skin infections, so antibiotics are often given for the first several weeks of treatment. Because the mite flourishes on dogs with suppressed immune systems, try to get to the root cause of immune system disease, especially if your Corgi is older when she develops demodectic mange.

Sarcoptic Mange (Scabies)

Also known as canine scabies, this is caused by the parasite *Sarcoptes scabiei.* This microscopic mite can cause a range of skin problems, the most common of which is hair loss and severe itching.

The mites can infect other animals such as foxes, cats and even humans, but prefer to live their short lives on dogs. Fortunately, there are several good treatments and it can be easily controlled.

In cool, moist environments, the mites live for up to 22 days. At normal room temperature they live from two to six days, preferring to live on parts of the dog with less hair. Diagnosing canine scabies can be somewhat difficult, and it is often mistaken for inhalant allergies.

The vet will take a skin scraping to make a diagnosis and there are a number of effective treatments, including selamectin (Revolution – again, some dogs can have a reaction to this), an on-the-skin solution applied once a month which also provides heartworm prevention, flea control and some tick protection. Various Frontline products are also effective – check with your vet for the correct ones.

One product is the **Seresto Flea Collar,** *pictured,* which provides full body protection for up to eight months against all fleas, ticks, sarcoptic mange, lice and other bloodsucking critters! The collar is waterproof. There are also holistic remedies for many skin conditions.

Because your dog does not have to come into direct contact with an infected dog to catch scabies, it is difficult to completely protect her. Foxes and their environment can also transmit the mite.

> **Chemical flea and parasite treatments, such as Seresto, Bravecto, Comfortis, Nexgard, Frontline, Advantix, Trifexix, etc. can trigger epilespy, other neurological disorders or strange behaviour in a very small percentage of dogs.**
> **Do your research, talk to your vet and consider all options, including natural alternatives.**

Fleas

Most Corgis get regular outdoor exercise and so are more likely to pick up parasites such as fleas and ticks than couch potato breeds.

When you see your dog scratching and biting, your first thought is probably: *"She's got fleas!"* and you may well be right.

Fleas don't fly, but they do have very strong back legs and they will take any opportunity to jump from the ground or another animal into your Corgi's lovely, thick, warm coat. You can sometimes see the fleas if you part your dog's hair.

And for every flea that you see on your dog, there is the stomach-churning prospect of hundreds of eggs and larvae in your home.... So, if your dog gets fleas, you'll have to treat your environment as well as the dog in order to completely get rid of them.

The best form of cure is prevention.

Vets recommend giving dogs a preventative flea treatment every four to eight weeks – although the Seresto Flea Collar lasts for eight months.

If you do give a regular skin treatment, the frequency depends on your climate, the season - fleas do not breed as quickly in the cold - and how much time your Corgi spends outdoors.

To apply topical insecticides like Frontline and Advantix, part the skin and apply drops of the liquid on to a small area on your dog's back, usually near the neck. Some kill fleas and ticks, and others just kill fleas - check the details.

 It is worth spending the money on a quality treatment, as cheap brands may not rid your dog completely of fleas, ticks and other parasites. There are also holistic and natural alternatives to insecticides, discussed later in this chapter.

Some breeders are opposed to chemical flea treatments. One added that when she found a flea, she simply washes all of her dogs, one after the other, and then washes every last piece of bedding.

Ticks

A tick is not an insect, but a member of the arachnid family, like the spider. There are over 850 types, some have a hard shell and some a soft one. Ticks don't have wings, they crawl. They have a sensor called Haller's organ that detects smell, heat and humidity to help them locate food, which in some cases is a Corgi.

A tick's diet consists of one thing and one thing only – blood! They climb up onto tall grass and when they sense an animal is close, crawl on. Ticks can pass on a number of diseases to animals and humans, the most well-known of which is **Lyme Disease**.

Lyme Disease

This is a bacterial illness passed on to dogs by ticks once they have been on the dog's body for one to two days. The ticks that carry Lyme Disease are most likely to be found in woods, tall grasses, thick brush and marshy ground.

In the UK, Lyme Disease is more prevalent in wooded areas, and in the US almost all cases are from the Northeast, Upper Midwest and Pacific coast. Typical symptoms include:

* Fever
* Loss of appetite
* Reduced energy
* Lameness (can be shifting, intermittent, and recurring)
* Generalised stiffness, discomfort, or pain
* Swelling of joints

Treatment includes antibiotics, usually for at least 30 days, which often resolves the symptoms. But in severe cases Lyme Disease can progress to fatal kidney failure, and serious cardiac and neurological effects can also occur. Your dog can't pass Lyme Disease on to you or other pets, but a carrier tick could come into your house on your dog's fur and get on to you.

 If your Corgi spends a lot of time outdoors in woodland or other high-risk areas consider having them vaccinated against Lime Disease.

One breeder added: "If ticks are removed quickly, they're not harmful. We use a tick tool which has instructions in the packet. You put the forked end either side of the tick and twist it till it comes out."

If you are not sure how to get a tick out of your dog's coat, have it removed by a vet or other expert. Inexpertly pulling it out yourself and leaving a bit of the tick behind can be detrimental to your dog's health.

Heartworm

Although heartworm does not affect the skin, we have included it in this section as it is a parasite. Heartworm is a serious and potentially fatal disease affecting pets in North America and many other parts of the world, but not the UK.

It is present in Mediterranean countries, so check with your vet if you're intending taking your dog there. *Leishmaniasis* is another parasitic disease that UK dogs can pick up in Europe. It's transmitted by a biting sand flea and causes skin lesions or organ infection.

The foot-long heartworms live in the heart, lungs and blood vessels of affected animals, causing severe lung disease, heart failure and damage to organs. The dog is a natural host for heartworms, enabling the worms living inside a dog to mature into adults, mate and produce offspring. If untreated, their numbers can increase; dogs have been known to harbour several hundred worms in their bodies.

Untreated heartworm disease causes lasting damage to the heart, lungs and arteries, and can affect the dog's health and quality of life long after the parasites are gone. For this reason, **prevention is by far the best option** and treatment - when needed - should be administered as early as possible.

When a mosquito *(pictured)* bites and takes a blood meal from an infected dog, it picks up baby worms that develop and mature into *infective-stage* larvae over 10 to 14 days. Then, when it bites another dog, it spreads the disease.

Once inside a dog, it takes about six months for the larvae to develop into adult heartworms, which can then live for five to seven years in a dog. In the early stages, many dogs show few or no symptoms. The longer the infection persists, the more likely symptoms will develop, including:

- **A mild persistent cough**
- **Reluctance to exercise**
- **Tiredness after normal activity**
- **Decreased appetite and weight loss**

As the disease progresses, dogs can develop a swollen belly due to excess fluid in the abdomen and heart failure. Dogs with large numbers of heartworms can develop the life-threatening caval syndrome, which, without prompt surgery, is often fatal.

Although more common in the south eastern US, heartworm disease has been diagnosed in all 50 states. The American Heartworm Society recommends that you get your dog tested every year and give your dog heartworm preventive treatment for all 12 months of the year. If you live in a risk area, check that your tick and flea medication also prevents heartworm. In the UK, heartworm has only been found in imported dogs.

Ringworm

This is not actually a worm, but a fungus and is most commonly seen in puppies and young dogs. It is highly infectious and often found on the face, ears, paws or tail.

This fungus is most prevalent in hot, humid climates but, surprisingly, most cases occur in autumn and winter. But it is not that common; in one study of dogs with active skin problems, less than 3% had ringworm.

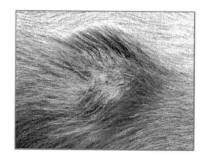

Ringworm, *pictured,* is transmitted by spores in the soil and by contact with the infected hair of dogs and cats, typically found on carpets, brushes, combs, toys and furniture.

Spores from infected animals can be shed into the environment and live for over 18 months, but most healthy adult dogs have some resistance and never develop symptoms. The fungi live in dead skin, hairs and nails - and the head and legs are the most common areas affected.

Tell-tale signs are bald patches with a roughly circular shape. Ringworm is relatively easy to treat with fungicidal shampoos or antibiotics from a vet.

 **Humans can catch ringworm from pets, and vice versa. Children are especially susceptible, as are adults with suppressed immune systems and those undergoing chemotherapy. Hygiene is extremely important.**

If your dog has ringworm, wear gloves when handling them and wash your hands well afterwards. And if a member of your family catches ringworm, make sure they use separate towels from everyone else or the fungus may spread.

As a teenager, I caught ringworm from horses at the local stables - much to my mother's horror - and was treated like a leper by the rest of the family until it cleared up!

Ear Infections

One of the Corgi's many advantages over some other breeds is that adult Pembrokes and Cardigans have pricked-up ears, *like this handsome Cardigan, pictured.*

This allows air to circulate more freely than in breeds with floppy ears and they are less likely to get ear infections. However, it doesn't mean that Corgis are completely immune to them.

Nearly all ear infections can be successfully managed if properly diagnosed and treated. But if an underlying problem remains undiscovered, the outcome will be less favourable.

Deep ear infections can damage or rupture the eardrum, causing an internal ear infection and even permanent hearing loss.

FACT **The fact that a dog has recurring ear infections does NOT necessarily mean that the ears are the issue – although they might be. If there is an underlying issue, it <u>must</u> be treated or the dog will continue to have ear infections.**

Dogs can have ear problems for many different reasons, including:

- Allergies, e.g. environmental or food allergies or intolerances
- Ear mites or other parasites
- Bacteria or yeast infections
- Injury, often due to excessive scratching
- Hormonal abnormalities, e.g. hypothyroidism
- Excess moisture in the ear
- Hereditary or immune conditions and tumours

Treatment depends on the cause and what - if any - other conditions your dog may have. Antibiotics are used for bacterial infections and antifungals for yeast infections.

Glucocorticoids, such as dexamethasone, are often included in these medications to reduce the inflammation in the ear. Your vet may also flush out and clean the ear with special drops, something you may have to do daily at home until the infection clears.

A dog's ear canal is L-shaped, which means it can be difficult to get medication into the lower (horizontal) part of the ear. The best method is to hold the dog's ear flap with one hand and put the ointment or drops in with the other, if possible, tilting the dog's head away from you, so the liquid flows downwards **with gravity**.

Make sure you then hold the ear flap down and massage the medication into the horizontal canal before letting go of your dog, as the first thing she will do is shake her head – and if the ointment or drops aren't massaged in, they will fly out.

Ear Cleaning

Check your Corgi's ears regularly - once every week or two weeks. Use a ball of damp cotton wool or baby wipe regularly to gently remove dirt and wax.

If your Corgi's ears look a bit waxy, you can also consider using an ear cleansing solution.

Squeeze a few drops of cleanser into the ear canal. Again, tilt your dog's head so the ear canal is pointing downwards, allowing gravity to help distribute the solution.

Massage the base of the ear for 15 seconds before allowing her to shake her head. Then dry the inside of the ear flap with cotton wool and gently wipe out any dirt and waxy build-up in the ear canal with cotton wool.

In both cases it is important to only clean as far down the ear canal as you can see to avoid damaging the eardrum. Keep your dog's ears clean and free from too much hair right from puppyhood and hopefully she will never get an ear infection. Visit YouTube to see videos of how to correctly clean without damaging them.

Canine ear cleaning solution is widely available, or you can use a mixture of water and white vinegar.

 When checking or cleaning your Corgi's ears, be very careful not to put anything too far down inside. DO NOT use cotton buds inside the ear, they are too small and can cause injury.

If your Corgi enjoys swimming or splashing about in water, towel dry the insides of the ears afterwards - and after bathing at home. There is more information in **Chapter 15. The Corgi Coat and Grooming.**

Nearly all ear infections can be successfully managed if properly diagnosed and treated. But if an underlying problem remains undiscovered, the outcome will be less favourable. Deep ear infections can damage or rupture the eardrum, causing an internal ear infection and even permanent hearing loss.

If your dog appears to be in pain, has smelly ears, or if their ear canals look inflamed, contact your vet straight away. If you can nip the first infection in the bud, there is a chance it will not return. If your dog has a ruptured or weakened eardrum, ear cleansers and medications could do more harm than good. Early treatment is the best way of preventing a recurrence.

 Ear infections are notoriously difficult to get rid of once your dog's had one, so prevention is better than cure. Check your Corgi's ears weekly when grooming, dry them after swimming and get the vet to check inside on routine visits.

Some Allergy Treatments

Treatments and success rates vary tremendously from dog to dog and from one allergy to another, which is why it is so important to consult a vet at the outset. Earlier diagnosis is more likely to lead to a successful treatment.

Some owners of dogs with recurring skin issues find that a course of antibiotics or steroids works wonders for their dog's sore skin and itching. However, the scratching starts all over again shortly after the treatment stops.

Food allergies require patience, a change or several changes of diet and maybe even a food trial, and the specific trigger is notoriously difficult to isolate – unless you are lucky and hit on the culprit straight away.

With inhalant and contact allergies, blood and skin tests are available, followed by *hyposensitisation* treatment (a series of vaccinations of the allergen(s) over weeks or months).

However, these are expensive and often the specific trigger for many dogs remains unknown. So, the reality for many owners of dogs with allergies is that they manage the condition, rather than curing it completely.

FACT ❭ While a single steroid injection is often highly effective in calming down symptoms almost immediately, frequent or long-term steroid use is not a good option as it can lead to serious side effects.

Our Experience With Max

According to our vet, Graham, more and more dogs are appearing in his waiting room with various types of allergies. Whether this is connected to how we breed or feed our dogs remains to be seen.

Our dog, Max, was perfectly fine until he was about two years old, when he began to scratch a lot. He scratched more in spring and summer, which meant that his allergies were almost certainly inhalant or contact-based and related to pollens, grasses or other outdoor triggers.

We decided not to have a lot of tests, not because of the cost (although they were not cheap), but because the vet said it was highly likely that he was allergic to pollens. Max was an active dog and if we'd had pollen allergy confirmed, we were not going to stop walking him two or three times a day.

Regarding medications, Max was at first put on to a tiny dose of Piriton *(pictured)*, a cheap antihistamine manufactured in the millions for canine and human hay fever sufferers. For the first few springs and summers, this worked well.

Allergies can change and a dog can build up a tolerance to a treatment, which is why they can be so difficult to treat. Max's symptoms changed from season to season, although the main ones were: general scratching, paw biting and ear infections.

One year he bit the skin under his tail a lot - he would jump around like he had been stung by a bee and bite frenetically. This was treated effectively with a single steroid injection, followed by spraying the area with cortisone once a day at home for a period. Localised spray can be very effective if the itchy area is small, but no good for spraying all over a dog's body.

Over the years we tried a number of treatments, all of which worked for a while, before he came off the medication in October when pollen levels fell. He was perfectly fine the rest of the year without any treatment at all.

Not every owner wants to treat his or her dog with chemicals, nor feed a diet that includes preservatives, which is why this book includes alternatives. Also, over a decade years ago, when we were starting out on the *"Allergy Trail,"* there were far fewer options than there are now.

We fed Max a high quality hypoallergenic dry food. If we were starting again from scratch, knowing what we know now, I'd look into a raw or home-cooked diet (which is what we fed him as he neared the end of his life in his teens), if necessary, in combination with holistic remedies.

One spring the vet put him on a short course of steroids, which were effective for a season, but steroids are not a long-term solution. Another year we were prescribed the non-steroid Atopica. The active ingredient is **cyclosporine**, which suppresses the immune system - some dogs can get side effects, although ours didn't.

The daily tablet was expensive, but initially extremely effective — so much so that we thought we had cured the problem completely. However, after a couple of seasons on cyclosporine he developed a tolerance to the drug and started scratching again. A few years ago, he went back on the antihistamine Piriton, a higher dose than when he was two years old, and this was effective.

Other Options

In 2013 the FDA approved **Apoquel** (oclacitinib) - *pictured* - to control itching and inflammation in allergic dogs. Like most allergy drugs, it acts by suppressing the immune system, rather than addressing the root cause.

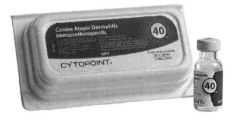

It has, however, proved to be highly effective in treating countless thousands of dogs with allergies. We used Apoquel with excellent results. There was some initial tweaking to get the daily dose right, but it proved highly effective.

The tablets are administered according to body weight — it's not cheap, but Apoquel can be a miracle worker for some dogs, including ours.

Side effects to Apoquel have been reported in some dogs. Holistic practitioners, Dogs Naturally magazine and others believe it can be harmful to the dog. Do your research.

Cytopoint, *pictured,* is another recent option that's proved to be highly effective for many dogs. It is given as an injection every four to eight weeks and starts working almost immediately. Dogs with seasonal allergies may only need the injections for part of the year.

FACT ▶ One added advantage of Cytopoint is that it is a biological therapy, not pharmaceutical, and does not suppress the dog's immune system. It contains engineered antibodies, similar to a dog's natural antibodies, which fight viruses and bacteria.

These antibodies have been specifically designed to target and neutralise a protein that sends itch signals to a dog's brain. This in turn helps to minimise scratching, giving the irritated skin chance to heal.

Allergies are often complex and difficult to treat; you should weigh up the pros and cons in the best interests of your own dog. Max's allergies were manageable; he loved his food, was full of energy and otherwise healthy, and lived a happy life into his teens. The Apoquel definitely helped him, but it's not for every dog.

Add fish oils, which contain Omega-3 fatty acids, to a daily feed to keep your dog's skin and coat healthy all year round – whether or not she has problems. A liquid supplement called Yuderm, *pictured,* (formerly Yumove Itchy Dog), which contains Omegas 3 and 6, golden flax and borage, is a good choice to add to your dog's daily feeds all year round.

When the scratching got particularly bad, we also bathed Max in an antiseborrheic shampoo twice a week for a limited time. This helped, although was not necessary once on Apoquel. Here are some other suggestions from owners:

Use an astringent such as witch hazel or alcohol on affected areas. We have heard of zinc oxide cream being used to some effect on dogs as well as babies' bottoms! In the human world, this is rubbed on to mild skin abrasions and acts as a protective coating.

Zinc oxide works as a mild astringent and has some antiseptic properties and is safe to use on dogs, *as long as you do not allow the dog to lick it off!*

Vitamins A and E also help to make a dog's skin healthy, and one added: "A couple of mine tend to have itchy legs and feet. I feed them a grain-free food and use anti-itch herbal remedies."

 Coconut oil used to be recommended (and still is in some places), but the latest research shows that it may contribute to inflammation and leaky gut in dogs.

Massage

Anybody can do it – we do – and your Corgi will love the attention! There are many videos on YouTube explaining techniques and showing very relaxed Corgis enjoying a massage from their owners.

 Massage can stimulate your dog's immune system and help to prevent or reduce allergies. It's also good for improving your dog's circulation and flexibility, reducing muscle and arthritis pain and other age-related problems.

Holistic practitioners also believe that *acupressure* can specifically help dogs with allergies. Type *"Acupressure for Dogs"* into Google to learn about the theory behind it and how to apply pressure at specific points on your dog's body.

Acupressure can also help nervous and elderly dogs.

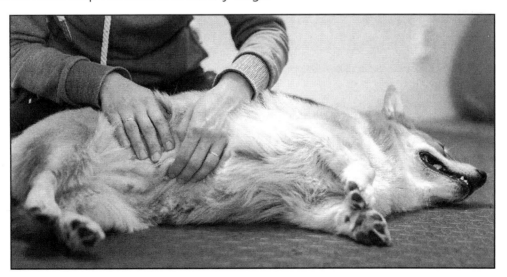

The Holistic Approach

Many owners of dogs with sensitivities find that their dog does well for a time with injections or medication, but then the symptoms slowly start to reappear.

More owners are now considering natural foods and remedies. A holistic practitioner looks at finding and treating the root cause of the problem, rather than just treating the symptoms.

Dr Sara Skiwski is an American holistic vet. She writes here about canine environmental allergies: "Here in California, with our mild weather and no hard freeze in Winter, environmental allergens can build up and cause nearly year-round issues for our beloved pets.

"Also, seasonal allergies, when left unaddressed, can lead to year-round allergies. Unlike humans, whose allergy symptoms seem to affect mostly the respiratory tract, seasonal allergies in dogs often take the form of skin irritation/inflammation."

Recurring Problems

"Allergic reactions are produced by the immune system. The way the immune system functions is a result of both genetics and the environment: Nature versus Nurture. Let's look at a typical case. A puppy starts showing mild seasonal allergy symptoms, for instance a red tummy and mild itching in Spring. Off to the vet!

"The treatment prescribed is symptomatic to provide relief, such as a topical spray. The next year when the weather warms up, the patient is back again - same symptoms but more severe this time.

"This time the dog has very itchy skin. Again, the treatment is symptomatic - antibiotics, topical spray (hopefully no steroids), until the symptoms resolve with the season change.

"Fast forward to another Spring...on the third year, the patient is back again but this time the symptoms last longer, (not just Spring but also through most of Summer and into Fall).

"By Year Five, all the symptoms are significantly worse and are occurring year-round. This is what happens with seasonal environmental allergies.

"The more your pet is exposed to the allergens they are sensitive to, the more the immune system over-reacts and the more intense and long-lasting the allergic response becomes. What to do?"

Root Cause

"In my practice, I like to address the potential root cause at the very first sign of an allergic response, which is normally seen between the ages of six to nine months old. I do this to circumvent the escalating response year after year.

"Since the allergen load your environmentally-sensitive dog is most susceptible to is much heavier outdoors, I recommend two essential steps in managing the condition. They are vigilance in foot care as well as hair care. What does this mean? A wipe down of feet and hair, especially the tummy, to remove any pollens or allergens is key. This can be done with a damp cloth, but my favorite method is to get a spray bottle filled with Witch Hazel *(pictured)* and spray these areas.

"First, spray the feet then wipe them off with a cloth, and then spray and wipe down the tummy and sides. This is best done right after the pup has been outside playing or walking. This will help keep your pet from tracking the environmental allergens into the home and into their beds. If the feet end up still being itchy, I suggest adding foot soaks in Epsom salts."

Dr Sara also stresses the importance of keeping the immune system healthy by avoiding unnecessary vaccinations or drugs: "The vaccine stimulates the immune system, which is the last thing your pet with seasonal environmental allergies needs.

"I also will move the pet to an anti-inflammatory diet. Foods that create or worsen inflammation are high in carbohydrates. An allergic pet's diet should be very low in carbohydrates, especially grains. Research has shown that 'leaky gut,' or dysbiosis, is a root cause of immune system overreactions in both dogs and cats (and some humans).

"Feed a diet that is not processed, or minimally processed; one that doesn't have grain and takes a little longer to get absorbed and assimilated through the gut. Slowing the assimilation assures that there are not large spikes of nutrients and proteins that come into the body all at once and overtax the pancreas and liver, creating inflammation.

"A lot of commercial diets are too high in grains and carbohydrates. These foods create inflammation that overtaxes the body and leads not just to skin inflammation, but also to other inflammatory conditions, such as colitis, pancreatitis, arthritis, inflammatory bowel disease and ear infections.

"Also, these diets are too low in protein, which is needed to make blood. This causes a decreased blood reserve in the body and in some of these animals this can lead to the skin not being properly nourished, starting a cycle of chronic skin infections which produce more itching."

Supplements

"After looking at diet, check that your dog is free from fleas and then these are some of Dr Sara's suggested supplements:

- ✓ **Raw (Unpasteurised) Local Honey** - an alkaline-forming food containing natural vitamins, enzymes, powerful antioxidants and other important natural nutrients, which are destroyed during the heating and pasteurisation processes.

  Raw honey has anti-viral, anti-bacterial and anti-fungal properties. It promotes body and digestive health, is a powerful antioxidant, strengthens the immune system, eliminates allergies, and is an excellent remedy for skin wounds and all types of infections. Bees collect pollen from local plants and their honey often acts as an immune booster for dogs living in the locality.

  Dr Sara says: "It may seem odd that straight exposure to pollen often triggers allergies, but that exposure to pollen in the honey usually has the opposite effect. But this is typically what we see. In honey, the allergens are delivered in small, manageable doses and the effect over time is very much like that from undergoing a whole series of allergy immunology injections."

- ✓ **Mushrooms** - make sure you choose the non-poisonous ones! Dogs don't like the taste, so you may have to mask it with another food. Medicinal mushrooms are used to treat and prevent a wide array of illnesses through their use as immune stimulants and modulators, and antioxidants. The most well-known and researched are reishi, maitake, cordyceps, blazei, split-gill, turkey tail and shiitake.

Histamine is what causes much of the inflammation, redness and irritation in allergies. By helping to control histamine production, the mushrooms can moderate the effects of inflammation and even help prevent allergies in the first place.

WARNING! Mushrooms can interact with some over-the-counter and prescription drugs, so do your research as well as checking with your vet first.

- ✓ **Stinging Nettles** - contain biologically active compounds that reduce inflammation. Nettles can reduce the amount of histamine the body produces in response to an allergen. Nettle tea or extract can help with itching. Nettles not only help directly to decrease the itch, but also work overtime to desensitise the body to allergens.

- ✓ **Quercetin** - is an over-the-counter supplement with anti-inflammatory properties. It is a strong antioxidant and reduces the body's production of histamines.

- ✓ **Omega-3 Fatty Acids** - help decrease inflammation throughout the body. Adding them into the diet of all pets - particularly those struggling with seasonal environmental allergies - is very beneficial. If your dog has more itching along the top of her back and on her sides, add in a fish oil supplement. Fish oil helps to decrease the itch and heal skin lesions.

- ✓ The best sources of Omega 3s are krill oil **(pictured)**, salmon oil, tuna oil, anchovy oil and other fish body oils, as well as raw organic egg yolks. If using an oil alone, it is important to give a vitamin B complex supplement.

Dr Sara adds: "Above are but a few of the over-the-counter remedies I like. In non-responsive cases, Chinese herbs can be used to work with the body to help to decrease the allergy threshold even more than with diet and supplements alone. Most of the animals I work with are on a program of Chinese herbs, diet change and acupuncture.

"So, the next time Fido is showing symptoms of seasonal allergies, consider rethinking your strategy to treat the root cause instead of the symptom."

With thanks to Dr Sara Skiwski, of the Western Dragon Integrated Veterinary Services, San Jose, California, for her kind permission to use her writings as the basis for *The Holistic Approach*.

Remember:

- ❖ A high-quality diet
- ❖ Maintaining a healthy weight
- ❖ Regular grooming and check-overs, and
- ❖ Attention to cleanliness

all go a long way in preventing or managing skin problems.

Tip If your Corgi does have a skin issue, seek a professional diagnosis <u>as soon as possible</u> before attempting to treat it yourself and it becomes entrenched. Even if a skin condition cannot be completely cured, almost all can be successfully managed, allowing your dog to live a happy, pain-free life.

15. The Corgi Coat and Grooming

Corgis have many advantages over other breeds: they are very adaptable, social, affectionate, lively and engaging. They have big personalities in small bodies, make good watchdogs and love a cuddle. Their intelligence and love of treats make them easier to train and housetrain than many breeds.

However, when it comes to grooming, most Corgis are NOT low maintenance! They love running free, digging and investigating everything with their noses and mouths. Couple this with them being so close to the ground and you begin to realise that keeping your dog in tiptop condition may require some effort on your part!

The Corgi Coat

Corgis were originally bred as herders and expected to work outdoors all day long in the harsh, damp conditions of Pembrokeshire and Cardiganshire in South West Wales – and their coats reflect that.

The Corgi has a thick double coat. The topcoat is designed to give the dog some inbuilt waterproofing. *Photo: Living the dream!*

Pembroke breeder and professional groomer Piotr Mazur-Jones explains the differences between the Pembroke and Cardigan coats: "In Pembrokes, coats should be medium length, straight with dense hair. The undercoat should never be soft or wavy.

"In Cardigans, coats should be short or medium with a hard texture. Both types are double coated and, as with other breeds, you do get a variety of coats depending on the breeding. These can vary from coarse/harsh to smooth/soft. Some coats can be more open where the hair is not as dense.

"In both breeds you can get *'fluffy'* coats, which is longer hair - this can be popular for some pet owners but isn't desirable in the show ring."

Tracy Irving, professional groomer and leading show breeder of both Pembrokes and Cardigans, added: "Both breeds are pretty much wash and go, in the sense that there is no trimming required for either breed (apart from the hair in between their foot pads). Pembrokes have slightly more length to the coat, while Cardigan lines have a much more dense, tighter type of coat

"The exception to this would be a *'fluffy.'* A lot of pet owners have the fluffy coats trimmed to make a neater, easier length to cope with." (More on *'fluffies'* later).

Shedding

There's no getting away from the fact that most Corgis do shed a lot of hair. This means that the breed is definitely not suitable for people with allergies. While most shed a little all year round,

Corgis *'blow'* their coat twice a year. This means that they get rid of one coat and grow another one, which will either be more or less dense, depending on the season. And for up to three weeks the hair just keeps on falling out.

During this time, your Corgi will need grooming every day, and he or she may look very dishevelled, but don't worry - it's natural and only temporary.

Piotr: "It is true, Corgis blow their coats twice a year. The timing can be determined by several factors, often seasonal with the coat coming out in spring and autumn. However, bitches post-litter will also blow their coats."

He has a few words of warning for owners who may be tempted into drastic action when their dog's coat blows: "Corgis have *'trousers'* (hair around their hind) - this is natural and how a Corgi should look: When they blow their coats, their trousers can look flared, or their collars look like an Elizabethan ruff - and their tails like a stick!

"This is all natural and a new coat will soon grow and make the coat full again. We've seen some sights - please do NOT be tempted to take scissors to a Corgi's coat - it's not needed!"

Factors affecting the amount of shedding include:

- Bloodlines
- Age
- Seasons
- Nutrition
- Whether the dog has been neutered. In some cases (more often reported in females) neutering can lead to a loss of sheen and coat condition, wooliness or increased shedding
- Sudden changes in temperature
- Allergies

Coat Colours

One of the nice things about Corgis is that they come in a range of different colours! The wording varies slightly between the US and UK Breed Standards, but basically these are the acceptable colours for Pembrokes in the US:

Red, Sable *(pictured)*, **Fawn** (a lighter shade of Red), **Black and Tan -** with or without white markings (with white they are known as a **Tricolour).**

White is acceptable on legs, chest, neck (either in part or as a collar), muzzle, underparts and as a narrow blaze on head.

UK: Red, Sable, Fawn, Black and Tan, with or without white markings on legs, brisket and neck. Some white on head and foreface permissible.

Sable is one of the rarest coats for a Pembroke, but nonetheless striking, making the dog look more like a wolf than a fox.

Sable is actually a pattern, rather than a colour; each individual hair has bands of colour with black or brown at the tip. Many Sables have a **'widow's peak'** (triangle of darker hair) on the top of their heads running down towards the eyes. Sable hair on their bodies - often on the back and shoulders - is known as a **'black cast.'**

You may also hear variations on the colours, such as red-headed tricolour or black-headed tricolour. These are all permissible colour combinations.

FACT ❭ If you ever see a **"merle Pembroke"** advertised, it is a mixed breed, most probably crossed with a Cardigan. There is no such thing as a purebred merle Pembroke as the breed does not carry the genes to produce a merle (mottled) coat.

NOTE: There is a rare Dilute (recessive) gene, also called a **Bluey,** which results in a Pembroke's colours being diluted – i.e. a smoky cast to the coat, liver or grey pigment on the nose and eye rims, and possibly one or two blue eyes.

If two Pembrokes carrying the Dilute gene are mated (perhaps by unscrupulous or ill-informed breeders trying to get a 'rare colour'), puppies can be born with the **Double Dilute (DD)** gene, which is associated with many health issues, including deafness and blindness. Pembrokes with one or two blue eyes may either have a single or double Dilute gene; health problems are only associated with the Double Dilute.

There are a few other rare colours that are regarded as faults in the show ring, but these Pembrokes make just as good companions as those with the "correct" colours: Whitelies (mostly white body colour), Bluies (mentioned above - as long as they don't have the DD Double Dilute gene), Mismarks (white patches on the back, sides or ears), Blackies (black with white markings but no tan).

The Cardigan has even more natural coat colours. In the US Breed Standard they are: "**Shades of Red, Sable and Brindle, Black,** with or without tan or brindle points. **Blue merle,** *pictured,* (black and gray; marbled) with or without tan or brindle points."

UK: Blue Merle, Brindle, Red, Sable, Tricolour with brindle points and **Tricolour with red points.**

The UK Breed Standard says: "All of the above with or without the typical white markings on head, neck, chest, underparts, legs and feet, white tail tip. White should not predominate on body or head where it should never surround the eyes. Nose and eye rims must be black. Liver and dilute colours highly undesirable."

Red and Sable are similar colourings to the Pembrokes. Black is accompanied by white, giving the dog a similar colouring to a Border Collie, although some black Cardigans have brindle or tan points.

Brindle, also known as the tiger coat, is another attractive colouring, with a brown base layer overlaid with black or dark brown stripes. The most unusual colour is Blue Merle which, like Sable, is a coat pattern rather than a colour.

The UK Breed Standard states: "One or both eyes pale blue, blue or blue-flecked, permissible only in blue merles." Other colours all have brown eyes; a blue merle can also have two brown eyes.

Blue merle is a natural colour for a Cardigan but, as you've read, not for a Pembroke.

Fluffies

What a wonderful name for a coat type! In short, a fluffy is a long-haired Pembroke or Cardigan - the name describes the look of the dog perfectly. They have a long, luxuriant coat with *'feathering'* under their belly and around their ears, chest, feet, legs and hindquarters.

The undercoat is actually less dense, so, despite the fluffy coat being longer, it may not be quite as warm or waterproof as the normal Corgi coat.

Photos: A fluffy puppy, left, and a trio of adult fluffies, below.

Fluffies can be born in the same litter as 'normal' Corgis and although they will never win any prizes in the show ring (due to the Kennel Clubs classing the fluffy coat as a 'Very Serious Fault'), they are highly-prized by many owners for their beautiful coat and rarity.

Fluffies are just as healthy and Corgi-like in every other way, it's just their coat that differs. This is due to a recessive gene called, appropriately, the *fluff gene* – or FGF5 if you're a scientist!

This gene is rare and recessive; BOTH parents have to have it for a puppy to be born with a fluffy coat. Even then, only one in four puppies with be a fluffy. And it's not possible to tell if a puppy is a fluffy until around the age of two to three weeks old when the coat begins to grow.

A few breeders have the fluff gene in their bloodlines - and usually a long list of people waiting to own one of their fluffy puppies. There is, however, a price to pay for the beautiful coat. Unlike regular Pembrokes and Cardigans, a fluffy will need a full trim - either by you or a professional groomer - every six to 10 weeks.

Piotr says: "Some groomers have been known to trim or clip Corgis at the request of the owner because of the hair - there is no need. The exception to the rule is with fluffies, as some coats can get very long. You can trim all over with a double-sided thinner to make them look like 'teddy bears.'

"Fluffies can get matted coats, which can become a welfare issue, so it is very important that they have regular coat maintenance to prevent matting. Dematting is painful and, if beyond recovery, a clip-off (shave) is the only solution."

Grooming Tips and Equipment

A healthy Corgi coat has a sheen and is a joy to behold, and regular brushing helps to keep the coat in tiptop condition. It also removes dirt and dead hair, stimulates blood circulation - which in turn helps to keep the skin healthy - and spreads natural oils throughout the coat.

A high-quality diet also helps, and some owners have found that feeding hypoallergenic kibble, or a raw or home-cooked diet can improve skin health and reduce shedding. Adding a daily squirt or spoonful of Omega 3 oil to a feed can also be beneficial.

Given many Corgis' innate love of all things muddy and the fact that they are so low to the ground, it might be worth investing in an outdoor tap. You can give your dog a hose down underneath and quick dry with a towel before letting him into the house - particularly useful on rainy days.

Rinsing your Corgi's paws and under his belly is also effective in reducing contact allergies.

 We recommend grooming your Corgi at least once a week and every day when the coat is blowing.

Routine grooming sessions also allow you to examine your Corgi's ears, tail, teeth, eyes, paws and nails for signs of problems. Older Corgis may need more regular checks from their owners. Time spent grooming is also time spent bonding with your Corgi. This physical and emotional inter-reliance helps bring us closer to our dogs.

Top Cardigan breeder and exhibitor Fran Fricker is devoted to her Cardis and says: "My dogs are groomed daily, it's their time with me.

"I always groom on a table; it's a brush-through and a check on eyes and ears, and weekly its nails with a Dremel. Pups are groomed when young and nails are cut at first and then progress to a Dremel.

"Dogs are always bathed before show days and dried and blasted; pups also get used to this. This keeps them in tiptop condition. Teeth are also checked, but I have never had an issue with dirty teeth."

Photo: Fran grooming Jac (Kerman on Parole, aged 2) before changing into her Sunday Best for his class at Crufts Dog Show.

 Corgis HATE having their nails trimmed until they get used to it – and even then, some are less than keen! They are complete cowards. Get your puppy used to being handled and groomed right from the beginning.

Corgi grooming can be done perfectly well at home. However, more and more owners are choosing to send their dogs to a professional groomer three or four times a year. Not only will your Corgi be bathed, 'blasted' (dried with a canine hair dryer) and brushed, nails will be trimmed, ears checked and, if you ask, anal glands squeezed.

Many groomers offer shorter puppy grooms at reduced rates to get a young dog used to the experience.

Regular Maintenance

Your puppy's coat starts to change at around six months, getting thicker and longer, and requiring attention. Hopefully, before then you will have got him or her used to being handled and groomed.

Here in a nutshell are a few basic tasks involved in regular maintenance of a pet Corgi:

1. Checking your dog's coat for mud and dirt (and ticks if he's often in woods).

2. Regular brushing to remove dead hair and stop the coat becoming matted.

3. Checking the insides of the ears are clean and not red or smelly (which could be a sign of infection) − see **Chapter 14. Skin and Allergies** for the best cleaning method.

4. Keeping your dog's teeth clean.

5. Nail trimming.

6. Trimming the hair between the foot pads.

Tip Excluding fluffies, the only hair that should be trimmed - i.e. cut with scissors - on a Pembroke or Cardigan is the hair that grows under the paw between the pads.

Photos: Professional Corgi trainer Maria Carter trimming the hair between Iucci's pads. Maria has trained her dogs to 'walk the plank' on to the grooming table... where a treat awaits!

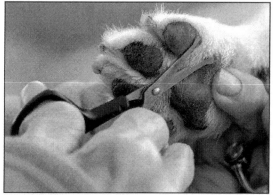

Piotr: "Brushing is an important part of a Corgi's well-being and, like humans, for whom brushing your hair can make you feel better, it's the same for Corgis.

"Regular, at least weekly, brushing is good coat maintenance. If you visit a groomer for bathing, etc. this should take place every six to 10 weeks.

"If you're doing it at home, I recommend a comb, **pictured above,** slicker brush and a rake. As a minimum, buy a good slicker brush.

"I have seen some promotion of **Furminators,** this is a definite NO for Corgis - including fluffies - as it damages the top layer and ruins the coat."

Here's what some others have to say, starting with Linda Roberts: "In an ideal world, the Pembroke should receive a full groom once a week. I recommend the use of a greyhound comb.

"During the course of grooming, particular care should be taken to ensure that the eyes are clear of any discharge, the teeth can be cleaned and the nails should be kept short. Check the intimate areas for any discharge or faeces.

"I bath my show dogs perhaps rather more than is ideal, but certainly a Pembroke would benefit from a full bath when changing coat or when extremely muddy after a walk, for instance. If you use a professional groomer, please remind them that this is not a trimmed breed, other than the hair between the pads on the foot. "

Kevin Dover: "Grooming should be done at least twice every week and, when moulting, should be done daily. A Corgi has a double coat and every six months or so they will shed the undercoat and some of the top coat. I personally use a twin pin steel comb as you can get right down to the skin to remove the loose hair.

"I don't overdo the bathing as this takes out the natural oils from the coat. An all-over bath may only be required every few months - unless they decide to rub themselves in something unsavoury!

"The fore chest and underparts can be washed when required, especially during the winter months when they will get very dirty - although if towel-dried after a walk any dirt will normally brush out once completely dry."

Carole Turner: "I groom mine every day and clean their teeth. Nails and ears are checked weekly. Bathing towards the end of the twice-yearly moult helps get the coat out. Using a zoom groom brush (**pictured**) in the bath helps to remove loose hair."

Margaret Leighton: "I just towel them off after a wet walk. I have a bad back and cannot groom my dogs, so they visit the groomer every three weeks. She also trims their feet.

"Corgis have a double coat and do shed a lot, but their grooming is very simple as they do not require special trimming - except under the pads on their feet. So it's relatively inexpensive at the groomers…. But I do use a Dyson cordless vacuum cleaner a lot at home!"

Jo Evans: "Corgis are very low to the ground, so get very muddy and are therefore used to being hosed off and towel dried. Mine seem to moult full-time, so I do groom them and I find a normal comb works as well as anything.

"They are double coated, so it's important to keep this natural coat. If we're going somewhere special, I may bath them beforehand. They do need their nails trimming often - and only a little at a time because they don't like it."

Lisa Thompson: "A quick daily brushing really helps. Give them baths as needed and seasonal deep grooming when they are blowing their coats. They hate nails being done!"

One breeder jokes: "Mine only shed once a year – from January 1st to December 31st!"

Lucy Badham-Thornhill: "I groom them and brush their teeth about four times a week for about 10 minutes and trim their nails weekly. Lettice has a phobia about having her nails done. She never bites or growls, but moans when I Dremel them! But they really do need their nails trimming.

"Twice a year their hair pours out – this time next week, mine will be nearly bald! It takes about a week for the coat to blow, and a fantastic amount of hair comes out."

Photo: A beautifully groomed Pembroke with a full tail.

Lucy added: "Good breeders remove the dew claws – or get a vet to do it – about two days after birth. Corgis are low to the ground and dew claws can catch and injure them."

A dew claw is the extra nail located on the upper, inner part of the dog's front foot. All Corgis are born with them and a tiny percentage also have them on their back legs. They are actually the remains of a prehistoric thumb!

....

Bathing

Too much bathing can rid the coat of its natural oils, so don't bathe your Corgi unless you think it necessary; a regular towelling or hosing down after a walk will suffice most of the time. However, if the coat and skin get too dirty it can cause irritation, leading to scratching and excessive shedding - it's all a question of getting the balance right.

 **If your Corgi is smelly, he needs a bath! A healthy Corgi coat should not have an unpleasant smell or any matting.**

NOTE: If you do notice an unpleasant smell (in addition to your Corgi's normal gassy emissions) and he hasn't been rolling in something unmentionable, then he may have a yeast infection or his anal glands may need squeezing.

 If your Corgi does needs a bath, only use a canine shampoo. A dog's coat has a different pH to human hair and shampoos made for humans can cause skin irritation.

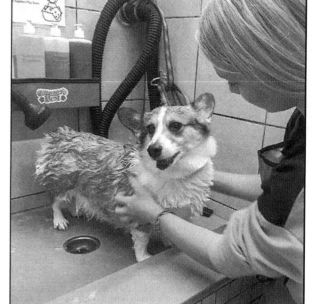

If your Corgi has skin problems or allergies, select a *medicated* shampoo with antibacterial, antifungal or anti-itching properties with antihistamines. It will help to get rid of bacteria and fungi without damaging the coat. Your vet will be able to recommend a suitable shampoo. They are also widely available in pet stores and online.

Photo: Happy Birthday! Lisa Thompson's daughter Natalie gives her beloved Roxie (Thompson's Foxie Roxie) a bath on her sixth birthday.

Before you bathe your Corgi, give him a good brush to remove all the dead hair.

 To help prevent water going right inside the ear canals, you might consider putting large wads of cotton wool inside the ears while bathing. Don't force the cotton wool in – and don't forget to remove them afterwards or your Corgi may be even deafer than usual to your commands!

You also have to be extremely careful with the eyes. Some owners put a drop or two of artificial tears in each eye to offer some limited protection against soap or chemicals in the shampoo.

There is a wide variation on how your Corgi will react to having a bath – some love the attention, while others are not so keen. Make sure you get everything ready before you start and, if your dog is resistant, keep the collar on so you have something to hold on to.

Use **lukewarm** water and spray it from the neck down to the tail until the coat is completely soaked, avoid wetting the face if you can, but gently wash the ear flaps without getting water in the ear canals. Work the shampoo into your dog's body and legs, not forgetting the underneath, and if it's a medicated shampoo, you may have to leave it on for a few minutes. This is not easy with a lively Corgi, so keep a firm hold or better still, have an accomplice hold the dog! It does get better as they get more used to it – especially if they get a treat at the end of the ordeal.

Rinse your dog thoroughly on top, underneath, on the legs, etc., making sure that all of the soap is out of the coat. Use your hand to squeegee excess water off the coat before putting him on an old towel on the floor and towelling him dry - again, be careful with the eyes. Then stand back as he gets his revenge by shaking and soaking you too!

Dry the coat as much as possible, a double-coated dog like the Corgi may take a while to dry naturally. You may want to use a hairdryer, put the heating on or find him a sunny spot.

One not uncommon reaction after a bath is for a dog to run around like a lunatic afterwards doing the *Zoomies* - as though they have just miraculously escaped the most horrific ordeal!

Piotr has some advice on bathing: "If you don't take your Corgi to a professional groomer then I'd recommend bathing every six to 10 weeks. A domestic hairdryer won't cut the mustard when it comes to the coat being blown, but you can buy *'blasters'* online at reasonable prices.

"Be warned - it will be a blizzard of hair! I would always recommend having this done in a salon; we are used to it.

"If you are bathing at home, my tips are to buy a decent dog shampoo, use very little as they all go a long way and it's very important to rinse well - especially under the armpits so as not to cause irritation."

Photo: Piotr at work.

"If you're showing your dog, you'll want your Corgi to look the best they possibly can. You should bath them two days before the show; this allows the coat to settle. Blast, brush, rake and comb the dead coat out, trim or shave the pads, Dremel the nails, clean the ears and then your Corgi is good to go to the ring!

"There are plenty of different products from finishing sprays to coat mousses you can apply, depending on the need of the coat. As a pastoral breed, the Corgi should be shown with no coat trimming."

Teeth Cleaning

Studies show that by the age of three, 80% of dogs show signs of gum or dental disease. Symptoms include yellow and brown build-up of tartar along the gum line, red inflamed gums and persistent bad breath (halitosis). If your dog suddenly stops eating his food, check his mouth and teeth.

Many owners keep their dogs' teeth clean by giving them an occasional raw bone (not chicken as it splinters), or regularly feeding bully sticks, Nylabones, Dentastix, etc.

However, it is important to take time to take care of your Corgi's teeth - regular dental care greatly reduces the onset of gum and tooth decay and infection. If left, problems can quickly escalate.

Without cleaning, plaque coats teeth and within a few days this starts to harden into tartar, often turning into gingivitis (inflammation of the gums). Gingivitis is regularly accompanied by periodontal disease (infections around the teeth). This can be serious as, in the worst cases, it can lead to infections of the vital organs, such as heart, liver and kidneys.

Even if the infection doesn't spread beyond the mouth, bad teeth are very unpleasant for a dog, just as with a human, causing painful toothache and difficulty chewing.

Maria brushes Ella's (aged 11.5) teeth.

If your Corgi needs a deep clean, remedial work or teeth removing, he will have to be anaesthetised, a procedure which is to be avoided unless it is absolutely necessary. Prevention is better than cure.

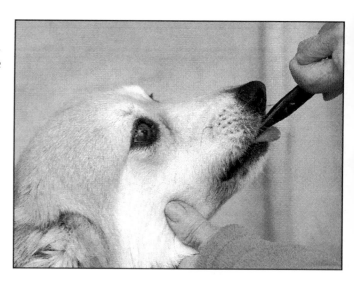

 If your dog has to be anaesthetised for anything, ask the vet to check and clean your dog's teeth while he's under.

Welsh Corgi League Breed Health Co-ordinator and show judge Linda Roberts adds: "Dental hygiene is often overlooked - I can confirm that from many judging appointments where we check the dentition. Bacteria from bad teeth can cause no end of systemic problems. I believe they can contribute to heart and kidney problems in seniors, so dental hygiene is an important part of their maintenance."

You can help to keep your dog's teeth clean by brushing them. There are also various tools owners can buy to control plaque, such as dental picks and scrapers. Start while still a puppy and take things slowly in the beginning, giving lots of praise. Once used to the process, many dogs love the attention - especially if they like the flavour of the toothpaste!

The real benefit comes from the actual action of the brush on the teeth, and various brushes, sponges and pads are available for dogs - the choice depends on factors such as the health of your dog's gums, the size of his mouth and how good you are at teeth cleaning.

Get him used to the toothpaste by letting him lick some off your finger when he is young. If he doesn't like the flavour, try a different one. Continue this until he enjoys licking the paste - it might be instant or it might take days.

Put a small amount on your finger and gently rub it on one of the big canine teeth at the front of his mouth. Then get him used to the toothbrush or dental sponge for several days - praise him when he licks it. The next step is to actually start brushing.

Lift his upper lip gently and place the brush at a 45° angle to the gum line. Gently move the brush backwards and forwards. Start just with his front teeth and then gradually do a few more. Do the top ones first.

Regular brushing shouldn't take more than five minutes - well worth the time and effort when it spares your Corgi the pain and misery of serious dental or gum disease.

Nail Trimming

FACT Most Corgis need regular nail trimming to keep the paws healthy. Overly-long nails interfere with a dog's gait, making walking awkward or painful and putting stress on elbows, shoulder and back. They can also break easily, usually at the base of the nail where blood vessels and nerves are located.

Be prepared: many Corgis dislike having their nails trimmed. It's best to get your dog used to having his paws inspected and trimmed from puppyhood. Use a nail grinder, called a Dremel, or specially designed nail clipper, *pictured.* Most have safety guards to prevent you cutting the nails too short. Do it before they get too long.

Tip If you can hear the nails clicking on a hard surface, they're too long. Trim only the ends, before *"the quick,"* (a blood vessel inside the nail). You can see where the quick ends on a white nail, but not on a dark nail.

Clip only the hook-like part of the nail that turns down. Start trimming gently, a nail or two at a time, and your dog will learn that you're not going to hurt him. If you accidentally cut the quick, stop the bleeding with some styptic powder.

Some dogs have tough nails that are harder to trim and a Dremel, *pictured,* may be less stressful for your dog, with less chance of cutting the quick. The grinder is like an electric nail file and only removes a small amount of nail at a time. Some dogs prefer them to a clipper, although others don't like the noise.

Piotr says: "Nail clipping and pad trimming should be done regularly; nails should be kept short to prevent pain or injury. Depending on your Corgi, nail trimming could be as often as every two weeks. Some of ours have that two-weekly need, others only need their nails trimming every six weeks.

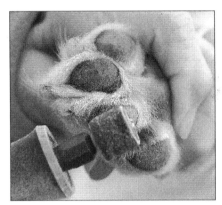

"I use a Dremel and also nail clippers. If you start at a young age, they soon get used to it. Not all like it, but it does have to be done and they soon get used to it.

"As a breeder, we do the pups' nails every two weeks from four weeks of age so they are used to it, and we encourage our forever families to continue this."

If you find it impossible to clip your dog's nails, or you are at all worried about doing it, take him to a vet or groomer and have it done as part of a routine visit - and check if your dog's anal sacs need squeezing, or "expressing," while he's there!

Anal Glands

While we're discussing the less appealing end of your Corgi, let's dive straight in and talk about anal sacs. Sometimes called *scent glands,* these are a pair of glands located inside your dog's anus that give off a scent when he has a bowel movement. You won't want to hear this, but problems with impacted anal glands are not uncommon in dogs!

When a dog passes firm stools, the glands normally empty themselves, but watery poop can mean that not enough pressure is exerted to empty the glands, causing discomfort. If they get infected, they become swollen and painful. In extreme cases, one or both anal glands can be removed – we had a dog that lived happily for many years with one anal gland.

If your dog drags himself along on his rear end - *"scooting"* - or tries to lick or scratch his anus, he could well have impacted anal glands that need squeezing, either by you if you know how to do it, your vet or a groomer. (Scooting is also a sign of worms).

Either way, it pays to keep an eye on both ends of your dog!

With special thanks to Piotr Mazur-Jones, professional dog groomer, and breeder and exhibitor of Creslow Corgis, for his invaluable assistance with this chapter.

16. The Facts of Life

Judging by the number of questions our website receives, there is a lot of confusion about the canine facts of life. Some ask if, and at what age, they should have their dog spayed or neutered, while others want to know whether they should breed from their dog.

Owners of females ask when and how often she will come on heat and how long this will last. Sometimes they want to know how you can tell if a female is pregnant or how long a pregnancy lasts. So here, in a nutshell, is a chapter on the birds and bees as far as Corgis are concerned.

....

Females and Heat

The female Corgi has an oestrus *(estrus* in the US) cycle which is similar to the human menstrual cycle. This is when she is ready (and willing!) for mating and is more commonly called **heat**, being **in heat**, **on heat** or **in season**.

Corgis usually have their first cycle any time between six months and over one year old. All dogs are different. Kennel Club Assured Breeder Fran Fricker, of Kerman Cardigan Welsh Corgis, has been involved with both types of Corgi for over 50 years and says of her Cardigans: "Their first season is from the age of six months, though it's not unheard of to come into season at five months.

"Their heat cycles are typically every six months, though this also can be every nine months. There are no set rules; each bitch is an individual."

Pictured is the beautiful Gucci (Kerman Guilty Party) aged six months, bred by Fran. Photo by Will Harris

Here's what some Pembroke breeders have to say, starting with fellow Assured Breeder Jo Evans, of Cerdinen Pembroke Welsh Corgis:

"My dogs' first season seems to happen in the second year. Often with a long break (nine months) until the next one. From then on, it's pretty regular every six months - February or March and then around September."

Assured Breeders Piotr and Johnathan Mazur-Jones, Creslow Corgis: "Their first season is usually around nine to 10 months, then typically every six to seven months.

"Obviously each dog is different - we have one who you can set your clock by and others who just go with what they like. Also, bitches do tend to sync their seasons when living together, so it's not unheard of to have one come into season and then shortly (days) after another to follow suit, and so on."

Linda Roberts, Breed Health Co-ordinator, Welsh Corgi League: "Mine come into season at approximately eight to 12 months of age, and then every five to seven months."

Exhibitor and international show judge Kevin Dover: "My bitches have normally come into season for the first time on or around six months of age, but I have had them be as late as eight or nine months. Their normal cycles are usually every six months, but again, one import I had many years ago was in season every four months, which is unusual but didn't affect her breeding later on."

Experienced owner and breeder Lucy Badham-Thornhill: "Mine come into season about every eight months and they are always very punctual with their own cycle, every six to eight months."

 Females often follow the patterns of their mother, so ask the breeder at what age the dam had her first season and how often they occur.

There is no time of the year that corresponds to a breeding season, so heat could occur during any month.

When a young bitch comes in season, it is normal for her cycles to be somewhat irregular - it can take up to two years for regular cycles to develop. The timescale also becomes more erratic with older, unspayed females.

A heat cycle normally lasts 18 to 21 days, the last days might be lighter in terms of blood loss - you might not even know that she is still in heat.

FACT ⟩ Unlike with women, the reproductive cycle does not stop when dogs reach middle age, although the heat becomes shorter and lighter. However, a litter takes a heavy toll on older females.

NOTE: Women cannot get pregnant during their period, while female dogs can ONLY get pregnant during their heat.

Here are some typical physical signs of heat:

- ❧ The pink bit under her tail (external sex organ called the vulva) becomes swollen and sometimes darker

- ❧ She loses some blood - the amount of blood varies from one dog to another - from "spotting," which is very light, to heavier bleeds

- ❧ She tries to lick the area under her tail

- ❧ She may urinate more frequently

The canine heat cycle is a complex mix of physical, hormonal and behavioural changes. Here are some behaviour changes to look out for - your Corgi may display none, one or several of these:

- ❧ Some dogs become more needy around you - or irritable, e.g. being less tolerant of other dogs and people, or more possessive with toys or food

- ❧ Others seem a little depressed and retire to their beds

- ❧ She may go off her food

- ❧ Some shed more hair when on heat

- ❧ Her hormones are raging and she may try to mount you, other dogs or even the furniture!

Some dogs clean themselves regularly, while others are less scrupulous on the personal hygiene front. If your girl has "heavy days" and is constantly on and off your furniture, put covers on your sofa (if she's allowed on there) during her heat - or invest in a couple of pairs of washable doggie pants for her heaviest days, **pictured.** Check the sizing, which is usually based on waist measurement.

Some dogs can get out of them pretty quickly, and even with pants on leakages occasionally occur - a few females will even take advantage and poo(p) in them.

The Cycle

There are four stages of the heat cycle (a female's season is **proestrus** plus **oestrus**):

Proestrus - this is when the bleeding starts and lasts around nine days. Male dogs are attracted to her, but she is not yet interested, so she may hold her tail close to her body. Her vulva becomes swollen. The blood is usually light red or brown, turning more straw-coloured or even colourless when she's ready to mate.

 If you're not sure if she's in heat, hold a tissue against her vulva or put a white sheet or cloth underneath when she lies down. Does any of it turn pink or red?

Oestrus - this is when eggs are released from ovaries and the optimum time for breeding. Males are extremely interested in her and the feelings are often very much reciprocated - her hormones are raging! If there is a male around she may stand for him and *"flag"* her tail (or move it to one side) to allow him to mount her. Oestrus is the time when a female CAN get pregnant and usually lasts around nine days, so roughly from Day 10-19.

Dioestrus - this is the two-month stage when her body produces the hormone progesterone whether or not she is pregnant. During this stage she is no longer interested in males. These hormones can sometimes lead to what is known as a *"false pregnancy."*

Anoestrus - this the period of rest when reproductive organs are inactive. It is the longest stage of the cycle and lasts around five-and-a-half months. If she normally lives with a male dog, they can return to living together again - neither will be interested in mating and she cannot get pregnant.

FACT ❯ When a female is on heat, she produces pheromones that attract male dogs. Because dogs have a sense of smell several hundred times stronger than ours, your girl on heat is a magnet for all the neighbourhood males. It is believed that they can detect the scent of a female on heat up to two miles away!

They may congregate around your house or follow you around the park (if you are brave or foolish enough to venture out there while she is in season), waiting for their chance to prove their

manhood – or mutthood in their case.

Don't expect your precious little princess to be fussy. Her hormones are raging when she is on heat and, during her most fertile days, she is ready, able and ... VERY willing!

As she approaches the optimum time for mating you may notice her tail bending slightly to one side. She will also start to urinate more frequently. This is her signal to all those virile male dogs out there that she is ready for mating.

Although breeding requires specialised knowledge on the part of the owner, it does not stop a female on heat from being extremely interested in attention from any old mutt!

To avoid an unwanted pregnancy, you must keep a close eye on her throughout her heat and not allow her to wander unsupervised.

Keep her on a lead if you go out on walks and whatever you do, don't let her run free anywhere that you might come across other dogs.

If you have a large garden or yard, you may wish to restrict her to that during her heat – but only if you 100% know it is safe. Determined male dogs can jump and scramble over high fences.

You can compensate for the restrictions by playing more games at home to keep her mentally and physically active.

It is amazing the lengths to which some entire (uncastrated) males will go to impregnate a female on heat. Travelling great distances to follow her scent, digging under fences, jumping over barriers, chewing through doors or walls and sneaking through hedges are just some of the tactics employed by canine Casanovas on the loose.

Tip Her hormones are raging and during her most fertile days (the oestrus), your female's instinct to mate will trump all of her training.

If you do have an entire male, you need to physically keep him in a separate place, perhaps with an understanding friend or even boarding kennels. His desire to mate is all-consuming and can be accompanied by howling or 'marking' (urinating) indoors. A dog living in the same house as a bitch in season has even been known to mate with her through the bars of a crate!

You can buy sprays that mask the natural oestrus scent. Marketed under such attractive names as *"Bitch Spray,"* these lessen, but don't eliminate, the scent. They may reduce the amount of unwanted attention, but are not a complete deterrent.

There is no canine contraceptive, so if your female is unspayed, you need to keep her under supervision during her heat cycle - which may be up to three or even four weeks.

If your female is accidentally mated (a *"mismating")*, there is an injection available in the UK called *Alizin* which blocks progesterone production.

It is used any time from the end of the season up to 45 days after the mismating. It is given as two injections 24 hours apart and has a low risk if used early on. If used late it causes abortion.

NOTE: Females tend to come back into season quite soon after the Alizin injections - usually one to three months, so take care not to get "caught out" at the next season. Alizin is also quite a painful injection for your girl.

Pregnancy

Regardless of how big or small the dog is, a canine pregnancy lasts for 58 to 65 days; 63 days is average. This is true of all breeds of dog from the Chihuahua to the Great Dane. Sometimes pregnancy is referred to as *"the gestation period."*

A female should have a pre-natal check-up after mating. The vet should answer any questions about type of food, supplements and extra care needed, as well as informing the owner about any physical changes likely to occur in your female.

There is a blood test available that measures levels of **relaxin**. This is a hormone produced by the ovary and the developing placenta, and pregnancy can be detected by monitoring relaxin levels as early as 22 to 27 days after mating. The levels are high throughout pregnancy and then decline rapidly after the female has given birth.

A vet can usually see the puppies (but not how many) using Ultrasound from around the same time.

Cara, aged three, with three of her puppies: Stella, Toby and Rooney, courtesy of Jo Evans.

Signs of Pregnancy

- After mating, many females become more affectionate. However, a few may become uncharacteristically irritable and maybe even a little aggressive!

- She may produce a slight mucous-like discharge from her vagina one month after mating

- Three or four weeks after mating, some females experience morning sickness – if this is the case, feed little and often. She may seem more tired than usual

- She may seem slightly depressed or show a drop in appetite. These signs can also mean there are other problems, so you should consult your vet

- Her teats will become more prominent, pink and erect 25 to 30 days into the pregnancy. Later on, you may notice a fluid coming from them. This first milk (colostrum) is the most important milk a puppy gets on Day One as it contains the mother's immunity

- Her body weight will start to increase about 35 days after mating

- Abdominal swelling may be just about noticeable from Day 40 and becomes more obvious from around Day 50, although first-time mums and females carrying few puppies may not show as much

- Many pregnant females' appetite will increase in the second half of pregnancy

- ❧ Her nesting instincts will kick in as the delivery date approaches. She may seem restless or scratch her bed or the floor - she may even rip and shred items like your comforter, curtains or carpeting!

- ❧ During the last week of pregnancy, females often start to look for a safe place for whelping. Some seem to become confused, wanting to be with their owners and at the same time wanting to prepare their nest. If the female is having a C-section, she should still be allowed to nest in a whelping box with layers of newspaper, which she will scratch and dig as the time approaches

 If your Corgi becomes pregnant - either by design or accident - your first step should be to consult a vet.

Litter Size

The size of Corgi litters varies a great deal. The number of puppies can be affected by factors such as bloodlines, the age of the dam and sire (young and older dogs have smaller litters), the health and diet of the dam, Mother Nature, and the size of the gene pool; the lower the genetic diversity, the smaller the litter.

This is what some of our experts said: "I have bred six litters and the range has been three to seven puppies. I have heard of litters of one and 11 in the Pembroke Corgi world."

"Most litters are six to eight pups; the largest litter I have had was 11."

"My litters have ranged from three for a first-timer to no more than six puppies born."

"Mine have been three to nine puppies; I have heard of 13 though!"

"When I first started, we normally had litters of around six or seven, although I personally like a litter of around five. I have had singleton puppies and my largest was a litter of 10."

"Our litters have been from one to 11 pups; the average is six. We have heard of a litter of 15, but that is a one-off."

False Pregnancies

Occasionally, unspayed females may display signs of a false pregnancy. Before dogs were domesticated, it was common for female dogs to have false pregnancies and to lactate (produce milk). She would then nourish puppies of the Alpha bitch or puppies who had lost their mother in the pack.

False pregnancies occur 60 to 80 days after the female was in season - about the time she would have given birth - and are generally nothing to worry about for an owner. The exact cause is unknown; however, hormonal imbalances are thought to play an important role. Some dogs have shown symptoms within three to four days of spaying; these include:

- ❧ Making a nest

- ❧ Producing milk (lactating)

- ❧ Appetite fluctuations

- Barking or whining a lot
- Restlessness, depression or anxiety
- Mothering or adopting toys and other objects
- Swollen abdomen
- She might even appear to go into labour

 Under no circumstances should you restrict your Corgi's water supply to try and prevent her from producing milk. This is dangerous as she can become dehydrated.

Occasionally, an unspayed female may have a false pregnancy with each heat cycle. Spaying during a false pregnancy may actually prolong the condition, so better to wait until it is over to have her spayed.

FACT False pregnancy is not a disease, but an exaggerated response to normal hormonal changes. Even if left untreated, it almost always resolves itself.

However, if your dog appears physically ill or the behavioural changes are severe enough to worry about, visit your vet. He or she may prescribe *Galastop*, which stops milk production and quickly returns the hormones to normal. In rare cases, hormone treatment may be necessary.

Generally, dogs experiencing false pregnancies do not have serious long-term problems, as the behaviour disappears when the hormones return to their normal levels in two to three weeks.

Pyometra

One exception is **Pyometra,** a serious and potentially deadly infection of the womb, caused by a hormonal abnormality.

It normally follows a heat cycle in which fertilisation did not occur and the dog typically starts showing symptoms within two to four months. It occurs most often in middle-aged females.

Commonly referred to as *"pyo,"* there are **open** and **closed** forms of the disease. Open pyo is usually easy to identify with a smelly discharge, so prompt treatment is easy.

Closed pyo is often harder to identify and you may not even notice anything until your girl becomes feverish and lethargic. When this happens, it is very serious and time is of the essence.

Typical signs of Pyometra are: excessive drinking and urination, vomiting and depression, with the female trying to lick a white discharge from her vagina. She may also have a temperature. If the condition becomes severe, her back legs will become weak, possibly to the point where she can no longer get up without help.

Pyometra can be fatal and needs to be dealt with promptly by a vet.

Standard treatment is emergency spay soon after starting intravenous fluids and antibiotics. In some milder cases, the vet may recommend Alizin injections plus antibiotics and (if needed) IV fluids, then spay as soon as possible after the pyo resolves.

Should I Breed From My Corgi?

The short and very simple answer is: NO! Not unless you do a lot of research, find a mentor for expert advice and then a good vet, preferably one experienced with Welsh Corgis.

Breeding healthy Corgi puppies with good temperaments is a messy, complex, time-consuming and expensive process and should not be approached lightly.

Unfortunately, lots of people with little or scant knowledge of Corgis have been tempted to breed their dogs to cash in on the rise in dog ownership and high price of puppies.

This can often lead to heartbreak for owners when the puppy has a temperament issue or later develops a disease or structural problem. Ultimately, it leads to badly-bred dogs entering the Corgi population and bringing unwanted traits with them.

The risk of breeding puppies with health issues is very real if you don't know what you are doing. Today's responsible breeders are continually looking at ways of improving the health of the Pembroke and Cardigan through selective breeding. See **Chapter 13. Corgi Health** for more information on health tests and ailments that can affect Corgis.

Another major consideration is that neither Pembrokes nor Cardigans are easy whelpers - meaning that many do not give birth straightforwardly and some cannot manage without veterinary help.

 According to the UK Purebred Dog Health Survey, 35.7% of Pembroke litters and 21.9% of Cardigan litters were born by Caesarean, or C-Section.

Typical veterinary fees for a C-section are in four figures and are not covered by normal pet insurance - and even then, a good outcome is not guaranteed. We know of several breeders of different breeds who have lost beloved dogs during or following C-sections.

Photo: A veterinarian performing a C-Section.

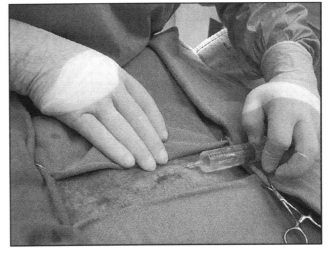

Corgi genetics are a complicated business that cover a multitude of traits, including structure, health, coat and colour, temperament and natural instinct.

Well-bred Corgi puppies fetch a high price. But despite this, you may be surprised to hear that many dedicated breeders make little or no money from the practice, due to the high costs of veterinary fees, health screening, stud fees and expensive special nutrition and care for the female and her pups.

Responsible breeding is backed up by genetic information and screening as well as a thorough knowledge of the desired traits of the Corgi. It is definitely not an occupation for the casual hobbyist.

 Breeding is not just about the look or colour of the puppies; health and temperament are at least as important.

Many dog lovers do not realise that the single most important factor governing health and certain temperament traits is genetics. Good breeders have years of experience in selecting the right pair for mating after they have considered the ancestry, health, temperament and physical characteristics of the two dogs involved.

They may travel hundreds of miles to find the right mate for their dog. Some of them also show or take part in other canine activities with their Corgis.

Anyone considering mating their dog should first ask themselves these questions:

- **Did you get your Corgi from a good, ethical breeder?** Dogs sold on general sales websites are seldom good specimens and can be unhealthy

- **Does your dog conform to the Breed Standard?** Do not breed from a Corgi that is not an excellent specimen in all respects, hoping that somehow the puppies will turn out better. They won't! Talk with experienced breeders and ask them for an honest assessment of your dog

- **Do you understand COI and its implications?** COI stands for Coefficient of Inbreeding. It measures the common ancestors of a dam and sire and indicates the probability of how genetically similar they are. This cannot be overlooked when breeding Corgis, due to the relatively small gene pool.

- **Have your dog and his or her mate both been screened** for genetic Corgi health issues that can be passed on to the puppies?

- **Have you researched his or her lineage** to make sure there are no problems lurking in the background? Puppies inherit traits from their grandparents and great-grandparents as well as from their mother and father

- **Are you 100% sure that your Corgi has no temperament issues** which could be inherited by the puppies?

- **Are you positive that the same can be said for the dog you are planning on breeding yours with?**

- **Do you have the finances** to keep the mother healthy through pregnancy, whelping, and care of her and the puppies after birth — even if complications occur?

- **Is your female two years old or older and at least in her second heat cycle?** Female Corgis should not be bred until they are physically mature, have had their joints screened, and are robust enough to whelp and care for a litter. Even then, not all females are suitable

- **Giving birth takes a lot out of a female - are you prepared to put yours through that?** And, as you've read, it's not without risk

- **Some females are poor mothers,** which means that you have to look after the puppies 24/7. Even if they are not, they need daily help from the owner to rear their young

- **Can you care for lots of lively puppies if you can't find homes for them?**

- **Will you be able to find good homes for all the puppies?** Good breeders do not let their precious puppies go to just any home. They want to be sure that the new owners will take good care of their dogs for their lifetime

- **Would you take back, or help to rehome, one of your dogs if circumstances change?**

Advice from the Experts

Piotr and Johnathan Mazur-Jones: "The true cost of raising a litter properly is huge. We often say it takes a litter size of four, under normal circumstances (no C-section, complications or other issues) to break even. If licensed, there are then other costs to consider.

"Commitment - it requires a lot if you are to do it properly: matching a mate, the mating, the pregnancy, whelping, raising the pups, socialisation, finding Forever Families etc. It isn't a question of boy meets girl, babies follow and then so does the cash!

"It should be done for love of the breed. Price is obviously individual. We wouldn't say: 'Don't breed,' we would say: 'Look into it as much as possible so you know what's involved. Read up as much as you can, especially on whelping; it can take hours!'"

Fran Fricker: "My advice to anyone thinking of breeding Corgis properly is to follow the breed, be interested in the breed and their health and welfare. Join a breed club, talk to responsible breeders and comply with all health testing. Providing the best care for a bitch and puppies costs money and it's not for the faint-hearted."

Linda Roberts: "Done properly, with all the costs of breeding, whelping and rearing the pups for 10 weeks, plus all the registration and vet fees, it is an expensive undertaking both financially and in terms of time. It is hard, hard work... and sometimes brings a great deal of heartbreak."

Jo Evans: "Breeding is hard work. Corgi puppies are small and easily lain on, starved or get cold. A great deal of attention is needed. Done properly, it can also be very rewarding."

Kevin Dover, who holds the UK breed record for the most Challenge Certificates (60) with his Pembroke, Magnus (Ch Pemcader Thunderball), *pictured:*

"In all my 45 years of breeding Corgis, I have never made a profit - even from the litter of 10, due to a very expensive C section and subsequent aftercare.

"I always ask people who wish to breed the following questions:

1. Why do you want your bitch to have a litter?
2. Do you have people waiting for puppies that can give them a happy and secure life for the next 15 years or so?
3. Are you prepared for the various problems that could arise during and after birth, i.e. the expense of a suitable stud and any veterinary fees should the bitch get into difficulty?
4. Do you have the time to spend with the puppies and mother day and night ensuring the puppies are feeding and the bitch is caring for them at least for the first two weeks?
5. Are you prepared to hand-feed should she not have enough milk or any milk at all?
6. Or the worst-case scenario: to lose the bitch whelping and have to hand-feed and clean each puppy every two hours for the first two weeks of life day and night.

"I can understand that some may want their bitch to be 'fulfilled,' but not all take to motherhood so I always say to think long and hard before committing to such a life-changing commitment.

"Even after 45 years I take no pregnancy or whelping as a 'matter of fact' issue. As a long-term devotee of the breed, I'm always personally happy to help and have helped many new people within the breed to have their first litters, giving advice as and when required."

Lucy Badham-Thornhill: "I would always go to somebody experienced before mating my bitch, especially the first litter. I made a very small profit once, otherwise not.

"Corgis are not guaranteed easy whelpers, and the minute you have any sort of problem, the vet costs spiral. In the Corgi world, the maverick breeders charge the most.

"My comment, which is not rocket science, is that if you want to make money, try another method!"

Photo of Lucy's Lettice and Mole relaxing at home.

Seek Advice

Having read all of that, it's also true to say that experts are not born, they learn their trade over many years.

Anyone who is seriously considering getting into the specialised art of breeding Corgis should first spend time researching the breed and its genetics.

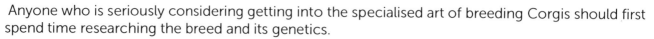

Make sure you are going into breeding for the right reasons and not primarily to make money - ask yourself how you intend to improve the breed.

Make contact with established breeders, visit dog shows or talk to owners and breeders of Corgis. Find yourself a mentor, somebody who is already very familiar with the breed.

To find a good breeder/mentor:

- ✓ **For Pembrokes in the UK,** visit The Welsh Corgi League website: www.welshcorgileague.org
- ✓ **For Cardigans in the UK,** visit The Cardigan Welsh Corgi Association website: www.cardiganwelshcorgiassoc.co.uk
- ✓ **For either breed,** visit The Kennel Club website and find an Assured Breeder in your area
- ✓ **For Pembrokes in the USA,** visit The Pembroke Welsh Corgi Club of America website: www.pembrokecorgi.org
- ✓ **For Pembrokes in the USA,** visit The Cardigan Welsh Corgi Club of America website: https://cardigancorgis.com/cwcca
- ✓ **For either breed,** visit the AKC website for a *Breeder of Merit,* or one who is a member of the *Bred with H.E.A.R.T.* programme

If you are determined to breed from your Corgi - and breed properly - do your research. Read as much as you can; one useful resource is *"Book of the Bitch"* by J. M. Evans and Kay White.

You may have the most wonderful Corgi in the world, but don't enter the world of dog breeding without knowledge and ethics. Don't do it for the money, the cute factor, to show the kids "The Miracle of Birth!" or because you want to breed the best show Corgi ever - you can't!

Breeding poor examples only brings heartache in the long run. Our strong advice is:
When it comes to breeding Corgis, leave it to the experts - or set out to become one yourself.

Neutering - Pros and Cons

There is a lot to think about before you make a decision on what's best for your Corgi. Show and most working dogs are not spayed or neutered, whereas dogs kept purely as pets often are. There is already too much indiscriminate breeding of dogs in the world.

However, there's mounting scientific evidence that spaying or neutering young dogs while they are still growing can have a detrimental effect on their future health. Then there is the very real threat of mammary cancer, as well as the life-threatening Pyometra in unspayed middle-aged females of all breeds.

As you will read in **Chapter 17. Corgi Rescue**, it is estimated that 1,000 dogs are put to sleep every hour in the USA alone. Rescue organisations in North America, the UK and Australia routinely neuter all dogs that they rehome. The RSPCA, along with most UK vets, also promotes the benefits of neutering; it's estimated that more than half of all dogs in the UK are spayed or castrated.

Another point is that you may not have a choice. Some breeders' Puppy Contracts may have a Spay/Neuter clause as a Condition of Sale. Others may state that you need the breeder's permission to breed your dog.

While early spay/neuter has been traditionally recommended, there is emerging scientific evidence that it is better to wait until the dog is through puberty before making the decision – whatever your vet might recommend.

The Science

It takes at least a full 12 months before Corgis skeletons mature and their growth plates close.

Based on the latest scientific studies, we recommend waiting until your Corgi is at least one year old before considering spaying or neutering.

This is because we now realise that the sex hormones play an important role in normal growth and development.

Veterinarian Dr Samantha Goldberg, says: "Testosterone and oestrogen are involved in some of the long bone formations in the body, so removing this too early can affect correct growth leading to prolonged growth and poorer quality bone with abnormal mechanical behaviours of the joints.

"Early neutering - i.e. before skeletal growth has finished - results in taller, leggier dogs as the closure of the plates in the long bones is helped by release of puberty hormones.

"There is also increased risk of cranial cruciate rupture, intervertebral disc disease (IVDD), hip dysplasia and patella luxation being cited in some breeds. The number of breeds listed as affected is likely to increase as we know more.

"Bitches may be sexually mature before the body has finished developing physically and mentally. Although they may be able to come into season, they have not finished growing if under 12 months and will certainly not have finished maturing mentally. Many vets will try to influence owners to spay their bitch at six months and often before a season. It is best to be patient and not just neuter to suit the human family."

Dr Goldberg added: "There is a lot of work looking at behavioural issues with dogs in rescues and when they were neutered. So far it seems likely that more dogs ending up in rescue with behavioural issues were neutered early – i.e. under 12 months.

"Neutering reduces metabolic rate and this means they need fewer calories or more exercise to balance it. Often neutering is carried out without the vet warning the owner of this.

"Thus we hear: 'She is overweight because she is spayed.' Actually not true - being overweight is caused by eating more calories than are expended.

"Overweight dogs have higher risks from many health conditions, e.g. Diabetes Mellitus and joint issues...and obvious things such as heart disease due to increased workload.

"Neutering male dogs directly reduces risks of increased prostate size due to testosterone (not the same as tumours) and in bitches removes the risk of Pyometra, a life-threatening uterine condition, and ovarian cancers. These effects are very positive.

"To summarise: Neutering should be carried out at the correct time to maximise health in your dog and afterwards their lifestyle may be changed a little, e.g. calorie control. Neuter to reduce risks of many health conditions, but do it at the right time to maximize the lifespan of your dog."

Spaying

Spaying is the term traditionally used to describe the sterilisation of a female dog so that she cannot become pregnant.

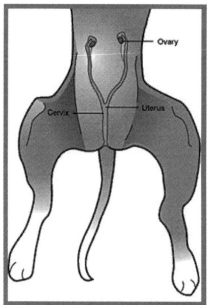

This is normally done by a procedure called an *"ovariohysterectomy"* and involves the removal of the ovaries and uterus, or womb. Although this is a routine operation, it is major abdominal surgery and she has to be anaesthetised.

One less invasive option offered by some vets is an *"ovariectomy,"* which removes the ovaries, but leaves the womb intact. It requires only a small incision and can even be carried out by laparoscopy, or keyhole surgery.

The dog is anaesthetised for a shorter time and there is less risk of infection or excess bleeding during surgery.

One major reason often given for not opting for an ovariectomy is that the female still runs the risk of **Pyometra** later in life. However, there is currently little or no scientific evidence of females that have undergone an ovariectomy contracting Pyometra afterwards. Pyometra affects females of all breeds.

However, unspayed middle-aged (over six years old) Corgi bitches have a higher risk of getting **mammary cancer** (the equivalent of breast cancer in humans) than spayed bitches.

FACT ❯ Spaying is a much more serious operation for females than neutering is for males. It involves an internal abdominal operation, whereas the neutering procedure is carried out on the male's testicles, which are outside his abdomen. Both procedures require a full general anaesthetic.

As with any major procedure, there are pros and cons.

Pros:

- ❧ Spaying eliminates the risk of Pyometra and significantly reduces the risk of mammary cancer. It also reduces hormonal changes that can interfere with the treatment of diseases like diabetes or epilepsy

- ❧ Spaying also prevents infections and other diseases of the uterus and ovaries

- ❧ You no longer have to cope with any potential mess caused by bleeding inside the house during heat cycles

- ❧ You don't have to guard your female against unwanted attention from males

- ❧ Spaying can reduce behaviour problems, such as roaming, aggression towards other dogs, anxiety or fear (not all canine experts agree)

- ❧ A spayed dog does not contribute to the pet overpopulation problem

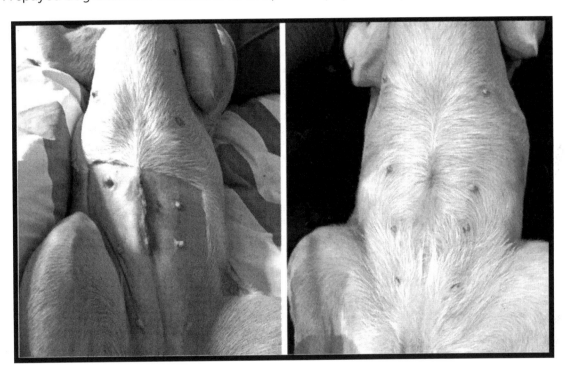

These photographs are reproduced courtesy of Guy Bunce and Chloe Spencer, of Dizzywaltz Labrador Retrievers, Berkshire, England. The left image shows four-year-old Disney shortly after a full spay (ovariohysterectomy). The right one shows Disney several weeks later.

Cons:

- ❧ Early spay (before the dog has finished growing) can lead to an increased risk of joint and other diseases

- ❧ Complications can occur, including an abnormal reaction to the anaesthetic, bleeding, stitches breaking and infections; these are not common

- ❧ Occasionally there can be long-term effects connected to hormonal changes. These include weight gain or less stamina, which can occur years after spaying

- ❧ Cost. This can range from £100 to £250 in the UK, more for keyhole spaying, and anything from $150 to over $1,000 at a vet's clinic in the USA, or from around $50 at a low-cost clinic, for those that qualify

❖ Urinary incontinence is more common in neutered females, especially if spayed early. One study found that urinary incontinence was not diagnosed in intact females, but was present in 7% of females neutered before one year old

Spaying during a heat cycle results in a lot of bleeding during the operation, which makes things messy for the vet and can make the operation riskier for the female.

Neutering

Neutering male dogs involves castration, or the removal of the testicles. This can be a difficult decision for some owners, as it causes a drop in the pet's testosterone levels, which some humans - men in particular! - feel affects the quality of their dog's life. Fortunately, dogs do not think like people, and male dogs do not miss their testicles or the loss of sex.

FACT ❭ Dogs working in the Services or for charities are often neutered and this does not impair their ability to perform any of their duties. NOTE: All male show Corgis are unneutered (entire).

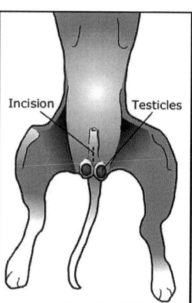

Technically, neutering can be carried out at any age over eight weeks provided both testicles have descended. However, as you've read, recent scientific studies are undoubtedly coming down on the side of waiting until the dog is one year or older.

Surgery is relatively straightforward, and complications are less common and less severe than with spaying. Although he will feel tender afterwards, your dog should return to his normal self within a couple of days.

When a dog comes out of surgery, his scrotum, or sacs that held the testicles, will be swollen and it may look like nothing has been done. It is normal for these to shrink slowly in the days following surgery.

Here are the main pros and cons:

Pros:

❖ Castration is a relatively straightforward procedure

❖ Unwanted sexual behaviour, such as mounting people or objects, is usually reduced or eliminated

❖ You cannot have an uncastrated male and unspayed female together when the female is on heat. A castrated male can live alongside a female all year round – although be aware he can still get a female pregnant up to three or four weeks after castration due to residual sperm in his tubes!

❖ Behaviour problems such as aggression, marking and roaming can be reduced

❖ Testicular problems such as infections, cancer and torsion (painful rotation of the testicle) are eradicated

❖ Benign prostatic hyperplasia (prostate gland enlargement) is much less likely after castration

❖ A neutered dog is not fathering unwanted puppies

Cons:

❖ Studies indicate that males neutered before one year old may be more susceptible to joint problems later in life comparted with those neutered after two years old

- As with any surgery, there can be swelling and redness around the wound. It's fairly routine for dogs to need 10 days of anti-inflammatory medication and to have to wear an E-collar afterwards

- Some prostate cancers are more likely after neutering

- In some cases castration can make behaviour problems worse. Pain, trips to the clinic and having testosterone removed can lead to a reduction in the dog's confidence

- There is evidence that some dogs' coats may be affected; this also applies to spaying

- Cost - this starts at around £120 in the UK. In the USA this might cost anything from $150 to $1,000 at a private veterinary clinic, depending on your state, or less at a low cost or Humane Society clinic

Urban Myths

Neutering or spaying will spoil the dog's character - There is no evidence that any of the positive characteristics of your dog will be altered. He or she will be just as obedient, playful and loyal as before. Neutering may reduce aggression or roaming in male dogs, because they are no longer competing to mate with a female.

A female needs to have at least one litter - There is no proven physical or mental benefit to a female having a litter.

Mating is natural and necessary - We tend to ascribe human emotions to our dogs, but they do not think emotionally about sex or having and raising a family.

Unlike humans, their desire to mate or breed is entirely physical, triggered by the chemicals called hormones within their body.

Without these hormones – i.e. after neutering or spaying – the desire disappears or is greatly reduced.

Photo: The best of friends – Owain (7), who is neutered, and Bubbles (12), who is spayed. Courtesy of Margaret E. Leighton

Male dogs will behave better if they can mate - This is simply not true; sex does not make a dog behave better. In fact, it can have the opposite effect. Having mated once, a male may show an increased interest in females.

He may also consider his status elevated, which may make him harder to control or call back.

⊘ **Do your own research. Many vets still promote early spay and neuter.**

17. Corgi Rescue

Not everyone who wants a Corgi gets one as a puppy from a breeder. Some people prefer to give a rescue dog a second chance for a happy life.

What could be kinder and more rewarding than giving a poor, abandoned dog a loving home for the rest of his life?

Not much really; adoption saves lives and gives unfortunate dogs a second chance of happiness. The problem of homeless dogs is truly depressing. It's a big issue in Britain, but even worse in the US, where the sheer numbers in kill shelters are hard to comprehend. In **"Don't Dump The Dog,"** Randy Grim states that 1,000 dogs are being put to sleep every hour in the States.

Reasons for Rescue

If you're thinking of adopting a Corgi, you'll need patience and commitment. They may arrive with some baggage and it can take time to train them, or retrain them out of any bad habits.

The internet is full of photos of cute Corgis, especially puppies. Media attention on Queen Elizabeth II, coupled with the popularity of TV series The Crown has led to Corgi ownership rapidly increasing over the last few years.

That gorgeous little bundle of fluff with the tiny legs, melt-your-heart eyes and giant ears looks so cute. And people rush out in their droves to buy them, with scant regard to the nature or health of the puppy they are buying.

Many expect a lapdog and realise too late what they've actually got is a smart dog with working instincts who likes a challenge - exercise, games, canine competitions, etc.

Well, if you don't provide a challenge for a Corgi, they will certainly provide a challenge for you! Behaviour is a common reason for dogs ending up in rescue. They may have become too vocal, demanding, anxious or badly-behaved. This is almost always due to a lack of socialisation, training or exercise, or all three - all of which are part of the bargain when you decide to get an engaged, people-loving breed like the Corgi.

Other reasons for Corgis being put into rescue include:

- ❖ The dog or owner develops health issues
- ❖ A change in work patterns, so the dog is left alone for long periods
- ❖ The dog has way too much energy and needs a lot more exercise and attention than the owner is able or prepared to give
- ❖ A change in family circumstance, such as divorce or a new baby
- ❖ Moving into smaller or rented accommodation

- He is barking, growling, chewing things he shouldn't or nipping (which may be due to his herding instinct)
- He makes a mess in the house - housetraining requires time and patience from the owner
- The costs of keeping a dog are higher than expected

The Pembroke Welsh Corgi Club of America Rescue Committee, says: "Most Pembroke Welsh Corgis come into rescue because of lack of attention, training or changes in the family situation. The majority of these dogs are two years of age or older. All rescue Corgis are spayed or neutered and their shots are current before being placed in a new home.

"Generally, the rescue Corgi is placed in a temporary home for evaluation of temperament, to ensure that a compatible match can be made between the individual dog and a new family. Many of these adopted Corgis have become very successful in obedience, agility, herding and therapy dogs."

There is a ray of sunshine for some of these dogs. Every year many thousands of people in North America, Europe and countries all around the world adopt a rescue dog and the story usually has a happy ending.

The Dog's Point of View...

If you are serious about adopting a Corgi, do so with the right motives and with your eyes wide open. If you're expecting a perfect dog, you could be in for a shock. Rescue Corgis can and do become wonderful companions, but much depends on you and how much effort you are prepared to put in.

If you can, look for a rescue group specialising in Corgis – and preferably one where the dog has been fostered out. They are more likely to be able to assess the dog and give you an idea of what you might be letting yourself in for. And if a dog has bad habits, the foster parents have probably already started working on some of them.

Corgis are extremely loyal to their owners. Sometimes those that end up in rescue centres are traumatised, others may have behaviour or health problems.

They don't understand why they have been abandoned, neglected or badly treated by their owners and may arrive at your home with 'baggage' of their own until they adjust to being part of a loving family again.

This may take time. Patience is the key to help the dog to adjust to new surroundings and family and to learn to love and trust again. Ask yourself a few questions before you take the plunge and fill in the adoption forms:

- Are you prepared to accept and deal with any problems - such as bad behaviour, unwanted barking, aggression, timidity, chewing, jumping up or eliminating in the house - that a rescue dog may display when initially arriving in your home?

- Just how much time do you have to spend with your new dog to help him integrate back into normal family life?

- Corgis are one of the longest-lived breeds. Are you prepared to take on a new addition to your family that may live for another decade?
- Will you guarantee that dog a home for life - even if he develops health issues later?

What could be worse for the unlucky dog than to be abandoned again if things don't work out between you?

Other Considerations

Adopting a rescue dog is a big commitment for all involved. It is not a cheap way of getting a Corgi. It could cost you several hundred dollars or pounds.

Depending on the adoption centre, you may have to pay adoption fees, vaccination and veterinary bills, as well as worm and flea medication and spaying or neutering. Make sure you're aware of the full cost before committing.

Many rescue dogs are older and some may have health or temperament issues. You may even have to wait a while until a suitable dog comes up. One way of finding out if you are suitable is to become a foster home for a rescue centre. Fosters offer temporary homes until a forever home comes along. It's shorter-term, but still requires commitment and patience.

And it's not just the dogs that are screened! Rescue groups make sure that prospective adopters are suitable. They also want to make the right match - placing a high-energy dog with an elderly couple or an anxious dog in a noisy household - could be storing up trouble. It would be a tragedy for the dog if things did not work out.

Most rescue groups ask a raft of personal questions - some of which may seem intrusive. But you'll have to answer them if you are serious about adopting. Here are some typical questions:

- Name, address, age
- Details, including ages, of all people living in your home
- Type of property you live in
- Size of your garden or yard and height of the fence around it

Photo: A Cardigan Welsh Corgi at home in the yard.

- Extensive details of any other pets
- Your work hours and amount of time spent away from the home each day
- Whether you have any previous experience with dogs or Corgis
- Your reasons for wanting to adopt
- Whether you have any experience dealing with canine behaviour or health issues
- Details of your vet
- If you are prepared for aggression/destructive behaviour/chewing/fear and timidity/soiling inside the house/medical issues
- Whether you are willing to housetrain and obedience train the dog
- Your views on dog training methods

- ❖ Whether you are prepared for the financial costs of dog ownership
- ❖ Where your dog will sleep at night
- ❖ Whether you are prepared to accept a Corgi cross
- ❖ Two personal references

If you go out to work, it is useful to know that UK rescue organisations will not place dogs in homes where they will be left alone for more than four to five hours at a stretch.

After you've filled in the adoption form, a chat with a representative from the charity usually follows. There will also be a home inspection visit - and even your vet may be vetted! If all goes well, you will be approved to adopt and when the right match comes along, a meeting will be arranged with all family members and the dog. You then pay the adoption fee and become the proud new owner of a Welsh Corgi.

It might seem like a lot of red tape, but the rescue groups have to be as sure as they can that you will provide a loving, forever home for the dog. It would be terrible if things didn't work out and the dog had to be placed back in rescue again.

All rescue organisations will neuter the dog or, if he or she is too young, specify in the adoption contract that the dog must be neutered and may not be used for breeding. Some Corgi rescue organisations have a lifetime rescue back-up policy, which means that if things don't work out, the dog must be returned to them.

Training a Rescue Dog

Some Corgis may be in rescue because of behavioural problems; how this manifests itself varies from one dog to another. The Corgi was bred specifically to work with humans and is a very smart breed, so when problems develop it's usually due to lack of training and attention from the owner. It does, however, mean that these dogs can be retrained - even when older.

As one rescue group put it: **"Rescue dogs are not damaged dogs; they have just been let down by humans, so take a little while to unpack their bags and get familiar with their new owners and surroundings before they settle in."**

If you approach rescue with your eyes wide open, if you're prepared to be patient and devote plenty of time to your new arrival, then rescuing a Corgi is incredibly rewarding. They are such affectionate and loyal dogs, you'll have a friend for life.

 Ask as many questions as you can about the background of the dog, his natural temperament and any issues likely to arise. You are better having an honest appraisal than simply being told the dog is wonderful and in need of a home.

Training methods for a rescue Corgi are similar to those for any adult Corgi, but it may take longer as the dog first has to unlearn any bad habits.

If the dog you are interested in has a particular issue, such as indiscriminate barking or lack of housetraining, it is best to start right back at the beginning with training.

 Don't presume the dog knows anything and take each step slowly. See Chapter 9. Basic Training for more information.

Rescue Training Tips

- Start training the day you arrive home, not once he has settled in

- He needs your attention, but, importantly, he also needs his own space where he can chill out. Put his bed or crate in a quiet place; you want your dog to learn to relax. The more relaxed he is, the fewer hang-ups he will have

- Show him his sleeping and feeding areas, but allow him to explore these and the rest of his space in his own time

- Using a crate may help speed up training, **but it's important he first learns to regard the crate as a safe place,** and not a prison. See **Chapter 6. Crate and Housetraining** for the best way to achieve this

- If you have children or other animals, introduce them quietly and **NEVER** leave them alone with the dog for the first few months – you don't know what his triggers are

- Maintain a calm environment at home

- Never shout at the dog - even if he has made a mess in the house - it will only stress him and make things worse

- Don't give treats because you feel sorry for him. Only give him a treat when he has carried out a command. This will help him to learn quicker and you to establish leadership

- Set him up to SUCCEED and build confidence – don't ask him to do things he can't yet do

- Socialisation is extremely important – introduce him to new places and situations gradually and don't over-face him. All new experiences should be positive or you may reinforce his insecurities. You want him to grow in confidence, not be frightened by new things. Talk reassuringly throughout any new experience

- Mental stimulation as well as physical exercise is important for Corgis, so have games, toys or challenges to keep your new dog's mind occupied

- Don't introduce him to other dogs until you are confident he will behave well - and then not while he is on a lead (leash), when the *'fight or flight'* instinct might kick in

- Getting an understanding of your dog will help to train him quicker - is he by nature submissive or dominant, anxious or outgoing, fearful or bold, aggressive or timid? If he shows aggressive tendencies, such as barking, growling or even nipping, he is not necessarily bold. His aggression may be rooted in fear, anxiety or lack of confidence

 The aim of training a rescue Corgi is to have a relaxed dog, comfortable in his surroundings, who respects your authority and responds well to your positive training methods.

Rescue Organisations

Rescue organisations are usually run by volunteers who give up their time to help dogs in distress. They often have a network of foster homes, where a Corgi is placed until a permanent new home can be found. There are also online forums where people sometimes post information about a Corgi that needs a new home.

USA Pembrokes: PWC Rescue Network https://pembrokecorgi.org/about-pembrokes/pwc-rescue-network for rescue info and a list of regional Pembroke rescue groups.

USA Cardigans: The Cardigan Welsh Corgi National Rescue Trust
https://cardigancorgis.com/cwcca/rescue

CorgiAid: https://corgiaid.com provides financial assistance for medical and other expenses to people who foster Pembrokes and Cardigans from shelters or other non-permanent homes. They also have the CorgiAid Cart Program for disabled Corgis.

UK Pembrokes and Cardigans: Welsh Corgi League Rescue
www.welshcorgileague.org/corgi-rescue

If you visit these websites, you cannot presume that all descriptions are 100% accurate. They are given in good faith, but ideas of what constitutes a "lively" or "challenging" dog may vary.

Some dogs advertised may have other breeds in their genetic make-up. It does not mean that these are worse dogs, but if you are attracted to Corgis for their looks, temperament, quirky character and other assets, make sure you are looking at a Corgi.

DON'T get a dog from Craig's List, Gumtree or any of the other general advertising websites that sell golf clubs, jewellery, old cars, washing machines, etc.

You might think you are getting a bargain, but in the long run you will pay the price. Good breeders with healthy dogs do not advertise on these websites - or sell to pet shops.

You may be storing up a whole load of trouble for yourselves in terms of health or temperament issues, due to poor genetics and/or environment.

If you haven't been put off with all of the above... **Congratulations**, you may be just the person that poor homeless Corgi is looking for!

If you can't spare the time to adopt - and adoption means forever - you might consider fostering. You could help by becoming a home inspector or fundraiser to help keep these very worthy rescue groups providing such a wonderful service. Or just make a donation.

How ever you decide to get involved, Good Luck!

**Saving one dog will not change the world,
But it will change the world for one dog.**

18. Caring for Older Corgis

When it comes to getting old, Corgis are the Peter Pans of the canine world! They have a longer lifespan than lots of other breeds, and if all goes well you can expect your puppy to live a dozen years - maybe even into the mid-teens if you're lucky.

Secondly, in their twilight years, Corgis often stay fitter, more active and younger at heart than many other dogs.

Lifespan can be influenced by genetics; and how you feed, exercise and generally look after your Corgi will also have an impact on his quality and length of life. But eventually all of them slow down to some extent.

....

Approaching Old Age

After having got up at the crack of dawn as a puppy, you may find your old Corgi now enjoys a lie-in in the morning. He may be a bit slower on his walks, stopping to sniff every blade of grass, and may not want to go quite as far.

Some Corgis seem to continue just as before, while others get slightly stiffer joints and sometimes organs, such as heart, kidneys or liver, may not function quite as effectively. They will probably sleep more and may seek out a place in the sunshine to rest their old bones.

Pictured looking very pleased with herself after winning Best Veteran and a large trophy at her local agricultural show is Mole, aged 10. Photo by Lucy Badham-Thornhill.

Your faithful companion might even become a bit grumpier, stubborn or a little less tolerant of lively dogs and children. You may also notice that he doesn't see or hear as well as he used to.

On the other hand, your old friend might not be hard of hearing at all. He might have developed that affliction common to many older dogs of *"selective hearing."*

Our 12-year-old Max had bionic hearing when it came to the word *"Dinnertime"* whispered from 20 paces, yet seemed strangely unable to hear the commands *"Come"* or *"Down"* when we were right in front of him!

FACT ❭ We normally talk about dogs being old when they are in the last third of their life. Dogs are classed as a "Veteran" at seven years old in the show ring – however fit they are.

You can help ease a mature dog into old age gracefully by keeping an eye on them, noticing the changes and adapting their lifestyle. This might involve:

- 🐾 Slowly reducing the amount or intensity of daily exercise
- 🐾 A change of diet

- Modifying your dog's environment – perhaps with an extra blanket, a warmer place and thicker bed for those old joints

- A visit to the vet for supplements and/or medications

Ageing varies greatly from dog to dog and bloodline to bloodline. However, it's VERY important to keep all Corgis at an optimum weight as they get older.

Their metabolisms slow down, making it easier for them to pile on the pounds. Extra weight places additional, unwanted stress on their joints, back and organs, making them all have to work harder than they should.

Physical Signs of Ageing

Here are some signs of Corgis feeling their age - a Corgi may show one or more of these:

- Grey hairs appear, particularly around the muzzle, and coat colour fades. As with humans, darker colours tend to show more grey

Photo: 11-year-old Cardigan Annie (Ch Swanpool Angelica at Huntsville) owned by Denise Hunt.

- They get up from lying down and move more slowly

- They slow down and some are not as keen to go for long walks - and perhaps a bit less keen to go out in bad weather

- They put on a bit of weight - or lose weight

- They may drink more water and/or pee more frequently

- They shed more hair

- Hearing deteriorates

- The foot pads thicken and nails may become more brittle

- One or more lumps or fatty deposits (lipomas) develop on the body

  One of our old dogs developed two small bumps on the top of his head aged 10 and we took him straight to the vet, who performed minor surgery to remove them. They were benign (harmless), but always get the first one checked out ASAP in case they are an early form of cancer - they can also grow quite rapidly, even if benign

- Old dogs often can't regulate body temperature quite as well as they used to and may feel the cold and heat more easily

- Bad breath (halitosis), which could be a sign of dental or gum disease. If the bad breath persists, get it checked out by a vet

- If inactive, they may develop callouses on the elbows, especially if lying on hard surfaces

- Eyesight may also deteriorate – if eyes appear cloudy they may be developing cataracts, so see your vet if you notice the signs. Most older dogs live quite well with failing eyesight, particularly as Corgis have an incredible sense of smell

Mental Signs of Ageing

It's not just dogs' bodies that may slow down; their minds may too. It's normal for a dog's memory, ability to learn and awareness to start to dim - although one of the Corgi's many assets is that they often remain engaged and interested in life, their family and surroundings right to the end.

If your dog's mind is starting to lose its sharpness, here are some signs to look out for; it's officially called *Canine Cognitive Dysfunction:*

❖ Sleep patterns change; older dogs may be more restless at night and sleepy during the day. They may start wandering around the house at odd times, causing you sleepless nights

❖ They bark more, sometimes at nothing or open spaces

❖ Forgetting or ignoring commands or habits they once knew well, such as the Recall and sometimes toilet training

❖ They stare at objects, such as walls, hide in a corner, or wander aimlessly around the house or garden (this could be a sign of a mini stroke)

❖ Increased anxiety or aggression

❖ Some dogs may become clingier and more dependent, resulting in Separation Anxiety. They may seek reassurance that you are near as faculties fade and they become a bit less confident and independent. Others can become a bit disengaged

Photo: Fit as a butcher's dog! Mole (10) showing Lettice (4) the way in the agility tunnel. Photo by Lucy.

Understanding the changes happening to your dog and acting on them compassionately and effectively will help ease your dog's passage through their senior years.

Your dog has given you so much pleasure over the years, now he needs you to give that bit of extra care for a happy, healthy old age.

 If your Corgi is starting to show signs of slowing down or disengaging, you can help him to stay mentally active by playing gentle games and getting new toys to stimulate interest.

Helping Your Dog To Age Gracefully

There are many things you can do to ease your dog's passage into his declining years. As dogs age they need fewer calories and less protein, so some owners feeding kibble switch to one specially formulated for older dogs. These are labelled *Senior, Ageing* or *Mature.*

Check the labelling; some are specifically for dogs aged over 10, others may be for 12-year-olds. If you are not sure if a Senior diet is necessary for your Corgi, talk to your vet on your next visit. Remember, if you do change brand or switch to a wet food, do it gradually over a week or so. Unlike with humans, a dog's digestive system cannot cope with sudden changes of diet.

Years of eating the same food, coupled with less sensitive taste buds can result in some dogs going off their food as they age.

If you feed a dry food, try mixing a bit of gravy with it; this works well for us, as has feeding two different feeds: a morning one of kibble with gravy and the second tea-time feed of home-cooked rice and boiled chicken or fish. Rice, white fish and chicken – all cooked – can be particularly good if your old dog has a sensitive stomach.

If you are considering a daily supplement, Omega-3 fatty acids are good for the brain and coat, and glucosamine and various other supplements help joints. Yumega Omega 3, Yumove and Joint Aid are used by lots of breeders with older dogs.

 One of the most important things throughout your Corgi's life is dental care - by regular tooth brushing and the occasional bone, bully stick or antler, etc. to gnaw on.

Photo: A long and happy life. Sadie (Ch. Cherastayne Snow Bride JW), aged 16-and-three-quarters, owned and bred by Linda Roberts. In her heyday, Sadie twice won Best of Breed at Crufts Dog Show.

Linda regularly brushes her Corgis' teeth and added: "Sadie had her first and only scale and polish at the vet's (and a tooth extraction at the same time) at the age of 15-and-a-half."

Not only is toothache painful and unpleasant, but a dog may lose weight due to being unable to eat properly. It can also be traumatic for dogs to have teeth removed under anaesthetic.

Some dogs can become more sensitive to noise as they age. We had one and the lead up to Bonfire Night was a nightmare. (November 5th in the UK, when the skies are filled with fireworks and loud bangs). Other dogs become more stressed by grooming or trips to the vet as they age.

There are medications, homeopathic remedies such as melatonin, and various DAP (dog appeasing pheromone) products that can help relieve anxiety. Check with your vet before introducing any new medicines.

If your old friend has started to ignore your verbal commands when out on a walk - either through *"switching off"* or deafness - try a whistle to attract his attention and then use an exaggerated hand signal for the Recall.

Once your dog is looking at you, hold your arm out, palm down, at 90 degrees to your body and bring it down, keeping your arm straight, until your fingers point to your toes.

Hand signals worked very effectively with our old Max. He looked, understood ... and then decided if he was going to come or not - but at least he knew what he should be doing! More often than not he did come back, especially if the visual signal was repeated while he was still making up his mind.

Weight - no matter how old your Corgi is, they still need a waist! Maintaining a healthy weight with a balanced diet and regular, gentler exercise are two of the most important things you can do for an old dog. Some Corgis can also lose weight when they get older. In such cases, try and tempt your dog with white fish, chicken and rice, which are all gentle on the stomach, or add tasty warm gravy to his meals.

 If your dog rapidly loses or gains weight without any obvious reason, consult your vet promptly to rule out any underlying medical issues.

Environment - Make sure your dog has a nice soft place to rest, which may mean adding extra padding to his bed. This should be in a place that is not too hot or cold, as they may not be able to regulate their body temperature as well as they used to.

They also need plenty of undisturbed sleep and should not be pestered and/or bullied by younger dogs, other animals or young children.

Photo: This'll do! Bubbles (Pemcader Black Glamour, aged 12) finds a comfy place for 40 winks, courtesy of Margaret E. Leighton.

Jumping on and off furniture or in or out of the car shouldn't be allowed. It's high impact for old joints and bones. He may need a helping hand to get on to the couch (if he's allowed on there) or a ramp.

We bought an expensive plastic ramp to get one old dog into the car, but it proved to be a complete waste of money as dogs are tactile and he didn't like the feel of the non-slip surface under his paws.

After a few tentative attempts, he steadfastly refused to set a paw on it and we donated the ramp to a canine charity! I have heard of breeders carpeting ramps to (successfully) persuade their dogs to use them.

If eyesight is failing, move obstacles out of their way or use pet barriers to reduce the chance of injuries.

Exercise - Take the lead from your dog, if he doesn't want to walk as far, then don't force him to go further. But if your dog doesn't want to go out at all, you will have to coax him out. ALL old dogs need exercise, not only to keep their joints moving, but also to keep their heart, lungs and joints exercised, and their minds engaged with different places, scents, etc.

Ears - Sometimes older dogs produce more ear wax, so keep checking that the inside your Corgi's ears are clean and not dirty or smelly.

Coat - Some Corgis' coats thicken with age and they require grooming more often.

Time to Get Checked Out

If your dog is showing any of these signs, get them checked out by a vet:

- Cloudy eyes, possibly cataracts
- Drinking and/or peeing far more frequently than normal, which could be a sign of diabetes, Cushing's disease or a kidney complaint
- Constipation or not peeing regularly, a possible symptom of a digestive system or organ problem
- Watery poo(p) or vomiting

- ❋ Decreased appetite - this is often one of the first signs of an underlying problem - especially with Corgis, who normally love their food

- ❋ Incontinence, which could be a sign of mental or physical deterioration

- ❋ Lumps or bumps on the body - often benign, but can occasionally be malignant (cancerous)

- ❋ Excessive sleeping or a lack of interest in you and his surroundings

- ❋ A darkening and dryness of skin that never seems to get any better, which can be a sign of hypothyroidism

- ❋ Any other out-of-the-ordinary behaviour for your dog. A change in patterns or behaviour is often your dog's way of telling you that all is not well

What the Experts Say

Carole Turner, longstanding breeder of Cottonfields Pembrokes: "My older Corgis seem to just go on without realising how old they are - both mentally and physically; I do think living with a younger dog or dogs helps.

"I feed Royal Canin but have never changed to a senior version. I don't usually feed supplements, but recently started giving 12-year-old Jessie, *pictured*, a joint supplement as, when I groomed her, I could feel a slight 'grating' in one of her front legs. It has since cleared up.

"I groom my dogs every day and clean their teeth, which gives me a chance to also check for any problems. I've not noticed any difference in their coats, apart from the changes in a neutered animal.

"I keep their nails short which helps mobility, and I'm trained in canine massage which can be especially useful for an older dog. I've not used any other complementary therapies, although I've seen the benefits of hydrotherapies for rehabilitation.

"I have seen a lot of older Corgis that are overweight and therefore less mobile, which is not good for them either mentally or physically.

"Mine usually insist on going out for walks with the younger dogs, but sometimes I'd leave an older one behind if I was going on a long and challenging walk.

"In terms of behaviour, I do think it can become more intense, i.e. if they were bossy before, then look out! (said with tongue in cheek). I think a Corgi's positive outlook on life is what keeps them going - while correct diet and exercise plays a huge part."

Karen Hewitt, Chairperson of the Cardigan Welsh Corgi Association (CWCA), says: "Ageing totally varies dog by dog, some are 'old' by eight or nine whilst others are still really fit and active at 12+. Signs are greying, especially round the face and a general slowing down.

"In terms of health issues, there's nothing that wouldn't be found in other breeds: wear and tear of joints, a bit of arthritis, etc. Similarly, there are very few behavioural changes in Corgis in my experience; they just do the same things more slowly and when they are very old, they sleep a lot.

"I personally don't change their diet. I discuss supplements with our vet and give whatever they recommend. Be guided by your dog with exercise, when they appear to be less active, ask less from them.

"I've found that coats do change in texture quite often, and some older Cardigans may need a bath a little more often. Generally, I'd advise owners to be observant and look out for the little signs of old age; don't try to make them walk further than they are comfortable with, etc."

Eileen Eby, committee member of the CWCA, says: "Cardis tend to live 14 to 17 years, and typically enter their senior years when they are over 10. Signs would be getting generally stiffer with a bit of arthritis, and sometimes cataracts. I don't think there are any health or behaviour issues that are particular just to Corgis.

"I feed a raw diet from puppy throughout life and add glucosamine/chondroitin when then get older. I may shorten the walks as they get older, but other than that, they don't usually need any special attention.

"I massage all my dogs when petting and stroking, "listening" with my hands and heart to where they think it would feel nice."

Photo: Fit For Function. Fang (Kilvroch Rackett, aged 10) bred and owned by Eileen.

Fellow Cardigan breeder Fran Fricker, Kerman Cardigans, says she has heard of them living to 18 or 19 years of age. She adds: "A dog of any breed becomes a veteran from the age of seven according to the Kennel Club. But for each individual breed, age is just a number and you can see dogs looking older than their age from four years onwards and dogs of 10 plus years still in their prime.

"Some start to go grey around the muzzle and eye area and maybe gain a little weight as they slow down. Coats can also change and become thicker. My Bertie (Multi Ch Pluperfect Merrymoon Proper Englishman) was still winning Challenge Certificates at 11 years old and he runs around with the youngsters showing no signs of his age.

"My dogs have an hour each day free running. My oldies are all still very active and run with the youngsters. They enjoy being part of the team and can be crafty at crossing the field, so they only run round half of it! If it's wet, it's important to make sure they are dried thoroughly when back home and have clean warm bedding to rest in.

"For nutrition, I stick with my Adult diet from Royal Canin and will add meat to it, also fish oil, glucosamine and chondroitin for joints, plus seaweed. Mine have all lived to a good age - 14 years plus, some living into their 17th year.

"They can still tell you when it's food time, they also know when it's show time and still enjoy the regular bathing and grooming. Coats can become thicker but my grooming routine and health check stays the same. It's important to know how they feel so you will recognise any lumps and bumps that suddenly appear and need checking out.

"Mine enjoy a massage in the bath with the warm water. It really relaxes the muscles and, again, when drying them the warm air can be therapeutic. For those who have spinal and joint issues hydro therapy has proved useful.

"The oldies may get a little stiff in their joints and perhaps develop cataracts from old age - and bitches may develop mammary tumours - but they all continue to live life to the full. My advice is to treat them as normal, be mindful of them and respect them in their later years."

Here are some more comments from Pembroke owners and breeders, starting with Wisconsin Bred With Heart Breeder Lisa Thompson, of Thompson's Corgis: "Most Corgis enter old age about 10 years old. They start slowing down and definitely sleep more. They can get a little cranky if they have aches and pains – it's important to listen to their signs.

"I usually continue feeding adult food, and if teeth are missing, it's important to soak the food. I always give joint supplements to my dogs; glucosamine is a great supplement to give all dogs, it will keep the joints lubricated. My advice is to keep on loving them; they will tell you when it's time to go."

Assured Breeder Jo Evans, of Cerdinen Pembroke Welsh Corgis, bred her first litter over 30 years ago and says: "I've always carried on as normal with my older Corgis. My current Corgis are aged two, four and seven, our previous Corgi, Sian, lived to 17.

"Sian had all sorts of unlucky things happen in life: she got hit by a car in her younger days and had a metal plate put in, but this never affected her. She also got pyometra when she was quite old and nearly died. This taught us to have our bitches spayed if not breeding from them.

"I think Corgis have the chance to live a long life if kept fit with plenty of exercise and without being allowed to get fat. Any problems in later life are probably due to something in earlier life, such as Hip Dysplasia, in which case supplements or other treatments start long before they get old."

Welsh Corgi League Breed Health Co-ordinator Linda Roberts: "There is no doubt that genetics can influence longevity. However, there is much to be said for keeping your Corgi slim and fit, and feeding according to the amount of exercise given.

"Even my Corgis who are well into their teens still love their outings; of course, the distance of the walk is always appropriate for that particular dog. I don't alter their diet as they age and I'm careful to look after their teeth (including regular tooth brushing and dentals as needed) so I haven't found the need to soak their complete food at any stage. I believe dental infections can contribute to heart and kidney problems in seniors, so it's an important part of their maintenance.

"If your Corgi is prone to stiffness there are very effective joint supplements on the market, and I have used Yumove with great success in the past. If stiffness is severe, your vet will be able to help with anti-inflammatory medication.

"It goes without saying that grooming and bathing routines should continue through the senior years and these are a good opportunity to spot any lumps or bumps at an early stage. You might find that nails need more attention if your senior isn't walking quite as far as when younger. I haven't experienced sight loss in my dogs, however one became very hard of hearing. She adapted very well.

"It is very important to me that my old dogs are still enjoying life day-to-day and I cherish the time I have with them. That said, I don't believe there's ever a good reason to keep an old dog going when their quality of life has diminished and I'm pretty strict with myself when the time is coming. It's important to always put the well-being of your Corgi first and a good relationship with a vet who knows your dog is helpful on these occasions."

The Last Lap

Huge advances in veterinary science have meant that there are countless procedures and medications that can prolong the life of your dog, and this is a good thing. But there comes a time when you do have to let go.

If your dog is showing all the signs of ageing, has an ongoing medical condition from which they cannot recover, is showing signs of pain, anxiety or distress and there is no hope of improvement, then the dreaded time has come to say goodbye. You owe it to your Corgi.

There is no point keeping an old dog alive if all that lies ahead is pain and death. We have their lives in our hands and we can give them the gift of passing away peacefully and humanely at the end when the time is right.

Losing our beloved companion, our best friend, a member of the family, is truly heart-breaking. But one of the things we realise at the back of our minds when we got that gorgeous, lively little puppy that bounded up to meet us like we were the best person in the whole wide world is the pain that comes with it.

We know we will live longer than them and that we'll probably have to make this most painful of decisions at some time in the future.

It's the worst thing about being a dog owner.

If your Corgi has had a long and happy life, then you could not have done any more. You were a great owner and your dog was lucky to have you. Remember all the good times you had together.

Try not to rush out and buy another dog straight away. Assess your current life and lifestyle and, if your situation is right, only then consider getting another dog and all that that entails in terms of time, commitment, exercise and expense over the next decade and more.

Whatever you decide to do, put the dog first.

Photo courtesy of Fran Fricker. Photographer Will Harris.

Contributors

Breeders

Kevin Dover, Pemcader Pembroke Welsh Corgis, Herefordshire, England

Linda Roberts, Cherastayne Pembroke Welsh Corgis, Lancashire, England

Piotr and Johnathan Mazur-Jones, Creslow Corgis, Somerset, England

Jo Evans, Cerdinen Pembroke Welsh Corgis, Ceredigion (Cardiganshire), Wales

Tracy Irving, Twinan Welsh Corgis (Pembrokes and Cardigans), Lancashire, England
www.twinancorgis.com

Alexandra Trefán-Török, Born To Be Corgis, Hungary www.borntobe.hu

Fran Fricker, Kerman Cardigan Welsh Corgis, Carmarthenshire, Wales

Karen Hewitt, Cardhew Cardigan Corgis, Warwickshire, England www.cardhew.co.uk

Eileen Eby, Kilvroch Cardigans Welsh Corgis, Northamptonshire, England www.kilvroch.co.uk

Lisa Thompson, Thompson's Corgis, Wisconsin, USA https://thompsonscorgis.weebly.com

Owners

Sue Hardy

Kevin Egan

Lucy Badham-Thornhill

Margaret E. Leighton

Carole Turner

Vicky Methuen

Robin Bruce

Corgi Trainers

Maria Carter, professional dog trainer, Cheltenham, Gloucestershire, England

Mary Ann Wehmueller, Fairyfyre Pembroke Welsh Corgis, Indiana, USA

Marian Your, Tri-umph Pembroke Welsh Corgis, Texas, USA

Useful Contacts

The Welsh Corgi League www.welshcorgileague.org

Pembroke Welsh Corgi Club of America, Inc www.pwcca.org

The Cardigan Welsh Corgi Club of America https://cardigancorgis.com/cwcca

The Cardigan Welsh Corgi Association www.cardiganwelshcorgiassoc.co.uk

Kennel Club (UK) Assured Breeders www.thekennelclub.org.uk/search/find-an-assured-breeder

AKC (American Kennel Club) www.akc.org/dog-breeds/pembroke-welsh-corgi (Pembroke) and www.akc.org/dog-breeds/cardigan-welsh-corgi (Cardigan)

RSPCA Puppy Contract https://puppycontract.rspca.org.uk/home

AKC Preparing a Puppy Contract www.akc.org/expert-advice/dog-breeding/preparing-a-contract-for-puppy-buyers

AKC Canine Good Citizen www.akc.org/products-services/training-programs/canine-good-citizen

KC Good Citizen Scheme www.thekennelclub.org.uk/training/good-citizen-dog-training-scheme

Association of Pet Dog Trainers UK www.apdt.co.uk

Association of Pet Dog Trainers US www.apdt.com

Canadian Association of Professional Pet Dog Trainers www.cappdt.ca

Useful info on dog foods (US) www.dogfoodadvisor.com (UK) www.allaboutdogfood.co.uk

Helps find lost or stolen dogs in the US: register your dog's microchip at www.akcreunite.org and www.petmicrochiplookup.com to trace a registered microchip

Corgi internet forums and Facebook groups are also a good source of information from other owners.

Disclaimer

This book has been written to provide helpful information on Pembroke and Cardigan Welsh Corgis. It is not meant to be used, nor should it be used, to diagnose or treat any medical condition. For diagnosis or treatment of any animal medical problem, consult a qualified veterinarian.

The author is not responsible for any specific health or allergy conditions that may require medical supervision and is not liable for any damages or negative consequences from any treatment, action, application or preparation, to any animal or to any person reading or following the information in this book.

The views expressed by contributors to this book are solely personal and do not necessarily represent those of the author. References are provided for informational purposes only and do not constitute endorsement of any websites or other sources.

Pet Care Tracker

Vet's Name: _ _ _ _ _ _ _ _ _ _ _ _ _   Groomer's Name: _ _ _ _ _ _ _ _ _ _ _ _ _

Vet's Phone: _ _ _ _ _ _ _ _ _ _ _ _   Groomer's Phone: _ _ _ _ _ _ _ _ _ _ _

Day Care: _ _ _ _ _ _ _ _ _ _ _ _ _   Holiday Sitter: _ _ _ _ _ _ _ _ _ _ _ _ _

Pet's Name	Date	Vet Visit	Groomer	NOTES

Printed in Great Britain
by Amazon

19641924R00149